Praise for *Enfleshing Freedom*, Second Edition

Shawn Copeland's *Enfleshing Freedom: Body, Race, and Being* responds to the perpetual Christian theological inquiry about the meaning of being human with a refreshing reclamation of liberation theology's foundational premise that Jesus calls disciples to know and to contest the wounding of persons. A womanist theological anthropology that uses accumulated traumas of Black women's bodies to unmask the depths of human horrors and divine love, *Enfleshing Freedom* identifies countering division and domination as what it means to truly be human. The human body, *Enfleshing Freedom* maintains, is a facilitator of divine revelation, a source of human relationality, and divine affirmation of diversity. Citing Black women's historic opposition to Black pain and contemporary #BlackLivesMatter practices as signs, *Enfleshing Freedom* asserts that Jesus calls disciples to enact assembly (*ekklesia*) and communion (Eucharist) through solidarity in "bodily living" that both combats indignities against persons within Christian communities and extends assembly and communion as the solidarity of combating indignity through wide-open welcome and camaraderie.

—Rosetta Ross, professor of religious studies, Spelman College

Enfleshing Freedom is a masterpiece—one of the most important works of Catholic theology since the Second Vatican Council. It speaks lovingly of our raced, gendered, wounded, and joyous bodies and unites them in the liberating body of Christ. This second edition features expanded treatments of Toni Morrison's *Beloved*, the historical context of Jesus of Nazareth, recent US immigration policy, evolving Catholic views on same-sex relationships, and the phenomenon of "neo-lynching." It also includes a stunning new chapter, "Enfleshing Struggle," that interprets #BlackLivesMatter and #SayHerName. It is a must-read!

—Andrew Prevot, Amaturo Chair in Catholic Studies,
Georgetown University, author of *The Mysticism of Ordinary Life:*
Theology, Philosophy, and Feminism

Impossibly, Copeland has lifted the second edition of *Enfleshing Freedom* to even higher heights than the first. Strongly theological and philosophical, the pastoral intent of her work is to center a womanist constructive theology to counter racist heterosexism. Copeland challenges and inspires all theological thinking to pay close attention to the metaphysics of raced being, the continuing violence of slaving histories, the exclusions of some bodies from ecclesial spaces, to fashion a theology, Christology, and ecclesiology that actively resist prejudice and bigotry. Constructively, the book is a nuanced and careful mapping of the urgent need for Christians to create and sustain complex solidarities that have the potential to transform the despair of hate and anger into communities "ordered by the Eucharist" of love and care.

—Susan Abraham, vice president of Academic Affairs and dean, Pacific School of Religion

In this timely second edition, *Enfleshing Freedom* continues to be germane and relevant well over a decade later. M. Shawn Copeland's insightful womanist and intersectional study spans the centuries and exposes the invisibility of Black women's bodily trauma from the historical accounts of slavery to the contemporary #BlackLivesMatter movement captured in an expanded new chapter. Few studies engage the depths of theological anthropology and analogize the sacrality of the suffering body journeys of Black people and the crucified Jesus as brilliantly as Copeland. Copeland's use of theology, history, Morrison's literature, and Holiday's blues commingle to advance a new Black body theology much needed in these times when Black bodies seek freedom, restoration, and re-memberance amidst a culture of social and civil violence, disposability, valuelessness. In *Enfleshing Freedom*, Copeland's authorial voice is distinguishingly theological, discerningly Catholic, and unabashedly womanist. A must-read for a serious study of race, religion, and the Black body.

—Tracey E. Hucks, Victor S. Thomas Professor of Africana Religious Studies, Harvard Divinity School, and Suzanne Young Murray Professor, Radcliffe Institute for Advanced Study; author of *Yoruba Traditions and African American Religious Nationalism* and *Obeah, Orisa, and Religious Identity in Trinidad, Volume 1, Obeah: Africans in the White Colonial Imagination*

ENFLESHING FREEDOM

ENFLESHING FREEDOM

Body, Race, and Being

Second Edition

M. Shawn Copeland

FORTRESS PRESS
MINNEAPOLIS

ENFLESHING FREEDOM
Body, Race, and Being
Second Edition

Library of Congress Control Number: 2023940352 (print)

Cover image: Uta Uta Tjangala, Snake woman dreaming. (detail) Acrylic on canvas.
Aboriginal art, 20th CE. © Aboriginal Artists Agency Limited. Jennifer Steele / Art
Resource, NY
Cover design: Brice Hemmer

Print ISBN: 978-1-5064-6325-4
eBook ISBN: 978-1-5064-6326-1

to the memory of

Black women
whose bodies were destroyed in the Middle Passage
whose bodies were abused and chewed up in the maw of slavery
whose bodies were tortured and lynched
whose bodies were defiled and discarded
whose bodies lie in unmarked and unattended graves
whose bodies were shattered in extra-judicial killings

and

to the memory of
my grandmother
Mattie Lucille Hunt Billingslea
whose bodily labor
made my freedom possible and makes it still

Contents

Preface to the Second Edition

Our demand is simple: stop killing us.

Johnetta Elzie[1]

Enfleshing Freedom is an exercise in *theology as political* that aims to meet the *exigences of systematic theology* in wrestling with concrete historical, cultural, religious, social, and existential circumstances riddled with sin and irrationality. This second edition takes into account the impacts of the devastating global *pax imperii*, with its cruel (re)production of abused, impoverished, depleted children, women, and men around the world who have been made migrants; of the unspeakable, reprehensible, recrudescent neo-lynchings of Black (and Brown) children, youth, women, and men; and of the ongoing vicious depredation of "the least of the least" (Matt 25:45), Black female human persons.

This new edition expands the discussion in chapter 1 of the abuse of South African Khoisan woman Sarah Baartman, not only to unmask more critically the European (British, French, and Dutch) colonial contexts in which White and Black or Colored men manipulated her body and assaulted her dignity, but also to learn from the new scholarship of Black South African and diasporic women. Chapter 4 grew out of the necessity to consider the withering spread of the *pax imperii*, the new sovereign (dis)order or empire as globalization. The new chapter 6 discusses two contemporary movements, #SayHerName and #BlackLivesMatter, that continue freedom's struggle to protect and honor the bodies, lives, and dignity of Black human persons; at the same time, this chapter takes seriously Black women's resistance to sexual assault during the slave trade and their marginalization in Black movements for freedom, civil rights, and social justice. In chapter 7, I expand the treatment of the cross and the lynching tree, borrow Angela Sims's nomenclature of neo-lynching, and bring to the fore the lynchings of Black women.

In the cultural matrix that is the United States, everything has changed since 1619, and nothing has changed. Johnetta Elzie's stark, declaratively imperative sentence simultaneously marks both a forced arrival of Black persons in the English-speaking sector of the "new world" and our continuing experience: "stop killing us." Yet Elzie's cry may well express the pain and agony of *all* children, youth, women, and men who are impoverished or minoritized because of race, ethnicity, culture, language, religion, gender, sex, or sexual orientation within the US matrix. And, amid this maldistributed, vicious, transgenerational social suffering, Christianity too often dissembles; if it arrives at all, it does so much too late and with little effect.

Everything has changed, and nothing has changed. Ours is a time of continuing struggle: the critique of experience and understanding, the dynamism of thought and challenge, the necessity of accountability, the responsibility of judgment and action; the move toward personal integrity or authenticity, not for self alone, but for community; resistance to presuppositions, stereotypes, prejudgments, stultifying pasts, violence, death-dealing; self-transcendence; the daily making and constituting of ourselves as *ikons* of the Holy, emanating centers of solidarity, of true and authentic value and love—*human* persons seeking to enflesh freedom.

Introduction

The wounds of my people wound me too.
Is there no balm in Gilead? Who will turn my head into a fountain
and my eyes into a spring of tears so that
I may weep all day, all night for the wounded out of my people?[1]

There *is* a balm in Gilead,
to make the wounded whole.[2]

It is not knowledge we lack. What is missing is the
courage to understand what we know and to draw conclusions.[3]

Enfleshing Freedom focuses the Christian question of what being human means on the body, quite particularly on the bodies of Black women.[4] For centuries, black female bodies have been bought and sold, used and defiled, discarded, quite literally, as refuse—simply because they are female and Black, Black and female. To privilege suffering bodies in theological anthropology uncovers the suffering body at the heart of Christian belief. Reflection on these bodies, the body of Jesus of Nazareth and the bodies of Black women, lays bare both the human capacity for inhumanity and the divine capacity for love.

Five basic convictions ground this discussion of theological anthropology: that the body is a site and mediation of divine revelation; that the body shapes human existence as relational and social (i.e., political, economic, technological); that the creativity of the Triune God is manifested in differences of gender, race, sex, and sexuality; that solidarity is a set of body practices; and that the Eucharist orders and transforms our bodies as the body of Christ. Privileging the Black woman's body makes these claims specific and particular. Rather than exclude or overturn or punish other bodies or persons, specificity and particularity insist that we *all* are subjects.[5] Since the fifteenth-century radical and expedient subjugation of Black peoples to demonized difference,[6] *all* human bodies have been caught up in a near totalizing web of body commerce, body exchange, body value. Taking the Black woman's body as a starting point for theological anthropology allows us to interrogate critically the impact of that demonization in history, religion, culture, and society.

The argument here covers difficult, often precarious, ground. This book makes slavery visible. This is *not* a book about slavery, but slavery holds a compelling role in its central claims. In the United States, chattel slavery or racialized enslavement of Black human beings was secured and protected by federal and state laws, defended by the United States Supreme Court. Historian Nell Painter writes that slavery's influence "calibrated values in core [American] institutions," including the family, religion, government, commerce, labor, education, and entertainment. Nor did "the implications of slavery stop at the color-line; slavery's theory and praxis" seeped into the whole of American society.[7] While chattel slavery was practiced widely in the southern states, critical historical scholarship has uncovered slaveholding in northern and western states and regions of the United States. In fact, historian Wendy Warren chronicles the importation, purchase and sale of African women and men in colonial New England eighteen years after the arrival of the *Mayflower*.[8] Not only was slaveholding practiced in Massachusetts, but also in Connecticut, New York, New Jersey, and Rhode Island. In the past decade, universities, colleges, and Christian churches have come to acknowledge that the stature and benefits they are reaping were made possible by the labor of enslaved women and men.[9]

So it is that in the United States, we Christian theologians live and work, teach and write in a house haunted by the ghosts of slavery.[10] In a country at once enthralled and impoverished by the dazzling innovations of technical rationality, by the arrogance of untrammeled acquisitiveness, by self-regarding selfishness, the political memory of the nation suppresses our deep entanglement in slavery. Without the painstaking, thorough, and passionately dispassionate intellectual courage of women and men of all races—especially historians, and literary, visual, and musical artists—the nation might have gone on overlooking the bodies "piled up"[11] outside our door, gone on concealing slavery behind narratives of innocence or masks of pretense.[12] But total erasure has never been possible, never will be. In searing, mournful, and lyric prose, a month after the lynching of George Floyd, Caroline Randall Williams declared:

> I have rape-colored skin. My light-brown-blackness is a living testament to the rules, the practices, the causes of the Old South. If there are those who want to

remember the legacy of the Confederacy, if they want monuments, well, then, my body is a monument. My skin is a monument. My very existence is a relic of slavery and Jim Crow.[13]

The most vivid reminder and remainder of slavery, then, remains the black body. These bodies of evidence cannot be explained away so easily. They constitute a structural embarrassment.[14] The suffering and death of Jesus of Nazareth rebuke our national amnesia, our forgetfulness of enslaved bodies, our indifference to living black bodies. The *memoria passionis* interrupts our banal resignation to a vague past, our smug democratic dispensation, our not-so-benign neglect. From the perspective of a contextual theology of social transformation,[15] the full meaning of human freedom (i.e., religious, existential, social, eschatological) can be clarified only in grappling strenuously with the "dangerous memory" of slavery.[16]

This book also makes visible black bodies in pain.[17] I have chosen to reproduce accounts of torture, sexual assault, and lynching. I do not do so casually. I am aware that such reiterations may serve to "reinforce the spectacular character of black suffering"[18] and to foster voyeuristic sentimentality.[19] Rather, as a theologian who is Black and a woman, I understand my task here as Toni Morrison understands her task as a writer who is Black and a woman: to move aside "that veil drawn over 'proceedings too terrible to relate.'"[20] These may be narratives not to pass on,[21] but to pass over these sorrows imperils humanity as well as theology. For my part, drawing back that veil is an obligation to memory: the subjects and the subject of my theologizing are the dead, the "Many Thousand Gone."[22]

In raising the aching memory of slavery, this work interrogates memory and history for the sake of freedom. Black women began the healing of their flesh and their human subjectivity in the *there-and-then*, in the midst of enslavement. But without romanticizing or uncritically celebrating their resistance, we may say that Black women sometimes opposed their condition through word (sass) and deed (fighting back, literal escape); at other times, "poache[d] on the power of the dominating class."[23] At still other times, unable to escape or to resist, Black women submitted or found ways to subvert "the rituals, representations, and laws imposed on them . . . by the dominant social order [and] deflected its power."[24] Theologically considered, Black women's absolute enfleshment of freedom, sown in the *there-and-then*, is caught up and realized in the abiding presence of the resurrected body of Jesus. As a theologian, I fulfill my responsibility to these dead by challenging the reader to "respect the dignity of suffering that has accumulated in history"[25] and to translate that respect into compassionate practices of solidarity—to critical, healing practices that address the crusted residue of slavery in contemporary and global reenactments of violence against black bodies.

Chattel slavery not only critiqued freedom but also raised fateful questions about the meaning of being human. Contemporary philosophers and theologians agree that traditional metaphysics is under siege from postmodernity's deployment of *difference*. There are advantages to that strategy for projects like this one. Yet, even if problematic, the "implicitly metaphysical"[26] character of Christianity cannot be dismissed. With these debates in mind, chapter 1 begins by engaging some of the difficulties in speech and representation of body and race and being. These difficulties coalesce in the case of Sarah Baartman, a nineteenth-century Khoisan woman from South Africa, whose body was displayed as titillating exotica passed off as "scientific curiosity."[27] The story of Baartman's abuse unfolds within a religious, historical, and socioeconomic context shaped by European (British, French, and Dutch) colonialism; by the repercussions of the transatlantic trade in Black human bodies; and by "the creative fusion of scientific investigation, Cartesian philosophy, Greek ocular metaphors, and classical aesthetic and cultural ideals."[28]

Chapter 2 adverts to the narrative of human creation in Genesis and Christianity's murky role in chattel slavery, then directly confronts the attempt to degrade the *imago Dei* through commodifying, objectifying, and sexually violating Black women's bodies. The freedom of the (human) subject is at stake here and so is the (human) subject of freedom. In history, the psychic, spiritual, physical wounds of chattel slavery were rarely healed; but Morrison's great novel *Beloved*[29] mediates a healing performative midrash on the incarnation of *imago Dei*.

The principal historical and social (i.e., political, economic, technological) contexts for thinking about bodies in exercises of imperial power—the ancient *pax Romana* and the contemporary *pax imperii*—that is, the new sovereign (dis)order or empire as the global regime that constitutes, organizes, remakes, and reorients human subjects for disposability, maximum utility and profit—are discussed in chapters 3 and 4. Chapter 3 concentrates on the body of the Jewish rabbi or teacher, Jesus of Nazareth. His body and faith praxis present a formidable entry point for the scandal of particularity in theological anthropology: formidable because of the marks of that body (gender, race, sex, culture); because of that body's openness to, turn toward, and solidarity with even radically different others (Matt 15: 26–27); and because of that body's pledge to be given and poured out for *all* others across time and space.

Chapter 4 focuses on some of the dehumanizing conditions of bodies in empire, in particular, the bodies of poor non-White women; thus, the chapter attends to race, sex, and migration. The disciples of Jesus are called to contest in their bodies and in their bodily living, assembly (*ekklesia*), and communion (Eucharist) any indignity against, any oppression of those children, youth, women, and men—members of his family who are hungry and thirsty, need welcome and care, clothing and shelter, companionship and solidarity (Matt 25:39). At the same time, the disciples of Jesus must extend this contestation, openness, and commitment to lesbian and gay and transgender bodies; for, too often, as church, we have humiliated and disparaged these members of Jesus's family and our brothers and sisters too. Hence, by virtue of its subjects, theological anthropology evokes the church and those bodies that it recognizes, and those bodies that it suspects. If the body, the flesh of Jesus is the "hinge of salvation,"[30] then the embrace of the church must swing open and wide, welcoming and solidaristic.

Against the backdrop of the Enlightenment's surrender to racial empiricism, chapter 5 outlines the emergence of theologies of liberation and connects the "new" subject of theological anthropology to the practice of solidarity. An Italian newspaper report of a Black (migrant) woman giving birth by the side of a road unmasks the personal and social sin that racism is in the breakdown of human solidarity. This breakdown uncovers the very loss of *humanum*, the loss of our humanness. Against this loss I argue for solidarity as an expression of the mystical body of Christ.

We descendants of the enslaved Africans in the United States frequently use the word *struggle* to signify our strenuous, transgenerational effort to wrest from God and religion, jurisprudence and legislation, culture and society the freedom to live a dignified human life. Chapter 6 presents an overview of two contemporary movements that enflesh struggle: #BlackLivesMatter and #SayHerName. These movements continue in the noble path of freedom's struggle, not only to hold the nation accountable for its defiance of its own laws and ideals, but also for its attachment to White racist supremacy, to hetero-patriarchy. Theologically stated, these movements contribute to the resetting of those bones broken within the body of Christ.

Chapter 7 returns to accounts of the abuse of Black female bodies and takes seriously lynching and neo-lynching. It has not been easy for theologians and ethicists to grapple with the sexual abuse of Black women during chattel slavery,[31] but fewer—even Black theologians—write about lynching. Prior to the publication of James Cone's *The Cross and the Lynching Tree*, only Anthony Pinn, Kelly Brown Douglas, and I had written about this rampant display of the prolonged power of slavocracy. More recently, Angela D. Sims has published a study of this vicious practice based on sensitive oral interviews with Black elders.[32] The abuse and torture that is lynching concocts a surd, the irrationality of evil. Soteriologically considered: in his suffering and crucifixion, Jesus embraces and proleptically unites the real suffering of black bodies to his own. His embrace neither diminishes nor empties, neither justifies nor obscures the horror and misery of Black suffering.[33] Rather, the proleptic embrace of the suffering crucified Jewish Jesus, who is the Risen Lord, interrupts the abjection of Black bodies and creates an horizon of hope that is "hope against hope": *He have been wid us, Jesus, / He still wid us, Jesus, / He will be wid us, Jesus, / Be wid us to the end.*[34] A meal at the "welcome table" makes this eschatological hope tangible and nourishing, makes Christ present among us. Thus, the cross and the lynching tree reorient the discussion through reflection on Eucharist—the body of Christ, the Black body, the body raised up in humanity by Jesus Christ for himself.

The Christian gospel invites us *all* to *metanoia*, to change; the standard against which that change may be measured is the life praxis of the Jewish Jesus of Nazareth. In other words, the gospel challenges us not merely to change our lives, but to transform our living. Lived transformation is discipleship, the practice of solidarity with and beside and among those marginalized among us as "the least." Theology that rises from the message of the gospel should disturb as well as provoke, encourage as well as console in the furthering of life in the Resurrected Christ. In spelling out the meaning and implications of life in Christ, this theology can neither ignore nor mitigate the experiences that complexify being human and the real questions these experiences instigate—whether those questions arise from history or culture or social (i.e., political, economic, technological) arrangements. Thus, a theological anthropology worthy of reclaiming Black women's bodies is worthy of reclaiming *all human* bodies. This is the task I have set for myself in *Enfleshing Freedom*.

CHAPTER 1

Body, Race, and Being

God saw everything that he [sic] had made,
and indeed, it was very good.[1]

O my body, make of me always [one] who questions.[2]

the body, as always, tells the round, bald truth
when my stomach grips to say, no cure in sight.[3]

The body provokes theology. The body contests theology's hypotheses, resists its conclusions, escapes the margins of its texts. The body incarnates and points beyond and to what is "the most immediate and proximate object of our experience,"[4] even as it mediates our engagement with others, with the world, with the Transcendent Other. The immediate imperatives of hunger or thirst, pleasure or pain, desire or revulsion are not merely the body's imperatives; rather, they are *your* imperatives, *my* imperatives.[5] For the body is no mere object—*already-out-there-now*—with which we are confronted: always the body is with us, inseparable from us, *is* us. But, always, there is a "more" to you, a "more" to me: the body mediates that "more" and makes visible what cannot be seen. "The body," Yves Cattin writes, "is that ontological impotence which prevents the human spirit from presenting itself as pure absolute spirit. And in being human, the body is an essential quality of the soul."[6] Spirit or soul and body, he continues, "are not two realities of which we are composed, [but] the originary totality that we are."[7] The body constitutes a site of divine revelation and, thus, a "basic human sacrament." In and through embodiment, we human persons grasp and realize our essential freedom through engagement and communion with other embodied selves.[8]

Cultural anthropologist Mary Douglas calls attention to the body's symbolic function in human culture, focusing on the body as a code or image for social reality. She distinguishes and relates the physical and social bodies: "The social body constrains the way the physical body is perceived."[9] In other words, while interaction and engagement with others is crucial to realizing essential freedom, that realization in large measure hinges upon cultural perceptions and social (i.e., political, economic, technological) responses (affirmation or rejection or indifference) to the physical body. So the social body's assignment of meaning and significance to race and/or gender, sex and/or sexuality of physical bodies influences, perhaps even determines, the trajectories of concrete human lives. Thus, a social body determined by the arbitrary privileged position and, therefore, power of one group may enact subtle and grotesque brutality upon different "others."

Taking Black women's bodies as a prism, this work considers the theological anthropological relation between the social body and the physical body. By doing so, it avoids the trap of detaching the embodied subject from historical or social or religious contexts, which would render the subject eternal, universal, absolute. Rather, it opts for the concrete and aims to do so without absolutizing or essentializing particularity or jeopardizing the notion of personhood as immanent self-transcendence in act. Attention to the concrete bodies and experiences of Black women provides an interrogation of the dynamic unfolding of created spirit in the struggle to exercise freedom in history and society.

Five sections comprise this first chapter, setting out themes and questions that modulate the body. Race, along with gender, sex, and sexuality, is inseparable from the body, even if at times these markers may be ambiguous, paradoxical, problematic. What *is* race? What *makes* a body black? What does *black* mean? What might *being* black mean? These questions unsettle and problematize the conventional agenda of theological anthropology, but they are necessary questions if we are to take being human seriously.

When we talk with one another about "race," we assume we have some idea of what it is, and we do. But our understanding tends toward opinion or what philosopher-theologian Bernard Lonergan names common sense.[10] Most of us have an opinion about race; many of us even have had experiences that involve explicitly adverting to race—either our own or someone else's. The first section follows the idea of race as it was constructed and promulgated by European Enlightenment thinkers, then turns to the poignant figure of South African woman Sarah Baartman, whose body was caricatured and objectified by influential men of nineteenth-century science. By including

Baartman here, I intend neither to reinscribe those "master narratives" that reduced her to salacious body parts nor to simply or simplistically "claim her for Diasporic sisterhood."[11] Yet, as Janell Hobson makes clear, what *all* Black women have in common is the "associations of black female sexuality with animalistic characteristics [that] emerge not just in pseudoscientific studies of human anatomy but also in popular culture."[12] The second section theorizes race—skin—through the notions of horizon and bias. Horizon connotes a worldview; bias may participate in the construction and control of it, but both govern meaning-making. From the perspective of phenomenology, the third and fourth sections extend the framework advanced through relating the notions of horizon and bias, uncover the damage that racism does to body and soul, and gesture toward a "critical ontology of the body."[13] The final section summarizes some categories that surface in theological anthropology's attention to the black female body.

MAKING A BODY BLACK: INVENTING RACE

When confronted with the writings on race by major thinkers of the European Enlightenment, contemporary philosophy too often blinks, dismissing these texts as minor or unrepresentative. Yet, Emmanuel Eze argues, "Enlightenment philosophy was instrumental in codifying and institutionalizing both the scientific and popular European perceptions of the human race."[14] In an age that has become synonymous with criticality, major Enlightenment thinkers, including Georges Léopold Cuvier, Johann Friedrich Blumenbach, David Hume, Immanuel Kant, and Georg Wilhelm Friedrich Hegel, played a key role in shaping White European sensibilities of national, cultural, and racial superiority vis-à-vis non-White non-Europeans.[15] Indeed, from the eighteenth century and well into the twentieth, their ideas about race reinforced discredited proslavery attitudes, sustained racial segregation and discrimination, and exerted subtle, perhaps devastating influence on metaphysics and ethics.[16] Recall the vile effort of the Nazi regime to dehumanize and exterminate the Jewish peoples of Europe or the brutal reign of racial apartheid in South Africa or protracted anti-Black racism in the United States.

Readers may be familiar with Hume's suspicion that Black people "are naturally inferior to the Whites,"[17] or with Kant's insistence that the differences between Blacks and Whites were fundamental and that differences in their skin pigmentation mirrored differences in their mental capacities,[18] or with Hegel's pronouncement that Africa was bereft of history and its inhabitants lived "in barbarism and savagery [without] any integral ingredient of culture."[19] The enervating and underside of Enlightenment evaluations that correlated white skin with reason, intelligence, civilization, goodness, beauty, and creativity also correlated non-white skin, black skin with unreason, ignorance, savagery, depravity, grotesquery, and mimicry. Further, these evaluations insinuated the idea that white skin functionally accorded absolute supremacy to White men over non-Whites and women, and legitimated imperial brutality, extermination, slavery, racism, biology as human destiny.

We may trace a direct and disastrous route between the visual and psychological perception and physical treatment of black bodies and the work of both Blumenbach and Cuvier. By expanding the racial taxonomy developed by his teacher Carolus Linnaeus,[20] Blumenbach shifted the four-race "canonical geometry of human order from cartography to linear-ranking, to a system based on putative worth."[21] Blumenbach's taxonomy set out a scheme in which first place was accorded to the "Caucasian . . . as the most beautiful race," with the American, Mongolian, Malay, and Ethiopian varieties of the human species "degenerating" from the ideal.[22] The evolutionary biologist Stephen Jay Gould contends that Blumenbach did not use the term "degeneration" in the "modern sense of deterioration, but the literal meaning of departure from an initial form of humanity at the creation."[23] Rather Blumenbach held that all humans shared a unitary origin and allotted differences in skin pigmentation and character to differences in geography and custom. Still his five-race taxonomy has proved tragic for non-White peoples, Black people in particular.

Sixteenth-century Belgian physician Andreas Vesalius, the founder of modern anatomy, maintained, "The violation of the body would be the revelation of its truth."[24] Georges Cuvier's interest in the body of Sarah Baartman directly connects the violation and degradation of the Black body to Enlightenment-spawned pornographic pseudo-science.[25] Sarah Baartman's story is rife with anguish and suffering, disappointment and loss, deceit and fabrication. It is quite impossible to encounter Sarah Baartman directly, in terms of her person: no records, not even judicial proceedings, preserve her voice;[26] we do not know her given name, although Ssehura is proposed as, perhaps, closest to it, and her surname is a supposition.[27] Given her social location as a Black female colonial subject, if the decisions that Baartman may have taken perplex, these never were as vicious and duplicitous as those of the men, White and Black, who used their racial privilege and economic status to profit from the commercial manipulation of her body.

Baartman was born in 1789 to a Khoekhoe family in colonial South Africa's eastern frontier. Her mother died when she was an infant, her father was a cattle drover. Baartman grew up during a tumultuous period of armed conflict over cattle and land between and among rival Indigenous peoples (including San, Khoikhoi, Zulu, Xhosa, Swazi, Ndebele peoples) and invading Europeans (including Portuguese, Dutch and German, French, and British)—traders, missionaries, adventurers, refugees from religious persecution, hunters, herders, and farmers. It is likely that Baartman spent at least some of her early years working for Dutch colonists on land they seized from Indigenous peoples. When she was seventeen or eighteen years of age, her father was murdered; perhaps, this loss left her disoriented or traumatized. Somehow Sarah Baartman met free Black trader Pieter Cesars, who persuaded her to move to Cape Town to work for his brother Hendrik and sister-in-law Anna Catharina (free Black people) as a servant and live-in nursemaid to their infant daughter.[28]

In 1810, when she was about the age of twenty-two, disgraced British physician Alexander Dunlop, along with his employee Hendrick Cesars, smuggled Baartman into England and marketed her as a "lucrative scientific curiosity."[29] It is quite unlikely that Baartman went willingly with the men; she may have been taken in by promises of financial security or she may have been threatened and coerced. By all accounts, she was not fully cognizant of just what would be expected of her beyond playing her *ramkie* (a type of guitar with three or four strings), singing folk songs and dancing. Dunlop and Cesars intentionally planned to display her in order to "demonstrate that Sarah's [physical build] was a bona fide physiological anomaly."[30] They sought to appeal to the prurient curiosity and sexual fantasies of White European men who had read travel accounts by other White European male travelers, whose fabricated exaggerations elided Black women with deviant and lewd sexuality. Baartman was exhibited "onstage and in a cage" as the "Hottentot Venus" in London and Parisian drawing rooms, private clubs, and museums to eager audiences.[31] The very notion of displaying human beings as "artifacts" or examples of cultural or historical interest outrages and offends our religious, philosophical, and modern neoliberal sensibilities and commitments to human integrity, human dignity, and human rights—not that as global citizens we live up to these well, if at all. But the "living exhibition" of people with so-called "physical oddities" and of non-White peoples was not uncommon in the nineteenth century.[32] "The so-called Hottentot Venus was the product of the colonial white gaze that had woven Sara(h) Ba(a)rtman(n) out of a thousand details, anecdotes, [and] stories, which thereby imprisoned her."[33] Sarah Baartman died in Paris in 1815 at about the age of twenty-five.

No one had been more eager to gaze upon, to examine, to measure Sarah Baartman's body than Georges Cuvier. After Baartman's death, he conducted the postmortem examination and dissection of her body, organized its casting, and prepared her brain and genitals for preservation.[34] At some time between 1822 and the 1850s, Sarah Baartman's skeleton, body cast, brain, and genitals were placed on public display at the Natural Museum of History, and kept there until the 1970s, when her remains and those of other human persons were removed from public exhibition.[35]

Contra Vesalius, the violation and display of Sarah Baartman's body would yield no *truths*, only spurious quasi-theories of Black degeneration, degradation, and sexual deviance. The pseudo-scientific White colonialist gaze objectifies, scales, and assesses an "item" in relation to some set of putative hierarchical standards. This gaze registers degrees of conformity to and divergence from those standards, it normalizes, hierarchizes, and excludes. Aesthetic value judgments leach into degradation of intelligence and morality that demand disciplining, restraining, and controlling the body. The pseudo-scientific gaze is pornographic: it positions and handles, fetishizes, and exaggerates. The Black female body emerges from this spectacle of inspection as *the* spectacular; her body is remade in the asymmetric dynamics of power for exhibition and display, for pleasure and profit. These ersatz-theories excised Black women from (*read* White) humanity, from (*read* White) womanhood. As artist and critic Lorraine O'Grady argues:

> The female body in the West is not a unitary sign. Rather, like a coin, it has an obverse and a reverse: on one side is white; on the other side is not-white or, prototypically black. The two bodies cannot be separated, nor can one body be understood in isolation from the other in the West's metaphoric construction of "woman." White is what woman is: not-white (*and the stereotypes not-white gathers in*) is what she had better not be.[36]

SKIN AS HORIZON: THEORIZING RACE AND RACISM

Contemporary scholarly efforts to define and theorize race coalesce in the consensus that race, as commonly understood, is a social construct with no basis in biology.[37] Thus, there is only *one race*—the human race. At the same time, scholars conclude that the cognitive mapping, interpretations, and practices of race emerge from historical and social construction and replication.[38] The putative meanings of "race" are transmitted through a series of "durable, transposable dispositions" that structure, (de)form, direct, and predispose an individual's "perception and appreciation" of social experience. French sociologist Pierre Bourdieu names this complex process of acculturation *"habitus."*[39] Both sociologist Eduardo Bonilla-Silva and historian James Sweet extend this notion to race, to racism. Sweet concludes: "The structures of a racialized *habitus*, based on perceived phenotypical distinctions . . . result in homogenizing processes that reduce social or cultural 'difference' to innate traits, or 'race.'"[40] In this reduction, ideologically construed, skin generates a privileged and privileging worldview; skin morphs into a horizon funded by bias.

By horizon, I mean, "a maximum field of vision from a determinate standpoint."[41] What and who is outside the range of that field is eliminated from my knowledge and interest, care and concern. Uncontested, the limited and limiting standpoint of skin as horizon reassures and is reassured in bias. Thus, insofar as the skin, the race of the "other" differs from my own, a racially bias-induced horizon hides the "other" from me and renders the "other" invisible. Lonergan formulates the notion of bias with precision, distinguishing it from a commonsense notion of simple preference or inclination of temperament. Bias, he explains, is the more or less conscious and deliberate choice, in light of what we perceive as a potential threat to our well-being, to exclude further information or data from consideration in our understanding, judgment, discernment, decision, and action.[42]

Transposed as a racialized horizon, the four principal forms of bias—dramatic, individual, group, and common sense—account for racism as psychic, affective, and intellectual *scotosis* or blindness.[43] The denial of affect (e.g., fear or disappointment or joy) and suppression of unwanted insights of self-knowledge in everyday life result in *dramatic bias*, but members of the privileged racial group are permitted to project personal inadequacies onto members of non-privileged racial groups. The privileged members not only damage themselves by resisting the invitation to self-transcendence; by interrupting human intersubjective spontaneity they inflict incalculable harm on "others."

Individual bias stems from conscious distortions in personal human development in intelligence and in affective and experiential orientation. In a cultural and social matrix bounded by a racialized horizon, those belonging to the racially privileged group all too easily and frequently overlook or refuse opportunities to encounter those who are "different" from them. In yielding to individual bias, these women and men not only stunt their personal affective and cognitive development, but their distorted experience becomes the foundation for aberrant understanding of others, impairs social relations, and affects cultural representation.[44] While individual bias potentially is operative in any cultural and social matrix, the distortions that deform the patterns of the social order cannot be attributed to individual bias alone. *Group bias* finds decisive, even violent, expression in ethnocentrism. Within a racially bias-induced horizon, members of the privileged group are conditioned to withdraw from unnecessary experiential contact with "other" non-privileged members of society, thereby depriving themselves of the possibilities of human and humane relationships. With its penchant for "the quick-fix" and the short-term solution, the *general bias of common sense* colludes with group bias to disregard innovative and good ideas that might come from nonprivileged groups. General bias regulates social arrangements to the immediate well-being of the dominant racial group and thereby despoils the common good.

When the texture of civilization, the fabric of culture provides a scaffold for the bias-induced horizon of a group, racism holds potent currency. Race functions as a "metalanguage in its discursive representation and construction of social relations"; race is "'the ultimate trope of difference'—artificially and arbitrarily contrived to produce and maintain relations of power and subordination."[45] A White, racially bias-induced horizon defines, censors, controls, and segregates different, other, non-White bodies. Ordinarily, these bodies are "invisible" in the processes of historical, cultural, and social creativity and representation, but should these non-White bodies step "out of place," they are subordinated literally to surveillance and inspection, discrimination and assessment and containment. Turning a phrase coined by Martinique-born psychiatrist, philosopher, and activist Franz Fanon, Paul Gilroy writes:

> Epidermalized thinking violates the human body in its symmetrical, intersubjective, social humanity, in its species being, in its fragile relationship to other fragile bodies and in its connection to the redemptive potential inherent in its own wholesome or perhaps its suffering corporeality, our being towards death.[46]

Intentional and unintentional structures of White, racially bias-induced horizons replicate and reinforce customary patterns and practices of racial stratification even as racial self-identification grows more fluid, more unpredictable.[47] Yet, even the most creative[48] and most public[49] contestation of these structures, patterns, and practices may deny affirmation, verification, and admiration to "blackness" and, thus, reinforce "the privilege of violence."[50]

SEEING BODY

Perhaps no thinker exceeds Fanon's ability to signify racial alienation, to explicate its crushing objectification,[51] to diagnose its ruthless hurt, to evoke its shock and shame. The following passage illustrates his skill at slicing open "instances of skewed racial visibility,"[52] that peculiar way in which within a racialized horizon Black bodies are made absent and present:

> My body was given back to me sprawled out, distorted, recolored, clad in mourning in that white winter day. The Negro is an animal, the Negro is bad, the Negro is mean, the Negro is ugly; look, a [Negro], it's cold, the [Negro] is shivering . . . shivering because he is cold, the little boy is trembling because he is afraid of the [Negro]. . . . I sit down at the fire and I become aware of my uniform. I had not seen it. It is indeed ugly. I stop there, for who can tell me what beauty is?[53]

Fanon employs phenomenology to unpack the disturbing aesthetics of scaling racialized bodies, the Manichaean ethics of the social construction of race: contrast, objectification, distortion, the dichotomy of absence-presence, anxiety, evasion, race/skin as costume, self-wounding. His question leads us into a philosophic minefield strewn with conceptual models and practices spawned by modernity's arrogance, and hemmed in by the disturbing aesthetics of race.

In theorizing Black invisibility, philosopher Lewis Gordon comments: "The body is our perspective in the world. This perspective has at least three dimensions—the dimension of seeing, the dimension of being seen, and the dimension of being conscious of being seen by others."[54] In the world that Fanon interprets, Black embodied consciousness picks over a familiar query: "How does it feel to be a problem?"[55] In a White, racially bias-induced horizon, blackness is aberration and defilement, a source of dread and intimidation; thus, the Black body must be hidden, concealed, spatially segregated. "How does it feel to be a problem?" In this bias-induced horizon, Black embodied consciousness is labeled dense, thick; only a twilight of "agent intellect" shines in and through this darkness.[56]

In this White, racially bias-induced horizon, the relation of presence to absence leads to skewed regulative logic. Rules of presence, being, and identity apply to bodies not as *human* right, but as racial privilege: hence, "black presence is absence and white presence is presence." Two applications of this flawed logic: First, although absent, the Black body takes on a "peculiar" and "perverted" form of presence that renders the individual Black human person anonymous.[57] In a White, racially bias-induced horizon, the Black body, overdetermined, is every, all, any Black; metonymically, the Black *is* crime, wanton sexuality, evil, and sin. Second, in such a bias-induced horizon, the Black body, when isolated, may be enticed to deny "other" Black bodies. The "only" Black body in a room among White bodies may be lulled into social comfort, and liberated from the "burden of blackness" to assume a false whiteness—until another Black body enters the room.[58] A calculus of pleasure and fear drive the dialectic of evasion: "Maintain[ing] the illusion of seeing-without-seeing,"[59] while maintaining the illusion and self-loathing pleasure of being-seen.[60]

James Baldwin captures the "existential violation of human personality that is the inexorable consequence of the hegemon[y]"[61] of racially bias-induced horizon: "Negroes . . . are taught really to despise themselves from the moment their eyes open on the world."[62] To resist pretense, self-deception, and complicity, to *be* human is to grasp reality not as given and promoted in bias, but in critical questioning of one's own thoughtless initiatives, in admitting to consciousness the tension between limitation and transcendence, in revising choices and values, and in habitually incorporating what is estimable in daily living.[63]

The passage with which the section began concludes with this breathtaking question: *"Who can tell me what beauty is?"* The question, asked within a White, racially bias-induced horizon, challenges any so-called objective or neutral discussion of aesthetics and ethics. This disquieting passage incriminates practices and speech regarding bodies, race, gender, and power. Any response to Fanon's question ought to begin by acknowledging that any appeal to the empirical or visual in the effort to understand human being is never innocent, never ahistorical, and never divorced from power. As the adage would have it, "Beauty is in the eye of the beholder"; but the eye must be tutored to see, coached to attribute meaning to line and curve.

Elaine Scarry distinguishes four key features of beauty: beauty is sacred, unprecedented, salvific, and intelligible.[64] The beautiful evokes awe and reverence, responses commanded by the encounter with the divine, the wholly Other; beauty is singular, even as it prompts mimesis and creativity. Beauty nourishes and restores interiority and incites a longing for what is true. But, within a White, racially bias-induced horizon, such a depiction of beauty erases blackness; the Black body *cannot* be beautiful. In this bias-induced horizon, the Black body is repulsive, hideous; it encodes the demonic, the disposable, the lost, and the vacant. Like the mythical Caliban, Black being "remains too heavily mired in nature for its uplifting powers of reason and civilization"—and beauty.[65]

"Who can tell me what beauty is?" To reply, "Black is beautiful!" disturbs the hegemony of a White, racially bias-induced horizon, shakes the foundations of its unethical deployment of aesthetics and power. To declare, "Black is beautiful!" states a disregarded theological truth, nourishes and restores bruised interiority, prompts memory, encourages discovery and recovery, stimulates creativity, acknowledges and reverences the wholly Other. To assert, *"Beauty is black"* exorcises the "ontological curse"[66] that consigns the Black body to the execrable, and claims ontological space: space to *be*, space to realize one's humanity authentically.[67] *Nigra sum et formosa!*[68]

"Who can tell me what beauty is?" Any reply to Fanon's question requires a response that, while transcending race, gender, sexuality, class, and culture, neither dismisses nor absolutizes the problematic ontologizing potential of these dimensions of concrete human existence. Beauty is consonant with human performance, with habit or virtue, with authentic ethics: Beauty is the living up to and living out the love and summons of creation in all our particularity and specificity as God's human creatures, made in God's own image and likeness.

BEING BLACK

In a negrophobic society, Black ontological integrity suffers compromise. On the one hand, massive, negative, transgenerational assault on Black bodies has ontological implications. In such a society, *blackness* mutates as negation, non-being, nothingness; blackness insinuates an "other" so radically different that her and his very humanity is discredited. Then, Black identity no longer offers a proper subject of sublation, of authentic human self-transcendence, but a bitter bondage to be escaped. Blackness becomes a narrative of marginality and a marginal narrative. On the other hand, to center "suffering and resistance and White racism [as] ontologically constitutive of black life, faith, and theology," ethicist Victor Anderson asserts, jeopardizes the intrinsic meaningfulness of that life, faith, and theology. Anderson rightly questions the *limitation* of Black experience to Black resistance and Black suffering, with its truncation of the (Black) human subject.[69] He takes aim at blackness as essentialized identity, with its "unresolved binary dialectics of slavery and freedom, Negro and citizen, insider and outsider, Black and White, struggle and survival" and denial of transcendence or fruitful mediation.[70]

This critique also uncovers the epistemic function of race (blackness) as a "concept constructed by metaphor and metonymy."[71] At stake is whether concepts result from understanding or understanding from concepts. As a mode of human knowing, conceptualism fails utterly in grasping the relation of the universal to the particular, of *human* to *this* (*Black*) *human*. With the intrusion of White racial bias, sensible data (i.e., Black *human* performance) is dismissed and *insight* (into universal common humanity) is suppressed.[72] What is *seen* are preconceived patterns or stereotypes of Black body, life, and being—promiscuous, loud, illiterate, diseased. Insofar as a Black woman accepts and chooses to act out and out of such negation and contents herself with such denigrated living, she "is swallowed up by [her] alienated existence."[73] She has learned to submit, to stop asking questions.[74] White women and men, who applaud or mock this performance, *see* only an object—although an object structured by White racial bias for White racial pleasure.

Postmodernism offers strategies through which Black women may disrupt Black humiliation as well as White racist pleasure, and exorcise the ontological overdetermination of the Black body.[75] In displacing metanarratives and affirming situated knowledge, contesting *a priori* foundations and recognizing plurality of discourse, disrupting fixed identities and asserting the fluidity of social locations or positionalities, postmodernity may support Black women's upending of biased notions of blackness. However, postmodernism is not uncomplicated. Essayist and cultural critic bell hooks offers this trenchant critique of postmodernism:

> It is sadly ironic that the contemporary discourse which talks the most about heterogeneity, the decentered subject, declaring breakthroughs that allow recognition of Otherness, still directs its critical voice primarily to a specialized

audience that shares a common language rooted in the very master narratives it claims to challenge.[76]

Similarly, cultural critic Stuart Hall questions postmodernism's insistence on collapsing "the real." In an interview, Hall observed: "Three-quarters of the human race have not yet entered the era of what we are pleased to call 'the real.'" And, further: "Postmodernism attempts to close off the past by saying that history is finished, therefore you needn't go back to it. There is only the present, and all you can do is be with it, immersed in it."[77] Philosophers Cornel West and Emmanuel Eze concur with Hall's critique of postmodernism's easy relativism, vague commitment to history, and sense of the present as serial and fragmented.[78]

Yet certain deployments of postmodern theory may incite Black women (and men) to courage and shore up resistance to subordination. First, postmodernism is patient of the notion of race as ideology and insists that the concept of race lacks all scientific and intrinsic merit. Second, because postmodern approaches resist the limitations of binary (black–white) racial formations, they call for a reframing of the racial problematic. Doing so not only exposes the toxic in biased social arrangements, it requires both reimagining and reimaging and constructing those arrangements differently. Third, as bell hooks has pointed out, postmodern critiques of essentialism allow for the decentering of racism and its effects. By attending, for example, to the impact of class mobility in "alter[ing] collective black experience . . . multiple black identities, varied black experience" may be affirmed.[79] According to hooks, such a critique "challenges imperialist paradigms of black identity which represent blackness one-dimensionally in ways that reinforce and sustain white supremacy. . . . Abandoning essentialist notions would be a serious challenge to racism."[80] At the same time, in the effort to embrace the integrity of Black multi-dimensional identity, no uncritical, simplistic, inclusionary practices may be indulged.

Fourth, postmodern approaches also invite analyses from perspectives drawn from differentiated standpoints, including those of gender, sexuality, class, culture, and interculturality. Given the legacy of forced and voluntary migrations (in the United States and, for example, in Brazil, South Africa, possibly Australia), critical attention to cultural diversity and the particularities of lived conditions may constitute rich possibilities for human solidarity in understanding, in insurgent discourse, and in action for justice on behalf of all those who suffer oppression.[81]

The Black struggle for authenticity is coincident with the human struggle to *be* human and reveals *Black-human-being* as a particular incarnation of universal finite human being.[82] Authentic incarnations of Black identity (neither imitative nor emulative) emerge in response to "the law of genuineness" in human development. As suggested above, living by this law requires the repudiation of a racially bias-induced horizon, the rejection of all pretense and self-deception. Thus, living by this law means that the Black human subject takes herself, her humanity, seriously and respectfully: she engages in critical questioning of her own initiatives, acknowledges the tension between potential and actualization, responds to new spontaneities with new habits and patterns, revises choices and values, and seeks a new way of being in the world. Moreover, her struggle acknowledges and affirms all "others" in their subjectivity and engages with them in a praxis of compassionate solidarity that intends the concrete realization of a world of goodness and beauty, truth and justice in which Being is at home.

BLACK BODY THEOLOGY

Theologians and ethicists of African descent explicitly address the position and condition of the Black body in Christian theological anthropology.[83] Not surprisingly, Black women thinkers—writers, literary and cultural critics, historians, ethicists, theologians, philosophers, and scientists—have spearheaded this effort; after all, Black women's bodies have suffered under racial and gender bias in the extreme.[84] Their critical analyses of the human condition and its incarnation in the Black human condition, particularly the experiences of Black female embodiment, imply new categories for theological anthropology.

These categories include blackness, being, body, incarnation, beauty; power and oppression; sin and grace; suffering and compassionate solidarity; history, memory, and freedom. Such a list cannot be exhaustive, nor can all of these categories be treated here. The next six chapters interrelate several of these, pausing over some with more concentrated attention, foregoing elaboration of others. Here I undertake to interpret the "opaque symbol of blackness" and the "opacity of black experience,"[85] to uncover the light of divine revelation in that experience, to honor the beauty and courage and dignity of Black being—to make this visible in Black women's enfleshing of freedom.

CHAPTER 2

Enfleshing Freedom

God created humankind in his [sic] image,
in the image of God he [sic] created them;
male and female he [sic] created them.[1]

Oh Freedom! Oh, Freedom! Oh Freedom, I love thee!
And before I'll be a slave, I'll be buried in my grave
and go home to my Lord and be free![2]

But if God does not enslave what is free,
who is he that sets his own power above God's?[3]

No Christian teaching has been more desecrated by slavery than the doctrine of the human person or theological anthropology. Theological anthropology seeks to understand the meaning and purpose of human existence within the context of divine revelation. The starting point for theological reflection is the Old Testament account of the creation (and fall) of the first human creatures (Gen 1–3). This intensely realistic narrative furnishes Christianity with a cosmic account of all creation, a history regarding the first individual human beings, and a paradigm of human nature. Three convictions central to theological anthropology derive from Christian interpretation of this narrative: (i) that human beings, created in the image and likeness of God (*imago Dei*), have a distinct capacity for communion with God; (ii) that human beings have a unique place in the cosmos God created; and (iii) that human beings are made for communion with other living beings.

Slavery deformed these convictions. It aimed to deface the *imago Dei* in Black human beings, constrain Black human potential, and debase Black *being-in-communion* with creation. Slavery sought to displace God and, thus, it blasphemed. Its sacrilegious extension in White racist supremacy has had fatal consequences for *all* people—Black people, especially, and Black women, in particular. As historian Deborah Gray White perceptively observes, Black women stand "at the crossroads of two of the most well-developed ideologies in America, that regarding women and that regarding [race]."[4] These two ideologies raise substantive issues for Christian reflection on being human.

To speak about theological anthropology in terms of Black female embodiment may seem overly concrete and, therefore, to jeopardize a thoroughgoing notion of personhood as immanent self-transcendence in human existence and action. The ambivalence with which Christian thought focuses on the *sex of the matter* may be traced to a persistent *somatophobia* or a fear of flesh.[5] This fear stems from a conceptual axis, which compounds *both* distortions of Neoplatonism, with its tendency to idealism, suspicion of ambiguity, and discomfort with matter *and* Pauline and Augustinian warnings about the flesh and its pleasures.[6]

However, speaking about theological anthropology in these terms interrogates the enfleshing of created spirit through the struggle to achieve and exercise freedom in history and society. To speak in this way is to recognize that the Black body is a site of divine revelation and, thus a "basic human sacrament."[7] The body is the medium through which the person as *essential freedom* achieves and realizes selfhood through communion with other embodied selves.

This chapter accords hermeneutical privilege to *Black-embodied-being-in-the-world*, specifically that of Black women. Our encounter with Black women's bodies has been shaped, although not determined, by the historical matrix of slavery. That matrix or slavocracy was complex, contradictory, and produced ideological, technical, and religious discourses in its defense. The matrix of slavery was interactive, if reductive, structured by differentials in status and power, and organized for profit. To understand this matrix from the perspective of enslaved Black women, we turn to slave narratives as a guide.[8] These written records or transcriptions of oral interviews conducted well after Emancipation do present difficulties for scholars, but they remain the best source for the history of the enslaved people as told from their perspective.[9] These narratives, James Scott writes, accord ample space to slavery's "practices and rituals of denigration, insult, and assault on the body."[10] Careful attention uncovers what Scott names "hidden transcripts . . . those offstage speeches, gestures, and practices that confirm, contradict, or inflect" the practices and ideology of domination.[11] These narratives contest the "public transcripts"[12] of slaveholders, offer a critical, even didactic, commentary in which the enslaved people put forward a counter-discourse, which recognizes and defends their humanity, subjectivity, and agency.

The narratives of emancipated women account for roughly 12 percent of collected memoirs. These reports provide a glimpse of the cruel intersection of sex, sexuality, and race. By attending to Black women's understanding and interpretation, judgment and evaluation of their condition, we may understand more adequately their determination to reclaim their bodies and those of their loved ones, and appreciate their love and struggle for freedom. Moreover, we may be better prepared to challenge contemporary stereotypes about Black women—especially those intellectual, moral, and aesthetic labels that objectify, exploit, and deface God's image in Black womanhood.

Slavery in the United States had an ambiguous beginning; it was the spawn of indentured servitude. Masters defaulted on time-bound contracts and attempted to extend their legal hold on men and women, White and Black; not surprisingly, indentured servants replied with rebellion. Historians are not in agreement, but around 1640, slavery came to be associated almost exclusively and exhaustively with Black bodies, and Black bodies became the sign of the slave.

Despite access to substantial critical scholarship, the contemporary view of slavery in the United States remains shaped by the film version of Margaret Mitchell's *Gone with the Wind*. Scholarship teaches us that, in practice, slavery was neither romantic, nor uniform; it was diverse in form and quite opportunistic—anyone, even free Blacks, who could own slaves, did.[13] Plantations and farms required overseers, drivers, field hands, cooks, housekeepers, nursemaids, weavers, domestic servants, blacksmiths, carpenters, craftspersons, and artisans. Slaveholders made money on their human property by leasing slaves to other Whites who owned small farms or businesses in urban centers. Further, slavery was never exclusively southern. At some time or another, prior to Emancipation, men and women who lived in New York, Massachusetts, Rhode Island, Ohio, and Wisconsin engaged in slaveholding or slave trading or slave ship building and provisioning. According to historian Marcus Rediker, in 1700 the first recorded merchant slaving voyage in America left Rhode Island, which became the hub of the American slave trade.[14] Slavery was a business, a way of life, but most basically, it was a lie. Nearly everyone touched by slavery learned to live with it by learning to live with that lie—a monstrous moral fiction that insulted God and human nature.

Early on, slavery in the Atlantic world was deeply entangled with Christianity.[15] David Brion Davis points out that "in 1488 Pope Innocent VIII accepted a gift of one hundred Moors from Ferdinand of Spain, and distributed them among the cardinals and nobility."[16] Albert Raboteau records the comments of fifteenth-century Portuguese chronicler Gomes Eannes de Azurara, who claimed conversion to Christianity as justification for enslavement. The Africans would benefit, de Azurara wrote, "for though their bodies were now brought into some subjection, that was a small matter in comparison of their souls, which would now possess true freedom for evermore."[17]

Christian baptism underwent mutation. English planters in the American colonies feared that under British law Christian baptism would require the manumission of enslaved people and refused missionary attempts at catechizing.[18] During much of the seventeenth century, Anglican clergy preached either freedom from slavery as a byproduct of baptism or the admonition that one Christian should not enslave another. But Christian conversion, historian Raboteau observes, "ran directly counter to the economic interest of the Christian slave owner."[19] Colonial legislation resolved the issue. In 1664, Maryland's then-legislative body drew up and affirmed "an Act obliging Negroes to serve *durante vita* . . . for the prevention of the dammage Masters of such Slaves must susteyne by such slaves pretending to be Christened."[20]

Colonial legislation attempted to resolve the issue, but it did not quell the debate. White planters and pastors continued to clash over the meaning and value of Christianity for enslaved Africans. Some planters insisted that the time needed for religious instruction of the enslaved people interfered with work routines in the fields or other employments. Other planters maintained that the Africans were too savage for Christianity; their "opaque bodies" could not have been made in the *image* of God; rather, they were created inferior, natural slaves.[21] Still other planters drew on biblical passages and alleged theological arguments as well as appeals to a notion of cultural superiority to support their views.[22] Further, Protestant and Catholic clergy, as well as members of Catholic religious orders of men and women, owned human property.[23] Yet there were pastors and missionaries who wanted sincerely to instruct and baptize the enslaved people and who defended their share in humanity.

However, the majority of slaveholders viewed the mere suggestion of common human nature to insinuate the possibility that, as Christians, the enslaved people might make a claim of fellowship upon them. Baptism represented a threat to the power differential, which sustained the positions of master and slave.[24] Missionaries tried to "build a wall" between the notions of equality as taught by Christianity and the master–slave hierarchy.[25] In this construction, the Bible was manipulated to legitimate and sanctify the bondage of Black bodies. To this end, many ministers advocated a Christianity that sought to unmake the God-image in Africans, to render them servile, docile, and acquiescent to a divine ordination of their subjugation to Whites. How sly to detach the New Testament admonition from its *Sitz im Leben* and to inscribe it onto the circumstances of the plantation: "Slaves, obey your earthly masters in everything, not only while being watched and in order to please them, but wholeheartedly, fearing the Lord. Whatever your task, put yourselves into it, as done for the Lord and not for your masters, since you know that from the Lord you will receive the inheritance as your reward; you serve the Lord Christ" (Col 3:22–24).[26]

While the duration and intensity of chattel slavery invest this dread experience with peculiar *gravitas*, slavery neither exhausts nor circumscribes African American experience. Yet we cannot ignore the trajectory that the institution of slavery set in motion. *All* of us—White or Red or Brown or Yellow or Black, *Mayflower* descendant or immigrant, rich or poor, southerner or westerner, northerner or easterner—live today in its wake. To paraphrase literary theorist Saidiya Hartman: We the people, the *entire people* of the nation, live in the time of slavery; we live presently in the future generated by chattel slavery. This is the "ongoing crisis of [our American] citizenship."[27] Rethinking theological anthropology from the experience of Black women holds substantial social and cultural, moral and ethical, psychological and intellectual consequences for us *all*. Such work promises not only recovery of repressed religious and social histories, but release of those "dangerous memories, memories that challenge . . . that flare up and unleash new dangerous insights for the present,"[28] memories that protest our forgetfulness of the human "other," our forgetfulness of what enfleshing freedom means.

This chapter, then, continues by interrogating slavery's objectification of Black women and its literal impact on their bodies. Next it considers some of the ways in which Black women understood themselves as made for freedom and reclaimed their bodies and those of their loved ones. The third section treats some characteristic features of personhood in womanist perspective.[29] This meditation on theological anthropology concludes with another story of creation, as told in Toni Morrison's great novel *Beloved*.[30]

OBJECTIFYING THE BODY

The reduction and objectification of Black women began with the seizure and binding of the body, the violent severing of the captive from community and personhood; imprisonment in dark and dank places below ground; packing and confinement in the slave ship; the psychic disorientation and trauma of the Middle Passage—suspended out of time and in "no place." More lessons in chattel slavery's idiom of power followed: handling and seasoning, bartering and selling. With chilling precision, literary critic Hortense Spillers writes of the idolatrous and terrifying unmaking of human being:

> The captive body is reduced to a thing, to *being* for the captor; in this distance *from* a subject position the captured sexualities provide a physical and biological expression of "otherness"; as a category of "otherness" the captive body translates into a potential for pornotroping and embodies sheer physical powerlessness that slides into a more general "powerlessness," resonating through various centers of human and social meaning.[31]

Thus, slavery rendered Black women's bodies objects of property, of production, of reproduction, of sexual violence.

Black Women's Bodies as Objects of Property

Chattel slavery was not just a kind of feudal system peculiar to southern plantation agriculture. Chattel slavery was structured, sanctioned, interpreted, and enforced by the laws of the United States. In a study of statutes and judicial decisions regarding slavery, William Goodell defined the slave as "one who is in the power of a master *to whom he [sic] belongs. The master may sell him [sic], dispose of his [sic] person*, his *[sic]* industry and his *[sic]* labor."[32] Further, slaves were "deemed, sold, taken, reputed and adjudged in law to be *chattels personal*, in the hands of their owners and possessors, and their executors, administrators, and assigns, *to all intents, constructions, and purposes whatsoever*."[33] These statutes and laws sought to "erase every feature of social and human differentiation," to reify African personality.[34]

In 1827, George Stroud published a compilation of state laws that pertained to the institution of slavery, *A Sketch of the Laws Relating to Slavery in the Several States of the United States of America*.[35] This summary illustrates the civil condition of slavery as social death: Slaves served the term of their lives, could not testify against any White person either in civil or criminal cases, could not be party to civil suits, were forbidden access to education and moral or religious instruction, were required to submit not only to the master but also to all White persons, had no recourse to self-defense against violence perpetrated by the master or other Whites. At the same time, enslaved men and women were not exempt from the penal codes of slave-holding states and could be "considered member[s] of civil society," chiefly for purposes of prosecution and trial upon criminal accusation. In these instances, enslaved women and men were to be treated differently from free White persons. This differential was, Goodell notes, "injurious to the slave and inconsistent with the rights of humanity."[36] These laws granted Whites near absolute power over Black bodies.

Enslaved Africans were "reputed and considered real estate; [and] shall, as such, be subject to be mortgaged, according to the rules prescribed by law, and they shall be seized and sold as real estate."[37] The laws of the United States permitted White men and women on whim or need to sell Black men, women, and children. Slave traders, slave pens, and the slave market served this function. Katie Rowe recalled how enslaved women (and men) were handled and inspected like cattle: "De white men come up and look in de slave's mouth jess lak he was a mule or a hoss."[38] Free born in the United States, kidnapped as an adult, held in a slave pen only blocks from the nation's capital, then sold into slavery, Solomon Northup confirmed this practice. Customers calling at the slave pen, he wrote, "would feel of our hands and arms and bodies, turn us about, ask us what we could do, make us open our mouths and show our teeth, precisely as a jockey examines a horse."[39] Buyers would tell slaves to roll up the legs of their pants or lift up their skirts in order to inspect for blisters, signs of disease, or scars from whippings that might indicate evidence of a slave's disposition toward rebellion.

Delia Garlic was one hundred years of age when asked about her suffering under slavery. Emphatically, she stated: "Slavery days was hell. . . . Babies was snatched from deir mother's breast and sold to speculators. Chillens was separated from sisters and brothers and never saw each other again. 'Course dey cry. You think they not cry when dey was sold like cattle?"[40] Mary Ferguson remembered the evening of her childhood when the plantation owner, Mr. Shorter, sold her away from her mother and father.

> Strange mens tuk me an' put me in de buggy an' driv' off wid me, me hollerin' at de top o' my voice an' callin my ma. Us passed de very fiel' whar Paw an' all my folks wuz wukkin' an' I calt out as loud as I could an' as long as I could see

'em. But [Ma] never heard me. An she couldn' see me, 'cause dey had me pushed down out o' sight on de flo' o' de buggy. I ain't never seed nor heard tell o' my ma an' paw, an' brothers, an' sisters, from dat day to dis.[41]

Whether Mary Ferguson was sold to settle a gambling debt or the payment of an overdue account, as Charles Johnson and Patricia Smith declare, a "master in need of money was a dangerous master to have."[42]

Black Women's Bodies as Objects of Production

For the sake of the profits of the plantation, enslaved women and men were reduced to instruments of labor. Black women and men worked from sunup to sundown, usually, six days each week, and sometimes for several hours on Sundays. On some plantations, field hands were supervised by Black drivers who, in turn, were under the direction of White overseers. On other estates, they worked the fields under the immediate supervision of White overseers, the plantation owner or a member of the owner's family.

When it came to heavy labor in the field, there was little gender differentiation. Harriet Robinson pointed out that "women broke in mules, throwed 'em down, and roped 'em. They'd do it better'n [some] men."[43] Writing of his travels in the Carolinas, Frederick Law Olmsted described "some thirty men and women" repairing a road:

The women were in majority, and were engaged at exactly the same labor as the men; driving the carts, loading them with dirt, and dumping them upon the road; cutting down trees, and drawing wood by hand, to lay across the miry places; hoeing and shoveling.[44]

Ferebe Rogers boasted that she "was a field hand," who had "come up twixt de plow handles. I weren't de fastest one with a hoe, but I didn't turn my back on nobody plowin'."[45] Fannie Moore recalled that her mother "work in the field all day and piece and quilt all night."[46] Sarah Gruder said, "I never knowed what it was to rest. I just work all de time from mornin' till late at night. I had to do everythin' dey was to do on de outside. Work in de field, chop wood, hoe corn, till sometimes I feel like my back surely break. I done everythin' 'cept split rails."[47]

Some emancipated people insisted that childhood under slavery had not been unpleasant, but there is ample evidence that children, male and female, worked in the fields at an early age. Katie Rowe told her interviewer:

These old eyes seen powerful lot of tribulations in my time, and when I shets 'em now I can see lots of li'l chillun toting hoes bigger dan dey is, and dey pore little black hands and legs bleeding whar dey was scratched by de brambledy weeds, and whar dey got whuppings 'cause dey didn't git done all de work de overseer set out for 'em.[48]

Madison Jefferson recalled that on George Neale's plantation, pregnant women were employed in heavy plantation labor within hours of child-birth.[49] And many freed people told of nursing mothers who carried their infants with them into the field, laying them under what shade they could find. Charles Ball explained that when the other slaves went to get water, the women "would give suck to their children, requesting someone to bring them water in the gourds, which they were careful to carry to the field with them."[50]

Black Women's Bodies as Objects of Reproduction

Black women labored in the making of the material of the plantation both through production and reproduction. Slavery thrived on the body of the Black woman, which became the site in which the planter's economic desire intersected with Black female sex, sexuality, and reproductive capability. Planters wanted to make sure that enslaved women would be prolific. This was more than cost cutting. When importation of Africans became illegal, the increase of plantation capital, its laborers or slaves, depended upon internal breeding. Biology bound the Black woman to capital accumulation.

Martha Jackson spoke of her aunt who was rarely beaten "'case she was er breeder woman en brought in chillum ev'ry twelve mont's jes lak a cow bringin' in a calf."[51] Given the custom of *partus sequitur ventrem*—the child follows the condition of the mother—slavery devoured the fruit of Black women's wombs. Fannie Moore maintained that "de 'breed woman always bring more money den de rest, even de men. When dey put her on de block dey put all her chillen around her to show folks how fast she can have chillen. When she sold, her family never see her again."[52]

Pressure to reproduce the human capital and labor for slavocracy meant that enslaved women frequently suffered miscarriages and that their children died young. The English actress Frances (Fanny) Kemble, whose husband Pierce Butler Mease owned a large plantation in the sea islands off the Georgia coast, recorded such losses in her diary:

Mile . . . had had fifteen children and two miscarriages; nine of her children had died; Die who had had sixteen children, fourteen of whom were dead [and] she had had four miscarriages: one caused with falling down with a very heavy burden on her head, and one from having her arms strained up to be lashed; Venus had had eleven children, five of whom died, and two miscarriages.[53]

Womanist ethicist Katie Cannon has denounced the exploitation and expropriation of Black women's procreative power and their reduction to "brood-sows."[54] Childbearing is a biological dimension of female nature, but enslaved Black women bore life only to surrender their children to the maw of the plantation,[55] to an order and culture of death. Black women were forced to sacrifice love, to yield their children to commercial objectification—the very "capitalization of life."[56] Black children were severed from their sacred humanity and deprived of person-identity, their bodies and spirits endangered and traumatized.

Black Women's Bodies as Objects of Sexual Violence

Many planters associated fertility with promiscuity and licentious behavior. Once they did so, enslaved women's bodies, sex, sexuality, and morality became topics of public conversation: "that which was private and personal became public and familiar."[57] Slavery made Black women's bodies sexually vulnerable and available.

White male slaveholders, their adolescent sons, slave traders, as well as patterrollers or slave-catchers, used Black women's bodies with impunity.[58] In 1841, representatives of the British and Foreign Anti-Slavery Society conducted an interview with Madison Jefferson, a fugitive, who had been held in slavery in Virginia. Jefferson confirmed reports that enslaved women who refused to submit to the sexual advances of White slaveholders or overseers were repeatedly whipped "to subdue their virtuous repugnance." Should this tactic fail, frequently the woman would be sold.[59] One former enslaved woman gave this description of the brutal beating her mother received for resisting the sexual advances of an overseer. The man

use to tie mother up in the barn wid a rope aroun' her arms up over her head, while she stood on a block. Soon as dey got her tied, dis block was moved an' her feet dangled, you know, couldn't tech de flo'. Dis ole man, now would start beatin' her nekked 'til the blood run down her back to her heels.[60]

And Mary Peters gave this account of her mother's ordeal.

> My mother's mistress had three boys—one twenty-one, one nineteen, and one seventeen. One day, Old Mistress had gone away to spend the day. Mother always worked in the house [and] while she was alone, the boys came in and threw her down on the floor and tied her down so she couldn't struggle, and one after the other used her as long as they wanted, for the whole afternoon.[61]

In a speech to an anti-slavery audience in Brooklyn, a man introduced as Lewis Clarke, who was fleeing Kentucky bondage, remarked that "a slave woman ain't allowed to respect herself, if she would."[62]

In his study of the antebellum slave market, historian Walter Johnson uncovers the link between money and pornographic fantasy. He traces the adjective "fancy" and its use to modify the word "girl," by referring to her appearance or manners or dress. But the sexual connotation of the word, Johnson points out, "describes a desire: 'he fancies.'"[63] White men purchased and acted out their "fantasies" in and on the body of a "fancy," a light-skinned adolescent (some as young as thirteen) or adult Black woman kept for purposes of sex or prostitution. "The essence of the transaction," Johnson remarks, "was the open competition of an auction—a contest between white men played out on the body of an enslaved woman."[64] Some of these "near-white victims" were auctioned off at "arbitrarily high prices," ranging from $2,000 to $5000.[65] This monetary value reflected the dominance of the White (Western) male's gaze, its capacity for sexual objectification, exploitation, and exoticization.

Whether dissuaded by the conventions of Victorian society or the indifference of arrogance, few White people associated with the slave trade spoke publicly about sex between slaveholding White men and the Black women whom they had enslaved. Mary Boykin Chestnut, whose husband was a slaveholder, confided the following to her diary:

> Like the patriarchs of old, our men live all in one house with their wives and their concubines; and the mulattoes [sic] one sees in every family partly resemble the white children. Any lady is ready to tell you who is the father of all the mulatto children in everybody's household but her own. Those she seems to think, drop from the clouds.[66]

This conspiracy of silence defended and supported White racist supremacy in the form of patriarchy. Hazel Carby has argued persuasively that the sexual ideology of the period spawned and validated "the dichotomy between repressed and overt representations of sexuality and . . . two definitions of motherhood: the glorified and the breeder."[67] The bodies of enslaved Black women were perceived with contempt and treated with contemptuous value. On the one hand, Black women were considered lascivious whores; yet their putative depravity made them good "breeders." On the other hand, those same characteristics were deployed to reinforce degrading stereotypes not only about the personal and collective morality of Black women but also about *their very being.* Sexual purity was the definitive quality of true, that is, White, womanhood; smeared as promiscuous, Black women were deemed incapable of chastity and, consequently, of true womanhood. Black women were not only dehumanized but also degendered and desexed.

Despite their silent collusion, the wives of slaveholders were angry and jealous at their husbands' sexual liaisons with Black women. Texas slaveholder Judge Maddox brought home a young, pretty mulatto girl whom he insisted was to help his wife with fine needlework. Mrs. Maddox was suspicious and would not believe him. She took out her fury on the girl, "cropp[ing her long black straight] hair to the skull."[68] Solomon Northup wrote movingly of the enslaved Patsey, who had "the unfortunate lot to be the slave of a licentious master and a jealous mistress."[69]

> [Patsey] shrank before the lustful eye of the one, and was in danger even of her life at the hands of the other, and between the two she was indeed accursed. Nothing delighted the mistress so much as to see her suffer. Patsey walked under a cloud. If she uttered a word in opposition to her master's will the lash was resorted to at once, to bring her into subjection; if she was not watchful when about her cabin, or when walking in the yard, a billet of wood, or a broken bottle perhaps, hurled from her mistress' hand, would smite her unexpectedly in the face. The enslaved victim of lust and hate, Patsey had no comfort of her life.[70]

Harriet Jacobs was never physically beaten or tortured, but she was psychologically and sexually harassed relentlessly. To elude the sexual advances of Dr. James Norcom, a prominent slaveholding physician (named Flint in her narrative), Jacobs hid in a cramped attic for nearly seven years. Eventually, she made her way north and wrote her story under the pseudonym of Linda Brent. Her narrative discloses the vulnerability of enslaved women's bodies. "Slavery is terrible for men," she asserted, "but it is far more terrible for women. Superadded to the burden common to all *they* have wrongs, and sufferings, and mortification's peculiarly their own."[71]

The libidinous economics of the plantation quite literally reduced Black women to body parts: parts that White men used for pleasure; parts that White men manipulated and sold for economic profit; parts that literally were coerced to nurse the heirs of White racist supremacy. Slavery laid the foundation for the bodily humiliations to which Black women have been exposed for centuries and against which Elizabeth Fox-Genovese maintains, "their men could not always protect them and from which their white 'sisters' continued to benefit. So long as [the master's] power persisted, the slave woman lived always on the edge of an abyss."[72]

THE SUBJECT OF FREEDOM

Slavery exacted a perverse intellectual, spiritual, psychological, and physical toll. By law and by custom, the enslaved people were deprived of the most rudimentary skills for meaningful, transformative education. Still, they risked beatings, mutilation, and disfigurement in order to learn to read and write. Verbally and physically intimidated, the enslaved people were coerced into a pantomime of survival—smiling when they wanted to weep, laughing when they boiled with anger, feigning ignorance when they brimmed with intelligence. Moreover, on many plantations, the enslaved people were forbidden to worship, to invoke the Spirit. Again, they risked abuse, assault, even martyrdom to withdraw to secret spaces in woods and gullies to commune with the Author and Source of Freedom. In seeking freedom and resisting domination, in striving for literacy, in cultivating counter-discourses and practices, in fixing themselves in the realm of the Spirit, the enslaved people nurtured a sense of themselves as subjects of freedom.

To some enslaved people, freedom was an awesome, perhaps unattainable condition. One man admitted, "I've heard [the slaves] pray for freedom. I thought it was foolishness, then, but the old-time folks always felt they was to be free. It must have been something [re]'vealed unto 'em."[73] Theologian Jamie Phelps asserts "black religious thoughts of freedom," irrupted from slavery's wound.[74] Inasmuch as the body is the medium through which human spirit incarnates and exercises freedom in time and space, enslaved women *fleshed* out the words of the Spiritual:

Oh Freedom! Oh, Freedom! Oh Freedom, I love thee!
And before I'll be a slave, I'll be buried in my grave
And go home to my Lord and be free!

Literally and metaphorically, Black women reclaimed their bodies and the bodies of their loved ones from bondage. They defied the degradation of chattel slavery and refused to internalize a devaluation of self. Literally and metaphorically, Black women chose struggle and death for the sake of life, for the cause of freedom in this life and the next.

Freeing the Mind

Slaveholders behaved toward their human property in contradictory ways, but never more so than with regard to the intellectual capacities of the enslaved people. Almost from the beginning, slaveholders and nearly all Whites assumed that these opaque bodies were incapable of the human functions of intellectual reflection and critique, culture-making, and cultural refinement. However, slaveholders believed that animal instinct and nature could be trained and directed by the master's will. At the same time, undermining their own arguments, slaveholders not only taught slaves complex operations and tasks but also benefited from their mental ingenuity and creativity.

The notion of freedom that slaveholders attempted to blot out from the minds of the enslaved people was the focus of their yearning, dreaming, and silent scheming. Northup contested the lie that slaves were happy with their lot and preferred it to freedom. If only, he said, White and Black free people would come to know

[the] *heart* of the poor slave—learn his [sic] secret thoughts—thoughts he [sic] dare not utter in the hearing of the white man. Converse with him [sic] in trustful confidence, of "life, liberty, and the pursuit of happiness," they will find that ninety-nine out of every hundred are intelligent enough to understand their situation, and to cherish in their bosoms the love of freedom, as passionately as [whites] themselves.[75]

In 1842, Lydia Marie Child published her transcription of a lecture given by a Lewis Clarke, perhaps the same fugitive mentioned above. Asked if he wanted freedom, Clarke offered this reply:

If some Yankee had come along and said, "Do you want to be free?" What do you suppose I'd have told him? Why, I'd tell him, to be sure, that I didn't want to be free; that I was very well off as I was. If a woman slave had a husband and children, and somebody asked her if she would like her freedom? Would she tell them yes? If she did, she'd be down the river to Louisiana, in no time; and her husband and children never know what become of her. Of course, the slaves don't tell folks what's passing in their minds about freedom; for they know what will come of it.[76]

Enslaved Black women and men disclosed a subtle, practical, and imaginative grasp of freedom, the conditions for its possibility, and its potential. They recognized that freedom was more than mere opposition to slavery. The abolition of slavery was a necessary condition if they were to enjoy autonomy, the exercise of choice, free will, and action. But escape, abolition, and emancipation, in and of themselves, were insufficient. Freedom required resources, chief among these the skills of reading and writing, tools critical for formal education. By depriving slaves of these rudimentary skills, slaveholders sought to curtail freedom's most basic domain—the mind.

Some slaves stole education. Through eavesdropping on young White school-age children reading aloud or reciting their lessons, some enslaved people gained a basic hold on literacy. In rare instances, the wife of a planter might teach the youngest enslaved children the alphabet. But other enslaved women and men slipped out at night to meet in gullies to study by dim torchlight, and some led free schools for the liberation of others.

The enslaved people guarded their literacy carefully since to display such attainments in front of Whites could result in beatings, disfigurement, or sale. Stressing the severity of reprisals by some slaveholders at attempts by slaves to read and write, one man compared White reaction to literacy to White reaction to murder. "For God's sake," he exclaimed, "don't let a slave be cotch with pencil and paper. That was a major crime. You might as well had killed your marster or missus."[77] Tom Hawkins said that when one slaveholding physician discovered that his carriage driver had learned to read and write, he had the driver's thumbs cut off. And Mary Ella Grandberry recalled:

De white folks didn't allow us to even look at a book. Dey would scold and sometimes whip us iffen dey caught us with our head in a book. Dat is one thing I surely did want to do and dat was to learn to read and write. Dey'd whip us iffen we was caught talkin' about de free states, too.[78]

Slavocracy attempted not only to prevent enslaved people from thinking about freedom but also to check their freedom of thinking. Actively and surreptitiously pursuing literacy, reflecting upon and imagining freedom, signaled fundamental protests against slavery's insistence that the slaveholder was human and the slave was not. If talk of freedom made some slaves uneasy, not even the most unlettered women and men could be convinced that they ought to be objects of property, bought and sold at whim; that they ought to relinquish a claim on humanity. This was true, even when necessity or self-preservation forced them to dissemble and to deny a love of liberty.

Freeing the Spirit

The enslaved people understood God as the Author and Source of freedom. They apprehended freedom as God's intention for them. Slaveholders tried to impose themselves between the slave and God and, to this end, manipulated Christian teaching. Anderson Edwards was ordered to preach to other slaves only what his master dictated:

> Marster made me preach to the other [slaves] that the Good Book say that if [slaves] obey their master, they would go to Heaven. I knew there was something better for them, but I daresn't tell them so, 'lest I done it on the sly. That I did lots. I told the [slaves]—but not so Marster could hear it—that if they keep praying, the Lord would hear their prayers and set them free.[79]

Womanist ethicist Joan Martin concludes that Christianity was a "*religious* battle-ground between slavocracy's attempt to define and control slaves, and the enslaved African/African Americans' self-definition of their own humanity and religious viewpoint."[80]

Delia Garlic remembered her mother's last words as she was sold away: "Be good and trust in de Lord." Garlic commented on that exhortation: "Trustin' was de only hope of de poor black critters in dem days. Us just prayed for strength to endure it to the end. We didn't 'spect nothin' but to stay in bondage till we died."[81] When Emancipation came, the enslaved people gave God the glory. Mary Reynolds mused:

> I sets and 'members the times in the world. I 'members now clear as yesterday things I forgot for a long time. I 'members 'bout the days of slavery and I don't 'lieve they ever gwine have slaves no more on this earth. I think Gawd done took that burden offen his black chillun and I'm aimin' to praise him for it to his face.[82]

If some slaveholders permitted enslaved people to worship without supervision, others punished them for praying and singing. Ellen Butler's master was among the latter and did not allow the enslaved people to attend church. The people prayed anyway: "Dey hab big holes out de fiel's dey git down in and pray. Dey done dat way 'cause de white folks didn' want 'em to pray. Dey uster pray for freedom."[83] Alice Sewell reported that many enslaved people in her area

> used to slip off in de woods on Sunday evening way down in de swamps to sing and pray to our own liking. We prayed for dis day of freedom. We come four and five miles to pray together to God dat if we don't live to see it, to please let our chillen live to see a better day and be free, so dat dey can give honest and fair service to de Lord and all mankind everywhere.[84]

What remarkable testament to the transcendent dimension of being human: enslaved people envisioned and prayed for a different future for their descendants. The unselfishness of such prayer astonishes and witnesses to hope, for the vast majority of Africans enslaved in the United States died in the bondage in which they were forced to live.

Redeeming the Body

Manumitted and fugitive slaves, abolitionists, and their associates frequently appealed in sympathetic newspapers and journals for financial assistance in redeeming enslaved people. Mrs. E. B. Wells publicized such a request in one of Frederick Douglass's newspapers. Mrs. Wells managed to emancipate herself and her mother, and was then raising money to redeem her only sister.[85] An enslaved woman with the surname of Jackson purchased her freedom by taking in washing and ironing in the evenings, after she had completed tasks assigned by the slaveholder. Once she gained her freedom, Jackson set about ransoming her sixteen-year-old daughter, who had been put up for sale. She could only offer four hundred dollars to counter a bid of nine hundred. This mother went so far as to offer her own body in mortgage-collateral to free her child, and the monetary assistance of sympathetic abolitionists helped her to redeem the girl.[86]

But some enslaved women, driven by the physical, psychological, and moral cruelties of slavery, considered death preferable. One woman described a scene of psychological and emotional turmoil, when slaveholder Jennings hired out her mother, Fannie. By the laws of slavery's universe, Fannie's offspring were not her own; she was ordered to leave her five children behind. But Fannie resolved to take her infant; Jennings objected. The woman recalled that her mother

> took the baby by its feet, a foot in each hand, and with the baby's head swinging downward, she vowed to smash its brains out before she'd leave it. Tears were streaming down her face. It was seldom that ma cried and everyone knew that she meant every word. Ma took her baby with her.[87]

Fannie's act appalls, but we cannot grasp the horror and suffering of her daily life, the terror and abuse her body may have absorbed, the dread that may have pressed her to threaten to murder her own child. For many enslaved women resistance to the death was the only real choice.

Some enslaved women physically fought with slaveholders or overseers. Fannie Moore may well have swelled with pride when she told her interviewer how her mother fought to protect her and her siblings.

> De old overseer he hate my mammy, 'cause she fight him for beatin' her chillen. Why she get more whippin' for dat dan anythin' else. She have twelve chillen. My mammy trouble in her heart about de way they treated. Every night she pray for de Lord to get her and her chillen out of de place.[88]

Thinking back to her youth, one former enslaved woman said that the "one doctrine of mother's teaching was that I should never let anyone abuse me. She would say, 'Fight, and if you can't fight kick; if you can't kick, then bite!'"[89]

Sometimes only running away could redeem the body. South Carolina abolitionist Sarah Grimke wrote with more than a little admiration of the persistent defiance of an enslaved woman whose attempts at escape earned her abuse:

> A handsome mulatto woman, about 18 or 20 years or age, whose independent spirit could not brook the degradation of slavery, was in the habit of running away; for this offence she had been repeatedly sent by her master and mistress to be whipped by the keeper of the Charleston workhouse. This had been done with such inhuman severity, as to lacerate her back in a most shocking manner; a finger could not be laid between cuts. But the love of liberty was too strong to be annihilated by torture; and as a last resort, she was whipped at several different times, and kept a close prisoner. A heavy iron collar, with three prongs projecting from it, was placed around her neck, and a strong and sound front tooth was extracted, to serve as a mark to describe her, in case of escape.[90]

Grimke contrasts this cruelty with the mistress's daily Scripture reading, direction of her family's worship, and solicitude for the poor. Such disparity in behavior stems from objectifying enslaved people, thus segregating them beyond the reach of human feeling. At the same time, historian Kerri Greenidge tells us that for all Sarah Grimke's

> sensitivity and compassion, [her] belief in the sinfulness of slavery rarely included a recognition of the lives of the enslaved. The sin was hers to bear and eventually atone for, but Black people themselves were mere objects within the constellation of sin that surrounded her.[91]

Enslaved women resisted bondage with as much intelligence and strength as they could muster. They drew on a variety of strategies in their struggle for the freedom of their communities, their families, their bodies, their very selves. The "everyday proximity to mistresses," Fox-Genovese writes, "permitted slave women special kinds of psychological resistance."[92] Sometimes, that resistance took the form of disrespect, slow performance of duties, impudence, backtalk or sass. Many enslaved Black women used sass to guard, regain, and secure self-esteem; to defend themselves from physical and sexual assault and to gain psychological distance in order to speak truth.

Incarnate spirit refuses to be bound. Escaping to freedom, purchasing one's freedom or that of a loved one, fighting for freedom, offering up one's own body for the life and freedom of another, dying for freedom, all were acts of redemption that aimed to restore Black bodily and psychic integrity. Living within a "system built on violence, disenfranchisement, and white supremacy" surely pushed some enslaved people to respond like contemporary victims of sexual and physical abuse—"with self-hatred, anger, and identification with the aggressor."[93] Still, many other enslaved women stocked their arsenal with wit, cunning, verbal warfare, daring, physical strength, and so-called uppity behavior. Freedom was the prize; they put their hands to its plow, and held on.

THE FREEDOM OF THE SUBJECT

Emancipation literally set Black women and men on new paths to life, to practical and existential liberation. Katie Rowe declared that she never forgot the moment and the significance of Emancipation. "It was de fourth day of June in 1865," she recalled, "I begins to live."[94] "Right off," Felix Haywood said, "the colored folks started on the move. They seemed to want to get closer to freedom, so they'd know what it wuz—like it wuz a place or city."[95] Robert Falls noticed that after freedom, "the roads was full of folks walking and walking along. Didn't know where they was going. Just going to see about something else, somewhere else."[96]

Not surprisingly, slaveholders would have been reluctant to announce the federal decree of Emancipation, but Buck Adams refused to do so. William Matthews said that the enslaved people on Adams's plantation learned of their freedom well after the war ended. "De freedom man come to [the] place an' read a paper what de Pres'dent had writ what said we was now free." Then, he continued, "dey make us git right off de place—jes' like you take an old horse an' turn it loose. . . . No money, no nothin'—jes' turn' loose without nothin.'" Matthews recalled that Adams's wife Mary told the people, "'Ten years from today, I'll have you all back 'gain.' Dat ten years been over a mighty long time, an' she ain' got us back yet."[97]

Meeting the practical demands of freedom could be daunting. Many freed people were drawn into sharecropping schemes that trapped them in debt peonage. But some people remained on plantations working for wages. Laura Cornish's parents, along with several other newly freed families, took up such an offer, remaining on the property for about two years, then acquiring land of their own.[98]

Charlie Davenport admitted that he "was right smart bit by de freedom bug for awhile. . . . But to tell the hones' trufe, mos' o' us didn' fin ourse'fs no better off. Freedom meant us could leave were us'd been born an' bred, but it meant too, dat us had to scratch for us own se'fs."[99] Patsy Mitchner considered slavery "a bad thing"; but without access to basic resources or employment or education, freedom also "was bad."[100] Ezra Adams echoed her sentiments: "freedom ain't nothin', 'less you got somethin' to live on and a place to call home. Dis livin' on liberty is lak . . . livin' on love. It just don't work."[101] Frustration, rejection, and fear needled some freed women and men to find freedom wanting. Thinking of the food, shelter, and clothing with which he had been provided, James Hayes said that he had been contented in slavery.[102] But Belle Caruthers aligned herself with Patrick Henry: "Some colored people say slavery was better, because they had no responsibility . . . but I'm like the man that said, 'Give me freedom or give me death.'"[103]

Freedom from enslavement was freedom for God. The enslaved people told of being beaten and whipped when they attempted to pray and to worship.

Relying on the biblical witness to God's engagement in history and their own critical reflection, the people fashioned for themselves "an inner world, a scale of values and fixed points of vantage from which to judge the world around them and themselves."[104] Slavocracy may have forced the enslaved people into a radical otherness, but their experience of God's acceptance and affirmation allowed them to perceive their authentic value and significance.

Freedom from enslavement was freedom for being human. Only by analogy could the words of the Emancipation Proclamation change the order of creation, but it did remove God's Black human creatures from the plantation ledger. Statutory freedom amended the social and political status of the enslaved people. It was now possible for enslaved women and men to begin to exercise essential freedom. The freed people now had the possibility of taking up the responsibility of human living without restraint. In sum, that responsibility was this: to be a human subject, to be a person; to be woman or man, who consciously and intentionally in word and in deed assumes and affirms her or his own personhood and humanity. This affirmation means that a human subject cannot consent to any treatment or condition that is intended to usurp the transcendental end or purpose for which human beings are divinely created. To do otherwise is to enter into a decreating negativity, which spoils the spirit and surrenders to *ressentiment*.

Freedom from enslavement was freedom for loving without restraint. Slavery dismissed marital love. Moses Grandy told of standing in a street and seeing a slave coffle pass by with his wife in chains. Desperate to find out why his wife was being sold, Grandy pleaded with the trader Mr. Rogerson. The slaveholder, Rogerson replied, wanted money. Then the trader drew his pistol, threatened Grandy, but allowed him to stand at a distance and talk with his wife. Grandy said, "My heart was so full that I could say very little. . . . I have never seen or heard from her from that day to this. I loved her as I love my life."[105]

Slavery devalued motherhood and mother-love. Enslaved mothers raged against the impediment their enslaved bodies imparted to their children. Audacious women, they fought overseers who beat their children, risked their bodies for the safety of daughters and sons, purchased their freedom, even mortgaged themselves for their lives. Toni Morrison depicts their condition with mournful outrage in her description of Baby Suggs, holy:

> In all of Baby's life men and women were moved around like checkers. Anybody Baby Suggs knew, let alone loved, who hadn't run off or been hanged, got rented

out, loaned out, bought up, brought back, stored up, mortgaged, won, stolen, or seized. What she called the nastiness of life was the shock received upon learning that nobody stopped playing checkers just because the pieces included your children.[106]

Freedom from enslavement was freedom for community and solidarity, for being human together. In the midst of oppression, the enslaved people forged community. Mothers relied on communal support and advice in sickness and in child rearing. Fugitive and emancipated slaves remembered and recounted not only their own experiences and suffering but also those of other enslaved women and men as well. Mary Prince spoke of her own commitment to their memory simply and eloquently: "In telling my own sorrows," she declared, "I cannot pass by those of my fellow-slaves—for when I think of my own griefs, I remember theirs."[107]

The possibilities and difficulties of community were manifold in the aftermath of emancipation. In this new situation, Black people who had been free for generations reached out to formerly enslaved Black people; White women and men of good will risked life and livelihood to offer assistance. Yet, even though the newly freed people faced sustained racial animosity and political and economic oppression, they came together in support of one another. Segregated by race and isolated by the "lingering badge of slavery," the freed people established churches, schools, hospitals, trades, and businesses—in some cases, whole towns.[108] They were present to one another in struggle, in shared understanding, and commitment; moreover, they were present to the future for the future's good.

For the enslaved woman in particular, freedom was linked inextricably and literally to the body. The White slaveholder had used "every part" of her body: "to him she was a fragmented commodity whose feelings and choices were rarely considered: her head and heart were separated from her back and her hands and divided from her womb and vagina."[109] In order to restore her body whole, the freed woman had to love her body; and to love her body meant dealing with the wounds of slavery. The Black woman's body had been treated as a slate upon which others had written. In the words of historian Stephanie Camp, the enslaved woman's body "served as a 'bio-text' on which slaveholders had inscribed their authority and, indeed, their very mastery."[110]

Slavery interfered radically with the enslaved peoples' psychological growth, development, and maturation. The enslaved body was not only a "vehicle of feelings of terror, humiliation, and pain," but also a source of vulnerability and uncertainty, anxiety and misery.[111] Black women had to cope with body memories of vulnerability, psychic and physical pain, to come to grips with internalized repercussions of violence and abuse. The damage done to the enslaved people's capacity for human flourishing can never be ignored; and not every Black woman or man survived in "lofty transcendence over racist adversity."[112]

Finally, the Black woman's body was subjugated to sexual and porno-graphic violence, even as her body was "a site of pleasure and resistance."[113] To love her body, the freed Black woman had to learn to claim and enjoy her body—her dress, her self-presentation, her comportment.[114] Loving her body, the freed woman took control of her sex and sexuality, denying neither sexual pleasure nor desire, resisting both coercion and intimidation. Loving her body, the freed woman fleshed out autonomy, self-determination, deci-sion, and action.

Freedom from enslavement was freedom for healing, for effecting psychic healing and growth. Freedom from enslavement was freedom for proper self-love, for loving black flesh, for loving black bodies. Slavery sought to desecrate and deform black bodies; freedom resacralized those bodies.

ENFLESHING FREEDOM—RETURN TO THE CLEARING

This chapter began by referring to the impact of the creation story in Genesis on Christian anthropology. The setting of that story is a garden lush with trees bearing food, life, and knowledge. The garden is for the human creatures, who are endowed with intelligence and free will, understanding and feeling. These human creatures are ordered to God and, in God, to one another and to all creation. Their decision and choice wounded their ordination to divine love, tore the web of relationships in which they have been created, and despoiled the garden. Christians read this account through the prism of creation-fall-redemption. Another choice in another garden and submission to another tree restores the whole.

Morrison's *Beloved* recapitulates the fate of the Black woman's body in slavocracy's (dis)order and desecration of creation as told through slavocracy. Some bodies were considered to have been made in the image and likeness of God; some bodies were not. The free decision and choice of some human beings tore the webs of relationships, destroying and desecrating some bodies.

Rituals of healing and (re)sanctification of black flesh sustain a redemption begun through emancipation.

Baby Suggs, holy, was an "unchurched preacher, one who visited pulpits and opened her great heart to those who could use it."[115] Her "sole qualification" for claiming responsibility and authority for this leadership was "the vision of grace that came with the recognition that her heart was already beating. Despite a lifetime of enslavement by Whites, her humanity was intact, her life holy, and wholly hers."[116]

Baby Suggs, holy, enfleshes a praxis of love that grounds and sustains authentic achievement of freedom. Every Saturday afternoon, she leads emancipated and fugitive slaves—Black children, men, and women to the "Clearing—a wide-open place cut deep in the woods nobody knew for what at the end of a path." She sits on a "huge flat-sided rock," gathers herself, and silently prays; the people wait and watch from among the trees.[117] Then, when ready, she puts down her staff and calls them forth into dignity, into life. The children are invited to laugh and, thus, to give joy to the mothers from whom they had been separated by slavocracy's pernicious economics. Children, who had picked cotton and plowed fields and cut sugar cane, children who had never been children, are called to be children. The men are summoned to dance, and thus to display their elegance and beauty to their wives and children. Men, from whom slavocracy had usurped the right to love and defend and protect their wives and children, are called to be husbands and lovers and fathers. The women are enjoined to cry for the living and the dead, and thus to disclose the depth and breadth of their sorrow and love. Women, who had built walls around their hearts to keep them from exploding at the pain of loss and the anguish of terror, are released to love. Baby Suggs preached the radical significance and power of love:

> Here in this place, we flesh; flesh that weeps, laughs; flesh that dances on bare feet in the grass. Love it. Love it hard. Yonder they do not love your flesh. They despise it. They don't love [it]. *You* got to love it, *you*! This is flesh I'm talking about here. Flesh that needs to be loved.[118]

Baby Suggs commands the people to love their flesh, to love their bodies, to love themselves and one another into wholeness. She names each bruised and tortured body part—eyes, hands, mouth, shoulders, arms, necks, feet, liver, lungs, womb, reproductive organs. Her naming re-members broken bodies, heals torn flesh. Baby Suggs prophesies deliverance of body and soul, flesh and blood, heart and mind through passionate love. Above all, she pleads, "love your heart. For this is the prize."[119] To reject one's heart is to reject all possibility and power of life, of freedom, of being human.

This sermon, Judylyn Ryan comments, "provides a detailed analysis of the self-hatred oppression generates"[120] and counters slavery's caricatures. Embedded in an incantatory healing ritual with "an epistemological core,"[121] the sermon announces a *new* commandment: Love of self, love of black flesh. Love your black flesh and through that love (re)member and caress all the torn and wounded parts of your black body. Baby Suggs urges the people to love all those body parts that slaveholders and Whites despise, parts they would pluck out, flay, chop off, break, lynch, and destroy. In calling the people to love their black flesh, she conjures children, men, and women *anew*—makes them *whole* again. This love of black flesh upends the equation of whiteness with goodness and blackness with evil, whiteness with domination and blackness with subservience, whiteness with beauty and blackness with ugliness. As Anita Durkin remarks, "Baby Suggs's sermon attempts to redefine African American identity through the flesh, to transform the inscriptions inflicted by whites into a radical self-love of the African American body."[122]

The sermon is rooted in the command of self-love: love what you have been taught not to love, for only authentic self-love can sustain and nurture community. The ritualized dancing of Baby Suggs and the people constitutes a (re)patterning of reality that supports personal and communal transformation and a "(re)construction of cultural and spiritual kinship."[123] Interconnectedness and sharing of roles and responsibilities become crucial: "Women stopped crying and danced; men sat down and cried; children danced, women laughed, children cried until, exhausted and riven, all and each lay about the Clearing damp and gasping for breath."[124]

Baby Suggs calls forth the children, women, and men *as a people* to new identity-in-community, to love of their own and others' black flesh, black bodies, Black selves. Slavocracy, colonialism, and empire "require[d] that all relations be accidental";[125] thus, any relations and relationships between and among enslaved and free Black peoples were deemed expendable and insignificant. For as bell hooks declares, "a culture of domination demands self-negation. The more marginalized, the more intense the demand."[126]

In Baby Suggs's sermon, the heart resonates as a sacred place, a sanctuary for the protection of what no one can take away: the *whole self*. The heart is the seat of self-dispossession, of humanity, of freedom. For here "freedom and humanity [are] conjured from the vantage point of the flesh and not based on its abrogation."[127] Baby Suggs, holy, changes the sour wine of shame and the rotting bread of resentment into the pure wine of joy and the nourishing bread of love.

This liturgy of Spirit descending and renewing once despised, used, abused flesh counters slavocracy's sacrilegious de-creation of black flesh. From deep in the woods among the trees, Baby Suggs speaks into new life God's image in black flesh. She voices the principle of life, which is love, and calls the freed people to *new identity-in-community*, to the demands of proper love of Black self, black body, black flesh.

The hermeneutical privilege this chapter accords to enslaved Black women's bodies incriminates theological anthropology and imposes a praxis of solidarity in the concrete, in the here-and-now. Moreover, on a global scale, bodies—especially poor, dark, black, brown, despised bodies—are forced through the winepress[128] and consumed by a totalizing dynamics of domination. The memory of these dead invokes dangerous memories, which protest our forgetfulness of human others, our forgetfulness of what it means to enflesh freedom in our time and place. But there is one who does not forget—Jesus of Nazareth, who is the Christ of God. He does not forget poor, dark, and despised bodies. For these, for all, for us, he gave his body in fidelity to the *basileia theou*, the reign of God, which opposes the reign of sin. Jesus of Nazareth is the paradigm of enfleshing freedom, he *is* freedom enfleshed.

CHAPTER 3

Marking the Body of Jesus, the Body of Christ (Part I)

In the beginning was the Word, and the Word was with God,
and the Word was God....
And the Word became flesh and lived among us.[1]

See what wonder Jesus done
Jesus make de dumb speak
Jesus make the cripple walk
Jesus give the blind sight
See what wonder Jesus done.[2]

The Word of God assumed humanity that we might become [like] God.[3]

Focus on the body, on flesh, is no novelty in theological anthropology. Christian teaching long has struggled to understand and interpret, then to maintain the truth that the eternal Word, the *Logos*, became flesh, became the bodily, concrete, marked, historical being, Jesus of Nazareth; that Jesus died, rather than betray his mission, his love for God and for human beings; that that fidelity, integrity, and love were vindicated, and his crucified body was raised glorious from the dead. This teaching promotes the value and significance of the body, which is never to be disregarded or treated with contempt.

The previous chapter drew on history and memories of enslavement to show just how brutally and easily the value and significance of the body may be undermined. For bodies are marked, made individual, particular, different, and vivid through race, sex and gender, sexuality, and culture. The protean ambiguity of these marks transgresses physical and biological categories, destabilizes gender identities, and disrupts ethical and relational patterns (*who is my brother, who is my sister*). These marks delight as much as they unnerve; they impose limitation: some insinuate exclusion, others inclusion, for the body denotes a "boundary" that matters.[4] But, in a finite and sinful context, some unnerved concrete historical human beings manipulate this ambiguity to violate in multiple vicious ways the bodies of others. Such violence overlooks just how these bodily marks ground intelligence, discovery, beauty, and joy; enable apprehension and response to sensible experience; and shape culture, society, and religion. Such violence ignores the ways in which culture, society, and religion in turn shape our bodies. Even if verbal self-disclosure is unnecessary, just as often, the body's marks complexify through creolization, *mestizaje*, and hybridity; just as often, these marks render self-disclosure confusing and frustrating, invigorating and alchemizing.

In theology, the body is a contested site—ambiguous and sacred, wounded and creative, malleable and resistant—disclosing and mediating "more." Further, given the "fact of [Christian] faith that when God desires to manifest"[5] the divine presence, God does so in human flesh, the body can never be simply one element among others in theological reflection. Yet any formulation of theological anthropology that takes body and body marks seriously risks absolutizing or fetishizing what can be seen (race and sex), constructed (gender), represented (sexuality), expressed (culture), and regulated (social order). Moreover, such attention to concrete, specific, nonetheless accidental, characteristics also risks "fragmenting"[6] human being. But what makes such risk imperative is the location and condition of bodies in empire; what makes such risk obligatory is that the body of Jesus of Nazareth, the Word made flesh, was subjugated in empire.

Since antiquity empire has been a form of political governance and different historical periods have produced different imperial iterations. Perhaps our most enduring point of reference is the Roman Empire, with its laws, building programs, aesthetic concerns, bestowal of citizenship, and vast territorial holdings in Europe, North Africa, and Western Asia. The *pax Romana* was achieved and secured through the might of the Roman legions, fighting men said to be without equal in training, discipline, and combat ability. Empire building may have produced splendor, but it could be cruel. Tacitus, the historian of Roman antiquity, records these words of a Caledonian chieftain to his fellow Britons:

> You have sought in vain to escape [the Romans'] oppression by obedience and submissiveness. [They are] the plunderers of the world. . . . If the enemy is rich,

they are rapacious, if poor they lust for dominion. Not East, not West has sated them. . . . They rob, butcher, plunder, and call it "empire"; and where they make desolation, they call it "peace."[7]

Three major sections follow. In the first, empire forms a principal context for thinking about the marked, that is, raced, sexed, gendered, regulated, body of Jesus of Nazareth. Jesus preached the *basileia theou*, the reign of God, as an alternative to the *pax Romana*; to put it sharply, he contrasted the future of bodies in God with the future of bodies in empire. In every age, the disciples of Jesus must take up his critique of empire and through *basileia* practices incarnate an alternative. Empire continues to serve as context for the second section as we consider Jesus's prophetic praxis that includes a welcome table. The third section considers his gender performance and embodied spirituality.

JESUS AND EMPIRE

Jesus of Nazareth was human: his flesh "suffused with blood, built up with bones, interwoven with nerves, entwined with veins"—born of a woman.[8] The Gospels, testaments of faith, confirm Mary and Joseph as his parents: the Matthean narrative relates a story of a marriage not yet consummated, a young pregnant girl, a man reassured in a dream about the woman of his heart and the name of the unborn child—Jesus (Matt 1:9–22). Then, Herod, the Roman-appointed client-king of Judea, grows restive and murderous: in a dream Joseph is warned to take his family and flee forty miles (or 65 km) across the border into Egypt. His family is safe, but surely the sad news from Ramah reaches them—Roman soldiers have killed dozens, perhaps hundreds of little boys two years of age and younger. Two additional dreams prompt Joseph to take his family to Nazareth, far from Herod's son, Archelaus (2:1–22). "Joseph's accepting Mary and naming the child makes him Jesus' legal father," writes Amy-Jill Levine. "He not only cares for this new family, but also turns his life upside for them: he moves to Egypt, then relocates from Bethlehem of Judea to Nazareth of Galilee, on their behalf."[9]

Jesus of Nazareth lived and died in subjugation to the Roman Empire. His flesh, his body was and remains marked by race, gender, culture, and religion: he was a practicing Jew in a territory controlled by Roman political, military, and economic forces. Jesus was and remains marked by sex, gender, and sexuality: he was male and, although we cannot speak about his sexual orientation, tradition assumes his heterosexuality.

In his flesh, in his body, Jesus knew refugee status, occupation and colonization, social regulation and control. The Matthean account of the flight into Egypt (2:13–23) may well be what John Dominic Crossan calls a "symbol-story,"[10] serving more theological than historical purposes, thus recapitulating Israel's exodus and sojourn in the desert. Nevertheless, argues Richard Horsley, the story insinuates breakdowns in "the social relationships and political conditions that prevailed in Jewish Palestine under Roman and Herodian Rule.... The Roman and Herodian troops would have created refugees, often hundreds and thousands at once, virtually every time they took military action to maintain or reassert their domination in a given area."[11]

Roman military intimidation and brutality, coupled with Herodian economic exploitation and taxation, uprooted and displaced many people from their ancestral lands, drove them into debt, and forced them into wage labor as carpenters or day laborers or servants or petty merchants.[12] Ordinary fishermen also found their enterprise disrupted by the policies of Herod Antipas, who erected the city of Tiberias on the Sea of Galilee. Crossan defines Antipas's aim as "Romanization by urbanization for commercialization,"[13] a strict monopoly on fishing and the sea's harvest. Under Antipas's taxation policies, ordinary peasant-fisherman "could no longer cast their nets freely from shore, could no longer own a boat or beach a catch, and probably had to sell what they caught to Antipas' factories."[14]

The village of Nazareth, in which Jesus grew up, is located in Galilee, about four miles from the city of Sepphoris, once a thriving city until Herod Antipas built Tiberias. Galilee was a place of racial and cultural mixture,[15] a frontier region that buffered the "crossroad of empire."[16] Galilee was also a site of "persistent resistance and rebellion" against overweening Roman domination that determined and controlled the political and economic conditions of ordinary life.[17] Although open revolt was rare, as a conquered people the Galileans never surrendered "their commitment to the covenantal principles of their traditional way of life," and demonstrated on more than one occasion their willingness to die, rather than transgress Mosaic Law.[18] Of particular note is a revolt in 4 BCE carried out after the death of Herod the Great by the Galilean leader Judas, who sacked the treasury and armory at Sepphoris. In retaliation, the Romans burned the city and sold its inhabitants into slavery.[19]

Nazareth likely had a population of roughly three hundred to four hundred people, most of whom were peasants working their own land or tenant farmers working land belonging to others, along with a few artisans and crafts persons and, perhaps, merchants. The "basic social unit of the village was constituted by a household working the land, or on a fishing boat on the Sea of Galilee."[20] Archaeological evidence suggests that in villages like Nazareth family dwellings consisted of one or two cramped rooms, covered with a thatched roof. Often three or four such houses would be joined by a common wall and faced a common open-air courtyard, forming a compound where extended family groups might live. The common courtyard functioned as a shelter for domestic animals as well as a kitchen, with its "shared oven, cistern that held water, and millstone for grinding grain." The villages surrounding Sepphoris likely would have benefited from trade with the city, but this neither erases nor eliminates "the unequal power structure between the city as the base for Herod Antipas and the local elite, on the one hand, and the villages on the other."[21] Yet the majority of the peasant population would have had to set aside and save "at least one fifth of the crop for next year's seed," and there were taxes: "land taxes on the harvest, poll tax on house members, and in all likelihood also tithes to the temple."[22]

Nazareth would have had a small synagogue where men and women gathered to pray, to listen to the reading and interpretation of Torah, and to receive instruction. More than likely, male heads of households led synagogue services and settled the community's disputes; but scholars maintain that in such small rural villages, women would have been active in synagogue and public life. Elizabeth Johnson surmises that "Celebrations of the life cycle, such as circumcisions, marriage feasts, and funerals would also [have entailed] the participation of women according to local tradition."[23]

According to Christian tradition, Joseph, the father of Jesus, was a carpenter. The gospels use the Greek term *tekton* to describe his work. This word implies more than those tasks and skills we recognize today as carpentry. Joseph and, perhaps, Jesus may have worked as stonemasons or builders, but as historian Maurice Casey observes, we have no idea whether or not Joseph worked "outside Nazareth to run a profitable business" or had clients in Sepphoris.[24] So, like every other peasant family in the village, Joseph and Mary would have supplemented their livelihood with a small plot of land for growing basic foodstuff.[25]

Jesus lived and carried out his mission in the palpable tension between resistance to empire and desire for *basileia theou*, the reign of God. This desire carried with it certain religious and political convictions: that the Messiah would lead the destruction of the Roman Empire, that YHWH would rule as king, and that Israel would be vindicated, justice established, peace and prosperity restored.[26] Jesus inserted his body into the tension between resistance and desire. With acts of healing, with images, stories, and parables of "welcome and warning,"[27] Jesus advanced a prophetic praxis on behalf of the reign of God. He sought not only a prophetic renewal of Israel but also denunciation of oppressive Roman rule.[28]

A PROPHETIC PRAXIS AGAINST EMPIRE

Jesus lived among common people, subjects of empire whose bodies were forced through the winepress of empire building. The old people in the small rural villages of Galilee to which he traveled carried in their bodies memories of brutality, of the Roman army burning their homes, raping women, "enslaving the able-bodied, killing the infirm."[29] These women and men knew forced labor, privation, and loss. They were shrewd and wary peasants, who had lived

> long enough at subsistence level to know exactly where the line is drawn between poverty and destitution. [They knew] all about rule and power, about kingdom and empire, but they [knew] it in terms of tax and debt, malnutrition and sickness, agrarian oppression and demonic possession.[30]

Thus, at the center of Jesus's praxis were the bodies of common people, peasants, economic and political refugees, the poor and destitute. They were the subjects of his compassionate care: children, women, and men who were materially impoverished as well as those who were socially and religiously marginalized or were physically disabled (the blind, paralyzed, palsied, deaf), lepers; those who had lost land to indebtedness, who were displaced through military occupation or religious corruption; those who were possessed and broken in spirit from ostracism and persecution.[31] Jesus did not shun or despise these women and men; he put his body where they were. He handled, touched, and embraced their marked bodies.[32] Jesus befriended them, but as Marcella Althaus-Reid observes not "to preach and show his compassion in a detached old-fashioned teaching mode. . . . 'Sinners' and prostitutes are human beings like anyone else. Like anybody else they may at times need compassion for their troubles, and at other times just friends for an intimate encounter, conversation and laughter."[33]

Through exorcisms and healings, Jesus decisively changed the village body. Men and women, shunned and isolated, particularly through demon possession or leprosy, hemorrhage or blindness were restored to synagogue and family, kin and friends. Those lost to human conversation and interaction, physical and affective intimacy were found; those abandoned or hidden because of deformity were restored to family life. The substantive impact of these miracles could not be ignored. The covenantal community was changed and renewed with the presence and potential participation of bodies formerly absent, and experienced an inflow of hope and joy. At the same time, Horsley suggests, the community was obliged to share perhaps already meager food stores, shelter, clothing, and work; and, "to take up the slack in light of the disintegration of some family units."[34] In his teaching and preaching, Jesus called upon these ordinary people to build up their community life, "to reestablish just egalitarian and mutually supportive social-economic relations" in their dealings with one another and with others.[35] Thus, Horsley argues, Jesus enacted a "larger program of social healing" that addressed "illnesses brought on by Roman imperialism,"[36] a program that would heal human bodies and the body politic.

The Welcome Table

Jesus demanded of his hearers and disciples personal conversion and new body practices of solidarity. Chief among these practices was the inclusion of new and "other" bodies at table. Crossan observes that commensality or table fellowship reproduces the prevailing "map of economic discrimination, social hierarchy, and political differentiation."[37] Even as the table includes, it excludes. With the parable of the Great Banquet (Luke 14:21–24; Matt 22:9–10), Jesus challenges the social and religious conventions surrounding commensality.

> The host replaces the absent guests with anyone off the streets. But if one actually brought in *anyone off the street*, one could, in such a situation, have classes, sexes, and ranks all mixed up together. Anyone could be reclining next to anyone else, female next to male, free next to slave, socially high next to socially low, ritually pure next to ritually impure.[38]

Jesus lived out this parable audaciously. He ate and drank with sinners: tax collectors, who made the already hardscrabble life of peasants even more so; lepers, whose diseased bodies threatened the bodily boundaries of "others"; women, who were forced to sell their bodies for survival; women who were accused of giving their bodies away in adultery.[39] Jesus acted out just how unrestricted neighbor love must be, just how much "other" bodies matter. The open table embodied egalitarianism, disrupted the "pleasures of hierarchy"[40] and domination, and abolished the etiquette of empire. The open table embodied the desire for and the design of the reign of God. *All* are welcome. God sets the table for the "little ones," for those denied access to restorative moments of celebration, to the material benefits of culture and society.[41] Jesus invites all who would follow him to abandon loyalties of class and station, family and kin, culture and nation in order to form God's people anew and, thus, to contest empire.

GENDER PERFORMANCE AND EMBODIED SPIRITUALITY

On the one hand, saying that the flesh of Jesus of Nazareth is marked by sex and sexuality, gender expectations and gender performance adds nothing to what we know about him; on the other hand, saying this uncovers what conveniently, too often, has been covered over. Jesus of Nazareth had and has a human body; his was and is a male body, he had and has the genitals of a male human being.[42] To refuse to speak about his sex and gender far too often leaves us unable to speak well and compassionately about sex, about gender, about sexuality, and, especially, about the lives of lesbian, gay, bisexual, transgender, and queer women and men.

The notion of sexuality always implies much more than genital sexual acts. Ethicist James Nelson long ago reminded us that sex refers to biology, sexuality to "our self-understanding and way of being in the world as male and female."[43] Sexuality, then, includes our formation in and appropriation of gender roles with their designation as masculine or feminine. Sexuality, writes Nelson, is "who we are as body-selves who experience the emotional, cognitive, physical, and spiritual need for intimate communion, both creaturely and divine."[44] A healthy appropriation of sexuality, then, includes reverence for "other" bodies and our own, a refusal to insult the beauty and dignity of sexual pleasure through narcissistic and dominative sexual repression, and a grasp of authentic freedom through which we realize our "body's grace."[45] In view of these considerations, two issues regarding the sex and gender of Jesus call for attention—his gender performance and his embodied spirituality.

Gender Performance: Feminist New Testament scholar Sandra Schneiders contends that the maleness of Jesus reveals nothing about the sex of the Godhead and cannot be used to divinize or deify human maleness.[46] Through his preaching and practices, living and behavior, Jesus performed masculinity in ways that opposed patriarchal expressions of maleness through coercive power, control and exploitation of "other" bodies, exclusion, and violence. He confronted this system through lived example, intentionally choosing courage over conformity, moral conflict over acquiescence, and boldness over caution. With all his heart and soul, mind and body, Jesus resisted religious and social attempts to reduce God's *anawim* to nobodies. Jesus made his body, his flesh available to others: he nurtured men and women with word and touch, bread and wine and water and fish. He reached out in compassion to the infirm, and took the lowly and forgotten, children and women to his heart.

Through his oppositional appropriation of masculinity, Jesus countered many gendered cultural expectations. He overturned the patriarchal family structure, releasing family members from their denotation as property of the male head of household.[47] He stretched solidarity far beyond the bonds and ties of blood and marriage, insisting on love of enemies, of the poor, of the excluded, of the despised.[48] Jesus "inaugurated a reform of male–female relationships," choosing women as disciples and teaching them as he taught the men, siding with and defending women against "men who questioned, attacked, or belittled them." Jesus affirmed women's agency over against narrow and constricting roles set for them by culture, religion, and empire. Jesus's performance of masculinity was *kenotic*; he emptied himself of all that would subvert or stifle authentic human liberation. In these ways, his maleness stood as contradictory signification, undermining kyriarchy and the multiple forms of oppression derived from it.[49]

In *Jesus, An Historical Approximation*, theologian and exegete José Antonio Pagola surmises that Jesus's neighbors and those he met in small Galilean towns may have frowned at his unmarried state.[50] Why was Jesus willing to forego the joys of sex and marriage? Pagola contends that neither Jesus's renunciation of sexual love nor his lifestyle stemmed from rigorous or exaggerated asceticism. Jesus ate and drank with putative sinners, talked openly with prostitutes, and did not live in fear of violating ritual purity, attended weddings, celebrated meals with friends. Nor did Jesus reject women. Pagola reminds us that

> Jesus accepted women in his group without hesitation, and did not shy away from their friendship, and responded tenderly to the special affection of Mary Magdalene. . . . If Jesus did not live with a woman, it was not because he disapproved of sex or belittled family. It was because he could not marry anyone or anything that might distract him from his mission of service to the reign of God.[51]

Embodied Spirituality: A healthy appropriation of sexuality is crucial to generous, generative, and full living. A fully embodied spirituality calls for the integration of sexual energies and drives, rather than repression or even sublimation. Comfortable in his body, sexuality, and masculinity, Jesus lived out of a "creative interplay of both immanent and transcendent spiritual energies."[52] A reclaimed notion of eros offers one way of thinking about such interplay.

We have poisoned eros, Raymond Lawrence contends. First, we have substituted sex for eros, then appropriated "a vision of sex as a fearsome and destructive force in human life."[53] Audre Lorde echoes his assessment. In "Uses of the Erotic: The Erotic as Power," she maintains that we have confused eros with "plasticized sensation or with its opposite, the pornographic."[54] Lorde seeks to release eros from the confines of the bedroom and to reconnect it with "lifeforce" and "creative energy." Eros, she proposes, is "the first and most powerful guiding light toward any understanding . . . the nurturer or nursemaid of all our deepest knowledge."[55]

Eros as embodied spirituality suffuses and sustains depth or value-laden experiences and relationships that emerge whenever we "shar[e] deeply any pursuit [whether] physical, emotional, psychic, or intellectual with another person."[56] Eros enhances our capacity for joy and knowledge, honors and prompts our deepest yearnings for truth and life, and validates our refusal of docility and submission in the face of oppression.[57] Eros steadies us as we reach out to other bodies in reverence, passion, and compassion, resisting every temptation to use or assimilate the other and the Other for our own self-gratification, purpose, or plan. Eros empowers and affirms life.

We can say, then, that Jesus had and has an eros for others; he gave his body, his very self to and for others, to and for the Other. Jesus lived out, and lived out of a fully embodied spirituality, an eros. In spite of themselves, the suspicious, the timid, the broken-hearted were attracted to his energy and joy. In spite of themselves, the arrogant, the smug, the self-satisfied were drawn to his authority and knowledge. In spite of themselves, hesitant men and women felt intense hope at sharing his struggle for the reign of God. Children, women, and men were attracted to his eros, and found themselves lifted up, made whole and new, open to "others."[58]

Finally, Jesus encouraged his followers to pray:

> Father sanctify Your name in the daily living of Your people. Let Your reign come in the way You dream and desire. Give us each day our daily bread. Forgive us our sins, take us to Your heart; we promise to forgive everyone who has sinned against us, to hold them as close as You hold us. Father deliver us from the time of trial and from the clutches of the evil one. (after Luke 11:2–4)[59]

This prayer comes from the depth of Jewish longing for the "reign of God" and expresses Jesus's own interpretation of what the "reign of God" meant. Given the context of Roman imperialism and colonization, for first-century Jews, this prayer, writes Amy-Jill Levine, "was profound and political . . . [it] promotes justice, consoles with future hope, and recognizes that the world is not always how we would want it."[60] Moreover, the address to God as Father uncovers a sharp political edge. "The Caesars on the throne in Rome were called 'father'. . . . By speaking of the 'Father in Heaven,' Jesus insists that Rome is not the 'true' father."[61] This prayer affirms the "reign of God" and resists the reign of Caesar and his lackeys or client kings.[62] Moreover, this prayer emerges from within an eschatological horizon, but it focuses on the historical boundary, the here and now, the point of change where the old order may give way to the new.[63] It is political prayer; it calls for concrete human action, even as it intimates irruption of divine action. The reign of God *shall* come. God *shall* overcome and tear down the structures of domination and subjugation, the needs of all human persons *shall* be met (daily bread), all shall dwell without fear and shall live in harmony with God and one another.[64]

Jesus of Nazareth is the measure or standard for our exercise of erotic power and freedom in the service of the reign of God and against empire. He is the clearest example of what it means to identify with children and women and men who are poor, excluded, and despised; to take their side in the struggle for life—no matter the cost. His incarnation witnesses to a divine destiny seeded in our very flesh. Jesus signifies and teaches a new way of being human, of embodied spirituality. Through his body marked, made individual, particular, and vivid through race, gender, sexuality, religious practice, and culture, Jesus mediates the gracious gift given and the gracious giving gift. His incarnation, which makes the Infinite God present, disrupts every pleasure of hierarchy, economy, cultural domination, racial violence, gender oppression, and abuse of sexual others. Through his body, his flesh and blood, Jesus of Nazareth offers us a new and compelling way of being God's people even as we reside in another imperial order.

CHAPTER 4

Marking the Body of Jesus, the Body of Christ (Part II)

"Lord, when was it that we saw you hungry or thirsty
or a stranger or naked or sick or in prison and did not take care of you?"
Then he will answer them, "Truly I tell you, just as you did not
do it to one of the least of these [a member of my family],
you did not do it to me."[1]

I am a poor wayfaring stranger traveling
through this world of woe.[2]

The poor and migrants are the faces of the new crucified
victims, exposing the scandal of a globalized world
that needs to be humanized.[3]

"Today's imperial peace, *pax imperii,* like that of ancient Rome is a false pretense of peace, that really presides over a state of constant war." So contend Michael Hardt and Antonio Negri.[4] At the turn of the century, these two political philosophers critically interrogated the geo-political-economic interactions between and among nation-states. They concluded that a new and different ordering of these relations was emerging, a new sovereign order, "empire."[5] We human beings of the twenty-first century are active witnesses to and participants in an "irresistible and irreversible globalization of economic and cultural exchanges [from which] has emerged a global order, a new logic and structure of rule—a new form of sovereignty,"[6] "empire." Whereas territorial expansion, control and domination of peoples and boundaries characterized *ancien régimes* (i.e., colonialism and imperialism), empire or globalization or the new sovereign (dis)order is "decentered and deterritorialized," capable of managing "hybrid identities, flexible hierarchies, and plural exchanges through modulating networks of command."[7]

Given the condition of bodies in empire, theological anthropology can never cease speaking of bodies: consider the global recrudescence of anti-Semitism, the near permanency of racisms (anti-Black racism in particular), of misogyny, of xenophobic reactions to "non-White" or "nonnational" others, to "illegal" or undocumented *anti-bodies* within the body of empire. Consider bodies raped, maimed, slaughtered, and displaced in wars mounted by pretenders to antiquated conceptions of empire—for example, Russia's occupation of Crimea and unprovoked war on Ukraine or armed civil conflicts in Myanmar or clashes between government forces of the Democratic Republic of Congo (DRC) and M_{23} rebel groups.

Consider the piles of bodies done to death by unchecked disease, AIDS, Ebola, and mutating viruses; bodies ravaged by hunger and thirst; bodies surveilled and tracked; bodies forced into and lost in migration, bodies sold into wage slavery, bodies abused and trafficked and prostituted, bodies ridiculed and reduced by breaking labor. Remember the body broken and resurrected for us: in memory of his body, in memory of the victims of empire, in the service of life and love, theological anthropology must protest any imperial word (*anti-Logos*) that dismisses his body and seeks the de-creation of human bodies.

Three large sections compose this chapter: In the first, we attend to the way in which this new sovereign (dis)order continues to debase and manipulate our body marks of gender and race, sex and sexuality, to separate, intimidate, and drive away bodies through poverty and precarity. In the second section, we attend to lesbian, gay, and transgender bodies and point to the difference that embracing those bodies might make to the body of Christ. Finally, in order to be worthy of the name of Jesus, the name in which it gathers, the church cannot help but open its heart and embrace *all* those bodies that the new sovereign order abuses, negates, and crucifies.[8] Thus, the third section calls for a (re)marking of the flesh of his church.

THE BODY IN THE NEW SOVEREIGN (DIS)ORDER

The new sovereign (dis)order arrogantly presides over the bones of the bodies of conquered children, women, and men. The bodies of the Indigenous peoples were the first to be sacrificed, eliminated, and contained; then the body of the Earth was raped and mastered; finally, the bodies of Yellow, Brown, poor White, and Black children, women, and men were squeezed through the winepress of new empire-building.

Globalization, the dominative process of empire, now cannibalizes the bodies and spirits, minds and hearts and imaginations, belonging and citizenship, labor and creativity, sexuality and generativity of global "others." In sacrilegious antiliturgy, agents of empire hand over Red, Yellow, Brown, White, Black, and poor bodies to the consuming tyranny of neoliberal globalized capitalism, to the idolatry of the market.[9]

Race, Gender, and Migration

"Globalization," sociologist Howard Winant argues, "is a re-racialization of the world."[10] Re-racialization does not rely on crude practices of lynching and cross burning, derogatory name-calling and physical or sexual assault, although these practices have not ceased altogether within the United States.[11] On a global scale, re-racialization turns on a range of practices nearly invisible and detached from the perpetrators; it relies upon an uncanny ability to mimic and co-opt antiracist social constructionist arguments. On the one side, the racism of empire, what Hardt and Negri denote as "imperial racism," replaces biological difference (race) with "cultural signifiers," which take on the essentialism once held by race. So, for example, should students of one race score consistently lower than students of another race on the same aptitude tests, the failure of the one and the success of the other are not linked to racial (biological) superiority, but to cultural values.[12]

On the other side, imperial racism "scramble[s] the spatial division of 'three worlds' . . . so that we continually find the First World in the Third, the Third in the First, and the Second almost nowhere."[13] To borrow a phrase from Zygmunt Bauman, this global system results in "a new socio-cultural hierarchy, a world-wide scale"[14] that correlates with the body's racial and gender markers: "the darker your skin is, the less you earn; the shorter your life span, the poorer your health and nutrition, the less education you can get."[15] The darker your skin is, the more likely you are to be incarcerated, a refugee, an undocumented worker; the darker your skin is, the more likely you are to migrate for survival from one outpost of empire to another. The darker your skin is, the more likely you are to become infected with HIV/

AIDS or Ebola or tuberculosis; and, if you are a woman, the darker your skin is, the more likely you will bury your infant.

Race and gender function as co-constituents of empire.[16] Women in empire continue to undergo multiple, intersecting oppressions.[17] For instance, within the domestic sphere, *all* women are subjected to heteropatriarchy; within the "globalized imperial" public sphere, *all* women are subjected to the economy, to the polity, to sexual intimidation and assault, to body control.[18] Sociologist Patricia Hill Collins maintains that, "Intersectionality's emphasis on intersecting systems of power suggests that distinctive forms of oppression will each have its own power grid, a distinctive 'matrix' of intersecting power dynamics."[19] Further, she points out that the constituent elements of the matrix will differ within each nation-state and in comparison to other nation-states given their differing and complex histories. Thus, while sexual and physical violence against women, whether in the United States or Brazil, India or Mexico, takes place within distinctive matrices of hetero-patriarchal power, within each matrix male domination not only is tolerated, but, even subtly, encouraged. At the same time, "the possibility for resistance and protest exists within political domination."[20]

The bodies of women, especially Red, Brown, Yellow, poor White, and Black women, bear the brunt of the cultivation and commercialization of material desire. In sweatshops and export processing zones, whether in Mexico, Indonesia, China, or India, poor women endure abuse, low wages, and indignities of every sort, even risk their lives, in order to support their children and families, in order to survive.[21] Pei-Chia Len observes, "Globalization has simplified the gendered household burdens for more privileged women even as it complicates the racial and class stratification of domestic work."[22] Each year, millions of impoverished bodies are driven from place to place, migrating from one sector of empire to another—from Bangladesh, India, Pakistan, Sri Lanka, or the Philippines to Hong Kong, Singapore, New York, Taiwan, or Qatar—seeking employment as nannies, domestic workers, nurses' aides, or caregivers. Such work can lead to starvation and death. Theologian Gemma Cruz recounts the abuse of Thelma Gawidan "whose ordeal left her with a body weight of sixty-four pounds, and Joanna Demafelis whose tortured lifeless body was dumped in a freezer by employers."[23] A pizza shop owner exploited his employees in what a *Boston Globe* reporter describes as "a harrowing campaign of abuse and intimidation that lasted years [according to] federal prosecutors." One immigrant from North Africa told authorities that he "worked as many as 119 hours each week," and said that he was assaulted by the shop owner several times and was once kicked "in the groin with such force he had to have surgery."[24]

Extreme global poverty remains a most serious problem and has been aggravated by some globalization policies. Nearly fifteen years ago, initial reports from the United Nation's International Forum on the Eradication of Poverty found that roughly 20 percent of the world's population live in extreme poverty, surviving on less than two dollars per day. Although poverty rates decreased in developing countries and in East Asia and the Pacific and South Asia, neither Latin America nor sub-Saharan Africa have made much, if any progress.[25] However, studies conducted in 2022 concluded that

> more than 70 percent of the world population now live in countries where *income inequality has increased* in the last three decades. Inequalities between social groups, including those based on age, gender, race, ethnicity, migrant status and disability are pervasive in developed and developing countries alike.[26]

Empire's global economic policies have aggravated poverty, enmeshing infants, children, youth, adults, elders in a web of "mutually reinforcing deprivations that prevent them from realizing their rights and perpetuate their poverty, including dangerous work conditions, unsafe housing, lack of nutritious food, unequal access to justice, lack of political power, and limited access to health care."[27] Some of those who are stranded in the Second World detect the scent of poverty outside their doors and react. They are frightened, anxious, and angry. Acting as individuals or as vigilante groups, they blame their frustration and experience of growing inequality not on the contradictory demands of company shareholders and investors for increasing profits, but on immigrants. In some instances, these drowning victims of globalization assault, maim, even kill migrants.[28] The global transfer of power and resources from the natural world to human control, from local communities to transnational and neocolonial elites, from local to transnational power centers, reduces life expectancy, increases infant and child mortality, compromises healthcare, ignores education and illiteracy, and distorts income distribution. So it is that "zones of social abandonment"[29] are to be found not only in Sao Paulo or Port-au-Prince or Diepsloot but also in London and Boston and Los Angeles.

In 2017, the US federal government implemented a "zero tolerance policy" aimed to deter unauthorized immigration, particularly along the southern border. This policy not only required the detention and criminal prosecution of each and every migrant, including asylum seekers but also sanctioned the separation of newly arriving adult migrants from the children who accompanied them. This policy separated approximately five thousand children from their parents, without developing a tracking process or keeping records that facilitate the reunion of parents and children. According to Caitlin Dickerson, a staff reporter for *Atlantic* magazine, "parents were told that if they agreed to their own deportation, they would get their children back. And of course they didn't. Reunifications of separated families didn't start in earnest until they were mandated in a federal court case."[30]

Family separation leaves children depressed and bewildered, parents daunted and frantic, more often than not lacking resources to reach their children. "In the aftermath of detention or deportation, families face major economic instability, and affected children suffer poor health and behavioral outcomes. Such foreseeable consequences violate fundamental norms regarding human dignity and care for the vulnerable."[31] These bodies on the move, these itinerant children, women, and men are claimed by Jesus of Nazareth as his brothers and sisters.

In the United States, national security strategies devised in response to the terrorist attacks of September 11, 2001, not only have spawned vigilante patrols of the western border with Mexico but also have increased racial profiling, government surveillance, and INS harassment and incarceration of immigrants, particularly Arabs, South Asians, and Muslims. Precedents for such hostility toward racially marked Brown, Yellow, and Black bodies are found, Winant argues, in the Nativism of the nineteenth-century assaults against the Irish, Catholics, and Asians; in the raids of the 1920s that "targeted eastern and southern Europeans and to some extent Caribbeans"; and in the internment of US citizens of Japanese descent during the Second World War.[32] As Winant comments, "race [has] offer[ed] the most accessible tool to categorize the American people politically: who is 'loyal' and who is a 'threat,' who can be 'trusted' and who should be subject to surveillance, who should retain civil rights and who should be deprived of them."[33]

Color-Blind Racism

Sociologist Eduardo Bonilla-Silva calls attention to the persistence of racism in the post–civil rights era, even though White people in the United States insist that they are not racist. Bonilla-Silva uses the familiar protestation, "I do not see color," to name this phenomenon as color-blind racism.[34] The four main frames of color-blind racism include:

- abstract liberalism, which involves ideas also linked to political and economic liberalism, such as equal opportunity, individualism, choice, and persuasion rather than compulsion in achieving social policy;
- naturalization, which "allows whites to explain away racial phenomena by suggesting that they are natural occurrences";
- cultural racism, which replaces the essentialism once held by biology to explain deviations from a putative White norm as the result of inferior culture and cultural norms; and
- minimization of racism, which downplays the role of racial discrimination as a "central factor affecting minorities' life chances."

Bonilla-Silva argues that when taken together "these frames form an impregnable yet elastic wall that barricades whites from the United States' racial reality."[35] He concludes that color-blindness remains the dominant and effective ideology of racism because it "binds whites together and blurs, shapes, and provides" the terrain and terms of the discourse for Blacks, Latinos, and East Asian, South Asian, and Middle Eastern diasporic communities.[36]

Inter-Racial and Intra-Racial Relations

We know that the emotion-laden, even vituperative, reactions of various nations, peoples and their cultures, and individuals to skin color as a signifier may be traced to pseudo-physiognomic taxonomies in which human beings are grouped, evaluated, compared, and hierarchized accordingly. Yet meanings attached to skin color can and have changed over time. Consider Francisco Bethencourt's probing question: "How is it that the same person can be considered black in the United States, colored in the Caribbean or South Africa, and white in Brazil?"[37]

The ongoing debate in the United States around immigration offers one way of examining, even in cursory fashion, the relations between and among differently marked racial groups. The results of a survey taken by the Pew Hispanic Center suggest that, in general, "African-Americans view immigrants more favorably than do whites, but they also believe more strongly than whites that immigrants take jobs from native-born workers."[38] But, even as ideological frames shift, the new racism reignites "old racism" issues of discrimination in employment, housing, and education, as well as stereotyping.

Let me pose three examples—*interracial* and *intraracial* relations. First: Consider that in 2005 in the aftermath of Hurricane Katrina, Mexicans and Brazilians were *imported* and employed to do repair work in New Orleans, while working-class, working-poor, and poor Blacks were *deported* from New Orleans.[39] With little or no financial means by which to return to the city, these men and women are deprived not only of the opportunity of employment but also of the personal and humanly re-creative satisfaction of participating in their city's recovery. But the situation in New Orleans ought to be read in a global context: the Migration Policy Institute (MPI) calculates that in 2019, roughly eleven million "unauthorized immigrants" were working and living in the United States. Forty-eight percent of these immigrants came from Mexico, 7 percent from El Salvador, 7 percent from Guatemala, 5 percent from India, and 4 percent from Honduras. Further, consider that immigrants constitute roughly 15.3 percent of the total population of the United States, while these women and men account for 88 percent of the total population of the United Arab Emirates.[40] This situation exposes the difficulties both countries have with "guest workers," the new "interiorized others."[41]

Second, sheer survival (food, medicines, clothing, shelter, escape from gang violence) pushes Mexicans and Brazilians, as well as peoples from Central and Latin America, Asia, and Africa, from one sector of empire to another.[42] These women and men enter empire's domestic economy at low wage rates and take on jobs that endanger their bodies, their lives.[43] Their immigrant labor is in high demand in slaughterhouses, meat-packing plants, canneries, food-processing plants, sweatshops, construction sites, and janitorial services. These places make "easy pickings" for raids by the Immigration and Customs Enforcement (ICE).[44] On May 12, 2008, the ICE carried out the largest raid against undocumented workers to date at Agriprocessors Inc., the nation's largest kosher slaughterhouse, located in Postville, Iowa. In this incident, nearly four hundred undocumented workers, most identified as illiterate villagers from Guatemala, were subjected to criminal charges (use of false Social Security cards or legal residence documents) rather than with immigrant violations.[45] The latter allegation would have ensured deportation, the former called for incarceration. A similar raid took place in Bedford, Massachusetts, at Michael Bianco, Inc., a leather manufacturer. Approximately 350 workers, predominantly immigrants from Guatemala and El Salvador, were taken into federal custody on charges of violating immigration laws and held for deportation.[46] The speed of the raid sent undocumented workers to detention centers with little or no warning, and an estimated 100–200 children were separated from their parents.[47] These raids continued during the decade that followed: for example, in 2019, ICE agents detained approximately 680 people in coordinated raids in six different cities across Mississippi.[48] What is most egregious is the way in which the lives of immigrants have been cheapened. Luis Ramierz, a twenty-five-year-old man from Guanajuato, Mexico, was beaten and kicked to death by three White teenaged youth in Shenandoah, Pennsylvania.[49]

Third and finally, displacement of Mexicans, Brazilians, and Blacks in New Orleans precipitates interracial resentment and forces some of the poorest subjects of empire to fight one another for crumbs. Let us consider comments taken from "Black Like Whom?" in which Lori Robinson interviews several racially Black immigrants. Robinson's aim is to identify and address differences about the meaning and function of *blackness* within the African diaspora. The first person Robinson interviews is Susan Peterkin-Bishop, who says flatly,

> Growing up in Jamaica, basically what I heard about African Americans was that they were lazy, didn't want to do any work, were just sitting there waiting for the White man to give them something. But when I came here, I realized that it was not true.[50]

The second woman, Miriam Muléy, who is Puerto Rican of African descent, born and raised in the Bronx, New York, says that she meets incredulity from African Americans whenever she declares her ethnic background. Muléy told Robinson that Blacks seem to be insulted by her claim of Puerto Rican identity. Muléy says that African Americans ask her pointedly, "You don't want to be an African American? You're disowning your Black roots?"[51] The third woman is Nunu Kidane, an Eritrean immigrant, whose encounters with African Americans are similar to those of Muléy. When Kidane insists that she is not Black, but Eritrean, African Americans say, "When was the last time you looked in the mirror? Sister, you're Black." Kidane says, "What was missing from our dialogue was the fact that to me 'Black' or 'race' was not an identity."[52]

Each of these comments pinpoints tensions between and among women and men whose skin pigmentation is dark—black. Such remarks also highlight the impact of racial formation as well as complicity with and resistance to this process.[53] Racial formation racializes all human subjects who, consequently, willingly or unwillingly, perpetuate and transmit racist ideologies and practices through uncritical acceptance of standards, symbols, habits, assumptions, and reactions rooted in racial differentiation and racially assigned privilege.

The comments by Peterkin-Bishop illustrate just how emphasis on the "hardworking" culture (and character) of immigrants and the "lazy" culture (and character) of African Americans reinforces cultural racism and undermines positive and humane relationships between African Americans and various immigrants. Stereotypes disguise the operation of racist ideology and racist (historical as well as current) practices that create and sustain political and economic conditions that continue to impede African American achievement and flourishing.

The statements made by Muléy and Kidane highlight the impact of racial formation on African Americans, who see and name race, but often overlook cultural and historical differences. On the one hand, the human legacy of the transatlantic slave trade in African bodies can be traced, seen, and heard in Belize, Brazil, Cuba, Haiti, Jamaica, Puerto Rico, Trinidad, and Venezuela.[54] In the United States, African Americans, who have had to learn (and are still learning) to love their Black selves, perhaps too quickly identify people of mixed African, European, and Indigenous ancestry as "Black," thus pulling them into a Black expressive culture that is really quite foreign to them. For in some of these geopolitical sites, despite pigmentocracy, the coalescing of class, culture, and language relativizes the meaning of dark skin, of blackness. On the other hand, Dominicans, Cubans, Eritreans, Egyptians, Ghanaians, Nigerians, Ugandans, the Congolese understand themselves in equally complex ways—nationality, ethnicity, cultural origins, ancestry, and village. To these women and men, use of the term *blackness* provides no meaningful point of reference. For many of these immigrants, blackness is not yet the "political identity" that Pan-Africanists on both sides of the Atlantic once desired so ardently.

Bonilla-Silva contends that the "new global racial reality will reinforce ... versions of colorblind racism."[55] A complex system of triracial stratification that mirrors race relations in Latin America will emerge: Whites, honorary Whites, and the collective Black, with phenotype taking a central role "determining where groups and members of racial and ethnic groups will fit." Yet this scenario will not dislodge White racist supremacy, only hide it from public view.[56]

At the same time, another and "new" African diaspora is emerging. In a blog post from the independent, nonpartisan think tank and publisher the Council on Foreign Relations (CFR), guest contributor Krista Johnson, associate professor and director of the Center for African Studies at Howard University, interrogates the "explicit incorporation of the African diaspora" in the Biden administration's African policy. Commenting on the visit of Vice President Kamala Harris to Ghana, Tanzania, and Zambia in early April 2023, Johnson takes note of the lack of widespread and in-depth media coverage and reporting of the vice president's visits. At the same time, Johnson points out that students from the Historically Black Colleges and Universities (HBCU) Africa Correspondents Corps did report on the meetings and gave particular attention to the clashing definitions of the notion of diaspora that emerged. Their reporting uncovered a "new narrative" aimed to depict a "'new' diaspora comprised of relatively recent, middle-class, economic migrants, as well as social and economic entrepreneurs." This new narrative decisively sidesteps the history and legacy of racial slavery in the United States, thus excluding the descendants of the enslaved Africans. "There's a danger," argues Johnson, "that the new US–Africa strategy may encourage not only siloed identities within the diaspora, but siloed opportunities and programs, some focused on the 'old' diaspora, and others on the 'new.'"[57]

Still, the actualization of both or either of these scenarios depends upon the refusal of re-racialized subjects within empire to form counterhegemonic alliances and to repudiate the bias that grounds and extends this process. Yet *not* sheer refusal alone. Jesus of Nazareth calls us to break bonds imposed by imperial design, to imagine and grasp and realize ourselves as his own flesh, as the body of Christ.[58]

Sex and Sexuality

Insofar as race and gender are co-constitutive in empire, they are governed by political and economic displays of power;[59] but sexuality in empire is subjugated through commercial exchange. Red, Brown, Yellow, poor White, and Black female bodies, violated and "occupied" in empire-building, poached in the process of globalization, function as exotic and standard commodities for trafficking and sex tourism, pornographic fantasy and sadomasochistic spectacle.[60] Red, Brown, Yellow, and, especially Black male bodies lynched and castrated in empire-building, mechanized in the process of globalization, now are caricatured as "sexually aggressive, violent, animalistic."[61] Empire's eager debasement of black flesh robs *all* human persons of healthy, dignified, and generative sexual expression. For in empire, the primary function of sex no longer entails human communication, embrace, and intimacy (not even procreation), but the heterosexual service of White male privilege. Sex is amusement; its imperial purposes are distraction, entertainment, dissipation. Thus, in empire, same-sex or transgender identification and relationships undergo particularly intense opprobrium. Empire entices and intimidates its *ordinary* subjects, and, perhaps especially, its most wretched subjects, to react to lesbian and gay and transgender persons with panic, loathing, and violence (malevolent homophobia); empire permits its *privileged* subjects to respond with curiosity, experimentation, and tokenism (benign homophobia). In empire, self-disclosure and self-disclosive acts by lesbian and gay and transgender persons are penalized by repression, expulsion, and, sometimes death.[62] The vulnerability and marginality of lesbian and gay and transgender persons makes a claim on the body of Jesus of Nazareth, on the body of Christ.[63]

The teaching of the Catholic Church on sex and sexuality manifests ambivalence and disquiet toward the body—female and lesbian and gay and transgender bodies, in particular. Church teaching signals a preference for celibacy and promotes marriage chiefly as a means for procreation. Certainly, church teaching acknowledges the presence of lesbian and gay and transgender persons, accords them equal human dignity with heterosexual persons, and urges pastoral compassion in their regard.[64] And, that teaching does little to contest the use and abuse of lesbian and gay and transgender persons in empire.

Church teaching distinguishes same-sex sexual orientation from same-sex sexual activity, and deems the latter "intrinsically disordered."[65] Same-sex sexual acts are deemed contrary to the natural law, and the *Catechism of the Catholic Church* declares that such acts "close the sexual act to the gift of life [and] do not proceed from a genuine affective and sexual complementarity."[66] This teaching admonishes lesbian and gay and transgender persons to repress or sacrifice their sexual orientation, to relinquish genital expression, to deny their bodies and their selves. But, if the body is a sacrament, if it is the concrete medium through which persons realize themselves interdependently in the world and in freedom in Christ, and if in Catholic sacramental economy, "to express is to effect,"[67] then, on Catholic teaching, in and through (genital) bodily expression, lesbian and gay and transgender persons are compelled to render themselves disordered. For on Catholic teaching, the condition of homosexuality constitutes a transgression that approximates ontological status. Can the (artificial) distinction between orientation and act (really) be upheld? What are lesbian and gay and transgender persons to do with their bodies, their selves?

Consider the response of *Homosexualitatis problema* to these questions:

> Fundamentally [homosexuals] are called to enact the will of God in their life by joining whatever sufferings and difficulties they experience in virtue of their condition to the sacrifice of the Lord's Cross. That Cross, for the believer, is a fruitful sacrifice since from that death come life and redemption. While any call to carry the cross or to understand a Christian's suffering in this way will predictably be met with bitter ridicule by some, it should be remembered that this is the way to eternal life for "all" who follow Christ.
>
> [The Cross] is easily misunderstood, however, if it is merely seen as a pointless effort at self-denial. The Cross is a denial of self, but in service to the will of God himself who makes life come from death and empowers those who trust in him to practise virtue in place of vice.
>
> To celebrate the Paschal Mystery, it is necessary to let that Mystery become imprinted in the fabric of daily life. To refuse to sacrifice one's own will in obedience to the will of the Lord is effectively to prevent salvation. Just as the Cross was central to the expression of God's redemptive love for us in Jesus, so the conformity of the self-denial of homosexual men and women with the sacrifice of the Lord will constitute for them a source of self-giving which will save them from a way of life which constantly threatens to destroy them.
>
> Christians who are homosexual are called, as all of us are, to a chaste life. As they dedicate their lives to understanding the nature of God's personal call to them, they will be able to celebrate the Sacrament of Penance more faithfully and receive the Lord's grace so freely offered there in order to convert their lives more fully to his Way.[68]

This is stern counsel: it calls for embrace of the cross, for bodily (sexual) asceticism, self-denial, and imposes strict abstinence. In a carefully argued analysis of the document, Paul Crowley affirms the meaningfulness of the cross not only for lesbian and gay and transgender persons but also for *all* Christians since the cross is *the* condition of discipleship. Crowley rightly objects to the peculiar application of "crucified living" (enforced abstinence) to the (sexual) fulfillment of lesbian and gay and transgender persons.[69] With regard to the last sentences quoted above, Crowley points out, "While penance is mentioned here as an aid to gay persons in attaining a chaste life, no mention is made of the graces accruing from one's baptism or from the life of the Eucharist."[70]

Regarding the command of abstinence, Xavier Seubert reasons that "to prescribe, in advance, abstinence and celibacy for the homosexual person simply because the person is homosexual is to say that, as it is, homosexual bodily existence stands outside the sacramental transformation to which all creation is called in Christ."[71] The writing of *Homosexualitatis problema* surely was motivated by deep pastoral concern. But it echoes with what James Alison describes as a reproachful sanctioning ecclesiastical voice, which commands: "Love and do not love, be and do not be." He concludes: "The voice of God has been presented as a double bind, which is actually far more dangerous than a simple message of hate, since it destabilizes being into annihilation, and thinks that annihilation to be a good thing."[72]

Church teaching repels lesbian and gay and transgender (anti)bodies to the periphery of the ecclesial body, and may well disclose just how afraid the church may be of the body of Jesus of Nazareth. Moral theologian Stephen J. Pope calls the magisterium's teaching about homosexual orientation "powerfully stigmatizing and dehumanizing."[73] That teaching, he continues:

> is also at least tacitly, if not explicitly, liable to be used to support exactly the kinds of unjust discrimination that the Church has repeatedly condemned. Describing someone's sexual identity as "gravely disordered" would seem to arouse suspicion, mistrust, and alienation. . . . One can understand why observers conclude that the magisterium's teaching about homosexuality stands in tension with its affirmation that each gay person is created in the *imago Dei*.[74]

Church teaching on homosexuality exposes us to the manipulation of agents of empire and coaxes our collusion in opposing and punishing lesbian and gay and transgender persons who refuse to internalize homophobia and who live their lives without self-censorship. This teaching feeds innuendo and panic; it nudges us to discipline the body's phrasing and comportment, the curiosity and play of our children; it disturbs our families and relationships; it rewards our disingenuousness as we praise, then mock, women and men whose talents enrich our daily lives and weekly worship.[75] Seubert poses a grave critique, one that incriminates the very mystery of the church: the "denial of the homosexual body as this group's basis of spiritual, relational, historical experience is tantamount to impeding access to the reality of Christ in a certain moment of human history."[76] This charge brings the church much too close to betraying the great mystery of love that suffuses it and stirs up continually a longing to realize itself as the marked flesh of Christ.

This situation provokes a most poignant, most indecent question, "Can Jesus of Nazareth be an option for gay and lesbian and transgender persons?" Some regional churches are beginning to answer this question affirmatively: In 2022, the Flemish-speaking bishops of Belgium opened their arms to lesbian and gay Catholics, creating a special outreach office within the Interdiocesan Family Pastoral Service that would support a ministry of "encounter and conversation" and authorizing prayer for committed couples.[77] In 2023, the German bishops voted to approve blessings for same-sex couples and the German church's synodal process voted to offer same-sex blessings to committed Catholic couples.[78] In the United States, bishops, presbyters, pastoral leaders, and theologians grapple with this question in a political context increasingly hostile to LGBTQ persons and their families. New Ways Ministry and Jesuit James Martin have actively sought to encourage listening and dialogue, "building bridges" to assist Catholics in understanding that "ministry to LGBT Catholics is not just ministry to LGBT people, but increasingly to the entire church."[79]

These affirmations of same-sex relationships stand in contestation to the Vatican declaration, "*Responsum* of the Congregation for the Doctrine of the Faith to a *Dubium* Regarding the Blessings of Unions of Persons of the Same Sex," that insists

> *Blessings* belong to the category of the *sacramentals*, whereby the Church "calls us to praise God, encourages us to implore his protection, and exhorts us to seek his mercy by our holiness of life." In addition, they "have been established as a kind of imitation of the sacraments, blessings are signs above all of spiritual effects that are achieved through the Church's intercession."

Consequently, in order to conform with the nature of sacramentals, when a blessing is invoked on particular human relationships, in addition to the right intention of those who participate, it is necessary that what is blessed be objectively and positively ordered to receive and express grace, according to the designs of God inscribed in creation, and fully revealed by Christ the Lord. Therefore, only those realities which are in themselves ordered to serve those ends are congruent with the essence of the blessing imparted by the Church.

For this reason, it is *not licit* to impart a blessing on relationships, or partnerships, even stable, that involve sexual activity outside of marriage (i.e., outside the indissoluble union of a man and a woman open in itself to the transmission of life), as is the case of the unions between persons of the same sex. The presence in such relationships of positive elements, which are in themselves to be valued and appreciated, cannot justify these relationships and render them legitimate objects of an ecclesial blessing, since the positive elements exist within the context of a union not ordered to the Creator's plan.[80]

On this account, lesbian and gay bodies are not "objectively and positively ordered to receive and express grace." Thus, on this position, gay and lesbian bodypersons remain ontologically disordered, unable to receive grace, unable to express grace, that is, unable to operate out of or act out of grace.[81]

We still ask: "Can Jesus of Nazareth be an option for gay and lesbian and transgender persons?" This question uncovers the pain, anguish, and anger that many lesbian and gay and transgender persons feel as we thwart their desire to follow Jesus of Nazareth, to realize themselves in his image. This question springs from the deep-seated feeling among many lesbian and gay and transgender persons that Jesus Christ is not an option for them, that he, as the embodied representative of God, hates them, and that they have no place in either Christ's church or the Kingdom of God he announced during his earthly ministry.[82]

If Jesus of Nazareth, the Christ of God, cannot be an option for gay and lesbian and transgender persons, then he cannot be an option. An adequate response to this concern requires a different christological interpretation, one in which we *all* may recognize, love, and realize our bodyselves as his own flesh, as the body of Christ.

MARKING THE (QUEER) FLESH OF CHRIST

This section pushes the boundaries of our thinking about the homosexual body further. The words "queer" and "Christ" form a necessary if shocking, perhaps, even "obscene" conjunction.[83] By inscribing a queer mark on the flesh of Christ, I *neither* propose *nor* insinuate that Jesus of Nazareth, the Christ of God, was homosexual. By inscribing a "queer" mark, I recognize that this mark poses epistemological challenges for theology: Have we turned the (male) body of Christ into a fetish or idol? In an effort to discipline *eros*, have we disregarded "God's proto-erotic desire for us"?[84] Can a Christology incorporate all the dimensions of corporality?

These questions target some of the discursive limits of sex, gender, and sexuality in Christianity and disturb cherished symbols. Just as a Black Christ heals the anthropological impoverishment of Black bodies so too a "queer" Christ heals the anthropological impoverishment of lesbian and gay and transgender bodies.[85] Because Jesus of Nazareth declared himself *with* and *for* others—the poor, excluded, and despised—and offered a new "way" and new freedom to *all* who would hear and follow him, we may be confident that the Christ of our faith *is* for gay and lesbian and transgender people. Conversely, if the risen Christ cannot identify with gay and lesbian and transgender people, then the gospel announces no good news and the reign of God presents no real alternative to the "reign of sin."[86] Only an *ekklesia*, that follows Jesus of Nazareth in (re)marking its flesh as "queer" as his own, may set a welcome table in the household of God.

Robert Goss takes the experience of homophobic oppression of lesbian and gay bodies in culture, society, and church as a starting point for a "queer" christological reflection.[87] He grounds this articulation in the "generative matrix" of the *basileia* praxis of Jesus and in the real suffering of gay and lesbian people.[88] The immanent and transcendent scope of that praxis allows Goss to detach the radical truth of Jesus Christ from all forms of hegemony and ideology—whether cultural, social, ecclesiastical, biblical, or theological—that might seek to master Infinite God present among us. Further, he constructs a "queer" biblical hermeneutics through which to unmask and discredit any heretical use of the Hebrew and Christian Scriptures to justify bigotry and violence against gay and lesbian people.[89]

Goss challenges the abusive use of the cross to justify explicit or implicit oppression and violence against gay and lesbian people as well as gay and lesbian acquiescence to interiorized oppression.[90]

> The cross symbolizes the political infrastructure of homophobic practice and oppression. It symbolizes the terror of internalized homophobia that has led to the closeted invisibility of gay and lesbian people. It indicates the brutal silencing, the hate crimes, the systemic violence perpetuated against us. The cross now belongs to us. We have been crucified.[91]

Crucifixion was the response of imperial power to Jesus's "*basileia* solidarity with the poor, the outcast, the sinner, the socially dysfunctional, and the sexually oppressed."[92] The death of Jesus "shapes the cross into a symbol of struggle for queer liberation" and Easter becomes the hope and fulfillment of that struggle.[93]

> From the perspective of Easter . . . God identifies with the suffering and death of Jesus at the hands of a political system of oppression. For gay and lesbian Christians, Easter becomes the event at which God says no to homophobic violence and sexual oppression. . . . On Easter, God made Jesus queer in his solidarity with us. In other words, Jesus "came out of the closet" and became the "queer" Christ. . . . Jesus the Christ is queer by his solidarity with queers.[94]

All Christology is interpretation and, in these passages, Goss articulates an understanding of the cross and resurrection from the perspective of the homophobic suffering of gay and lesbian persons. His theological analysis turns on the scandal of the body particular: Jesus of Nazareth in all his marked particularity of race, gender, sex, culture, and religion teaches us the universal meaning of being human in the world.[95] In Jesus, God critiques any imperial or ecclesiastical practice of body exclusion and control, sorrows at our obstinacy, and calls us all unceasingly to new practices of body inclusion and liberation. In Jesus, God manifests an eros for us *as we are* in our marked particularity of race, gender, sex, sexuality, and culture.

In contrast to christological formulations that avoid or distort sexuality and sexual desire, Goss's work offers an opportunity to honor what Sarah Coakley calls the "profound entanglement of our human sexual desires and our desire for God."[96] For, as Sebastian Moore insists, sexual desire is always a "hint of the ultimate mystery of us that is love."[97] A "queer" Christ is not scandalized by human desire, but liberates that desire from cloying common-sense satisfaction, misuse, and disrespect.[98] This liberation begins in regard and esteem for the body and comes to proximate fulfillment in authentic love of the body, as authentic love and loving.[99] Thus, a "queer" Christ embraces *all* our bodies passionately, revalorizes them as embodied mystery, and reorients sexual desire toward God's desire for us in and through our sexuality. This is not a matter of fitting God into our lives, but of fitting our lives into God. Homosexual and heterosexual persons are drawn by God's passionate love for us working in us to bring us into God's love.[100] To live in and live out of this reorientation demands refusal of isolating egoism, of body denial, and of whatever betrays spiritual and bodily integrity. Moreover, living in and out of this reorientation leads us, even if fitfully, toward virtue, helps us to grow lovable and loving, and, in fulfillment, we are gift and gifted with and in love.

In his relationships with women and men, Jesus embodied openness, equality, and mutuality. In his suffering and death on the cross, Jesus showed us the cost of integrity, when we live in freedom, in love, and in solidarity with others. In his resurrection, Jesus became the One in whom "God's erotic power"[101] releases bodily desire from the tomb of fear and loathing, the One who fructifies all loving exchange, the One who, in his risen body, quiets the restless yearning of our hearts.

(RE)MARKING THE FLESH OF THE CHURCH

If theological reflection on the body cannot ignore a Christ identified with Black, Brown, Red, Yellow, poor White, and queer folk, neither can it ignore reflection on "the flesh of the Church."[102] For, as Gregory of Nyssa tells us, whoever "sees the Church looks directly at Christ."[103] And as the flesh of the church is the flesh of Christ in every age, the flesh of the church is marked (as was his flesh) by race, sex, gender, sexuality, and culture. These marks differentiate and transgress, they unify and bond, but the flesh of Christ relativizes these marks in the flesh of the church. These marks may count, but the mark of Christ, the baptismal sign of the cross, counts for more, trumps all marks. Still, counting and trumping marks in the body of Christ must give way before *basileia* praxis. These acts of justice-doing, empire critique, love, and solidarity mark us as his flesh made vivid leaven in our world.

In a letter to followers of "the way" at Corinth, Paul hands over the gift he has been given: "For I received from the Lord what I also delivered to you, that the Lord Jesus on the night when he was betrayed took bread, and when he had given thanks, he broke it and said, 'This is my body which is for you.' Do this in remembrance of me" (1 Cor 11:23–24). This is the Tradition: the body of the Lord is handed over to us, handled by us as we feed one another. Further on Paul declares: "You are the body of Christ and individually members of it" (1 Cor 12:27). We are the body raised up by Christ for himself within humanity; through us, the flesh of the crucified and resurrected Jesus is extended through time and space.

In the very act of nourishing our flesh with his flesh, we women and men are made new in Christ, emboldened to surrender position and privilege and power and wealth, to abolish all claims to racial and cultural superiority, to contradict repressive codes of gender formation and sexual orientation. In Christ, there is neither Brown nor Black, neither Red nor White; in Christ, there is neither Creole nor *mestizo*, neither senator nor worker in the *maquiladoras*. In Christ, there is neither male nor female, neither gay/lesbian nor straight, neither transgender nor heterosexual (after Gal 3:28). We are all transformed in Christ: *we are his very own flesh.*

If my sister or brother is not at the table, we are not the flesh of Christ. If my sister's mark of sexuality must be obscured, if my brother's mark of race must be disguised, if my sister's mark of culture must be repressed, then we are not the flesh of Christ. For, it is through and in Christ's own flesh that the "other" is my sister, is my brother; indeed, the "other" is me (*yo soy tu otro yo*). Unless our sisters and brothers are beside and with each of us, we are not the flesh of Christ. The sacramental aesthetics of Eucharist, the thankful living manifestation of God's image through particularly marked flesh, demands the vigorous display of difference in race and culture and tongue, gender and sex and sexuality. Again, Gregory of Nyssa: "The establishment of the Church is re-creation of the world. But it is only in the *union of all the particular members* that the beauty of Christ's Body is complete."[104]

The body of Jesus the Christ, both before and after his death, radically clarifies the meaning of be-ing embodied in the world. His love and praxis releases the power of God's animating image and likeness in our Red, Brown, Yellow, White, Black bodies—our lesbian and gay and heterosexual bodies, our transgender bodies, our HIV/AIDS-infected bodies, our starving bodies, our prostituted bodies, our yearning bodies, our ill and infirm bodies, our young and old and joyous bodies. To stand silent before war and death, incarceration and torture, rape and queer-bashing, pain and disease, abuse of power and position is to be complicit with empire's sacrilegious antiliturgy, which dislodges the table of the bread of life. That desiccated antiliturgy hands us all over to consumption by the corrupt body of the "Market."

The only body capable of taking us *all* in as we are, with all our different and differentiated body marks—certainly, the mark of same-sex orientation—is the body of Christ. This taking us in, this in-corporation is akin to sublation, not erasure, not uniformity: the *basileia praxis* of Jesus draws us up to him. Our humble engagement in his praxis revalues our identities and differences, even as it preserves the integrity and significance of our body marks. At the same time, those very particular body marks are relativized, reoriented, and reappropriated under his sign, the sign of the cross. Thus, in solidarity and in love of others and the Other, we are (re)made and (re)marked as the flesh of Christ, as the flesh of his church.

We have drawn out some implications of the relation between Christology and anthropology by focusing on the marked body of the Jew Jesus of Nazareth. Jesus was born of people subjugated by the Roman Empire; an itinerant and charismatic preacher and teacher, his strenuous critique of oppressive structures, whether political or religious or cultural, along with his fearless love of ordinary people, provoked those in authority to brand him a criminal. Jesus mediated God's presence among us through a body marked by race, gender, sex, sexuality, culture, and religion. His radical self-disclosure constitutes the paradigm for all human self-disclosure in contexts of empire and oppression, exclusion and alienation, slavery and death.

The body of Jesus provokes our interrogation of the deployment and debasement of bodies in this new sovereign (dis)order. The flesh of his church is multilayered. Pulling back layer after layer, we expose the suffering and groaning, outrage and hope of the victims of history. In them we glimpse the flesh of Christ and we are drawn by that eros, his radiant desire for us, and we too seek to imitate his incarnation of love of the Other, love of others. The body of Jesus of Nazareth impels us to place the bodies of the victims of history at the center of theological anthropology, to turn to "other" subjects.

CHAPTER 5

Turning the Subject

... who, though he existed in the form of God,
did not regard equality with God as something to be grasped,
but emptied himself taking the form of a slave. ...
And being found in appearance as a human, he humbled himself
and became obedient to the point of death—even death on a cross.[1]

You got a right to the tree of life
Come to tell you, you got a right to the tree of life.[2]

Humanity is becoming tangible ... in its inhumanity.[3]

In the context of the European Enlightenment, the "turn to the subject" was intended to be emancipatory.[4] It aimed to release humanity to dare to rely upon reason, rather than revealed truth, as the authority by which to judge, decide, and act. But humanity's "exit"[5] from what Immanuel Kant named its "self-incurred immaturity"[6] was no progress, and, certainly not for many of God's human creatures. From the middle of the fifteenth century forward, a totalizing dynamics of domination, already obvious in anti-Semitism and misogyny, impressed itself upon the so-called "new worlds." Charles Long, Cornel West, David Theo Goldberg, Emmanuel Eze, Sylvia Wynter, and Michelle Wright, among others, have traced the relation between these oppressive dynamics and the Enlightenment's enervating failure of criticality.[7] These scholars have exposed how key categories in epistemology, ontology, ethics, and aesthetics were pressed to legitimate racism and genocide, expropriation and exploitation, cultural imperialism and colonialism, and now a new *pax imperii*.[8] Under the impact of these dynamics, Christianity buckled. At times willingly, ambivalently, silently, Christianity partnered domination; now, "human authenticity [could] no longer be taken for granted."[9] This complicity, as chapter 4 has shown, compromised Christian thinking about the meaning of human being.

A NEW ANTHROPOLOGICAL QUESTION

The involvement of Christianity in the dynamics of domination set the stage for the performance of tragic narratives, which have eaten the heart out of Western civilization. These master narratives originated in quest, but ended in conquest, in "cynicism, and violence."[10] They boasted of the means through which certain human beings were made masters and possessors and other human beings were made slaves and objects of property.[11] Few theologies responded to this tragedy or probed the effect of the dynamics of domination on God's human creatures. Rather as Johann Baptist Metz contends, they preferred to speak in general terms about "the person" or "the human subject" or "the modern subject." However, it has become clear that such speech served "as camouflage for a specific subject"[12]—the White, male, bourgeois European subject. Such speech failed theology's vital task of abstraction: grappling with concrete data to discern, understand, and evaluate their emerging patterns in order to interpret their meanings.

Since the early 1960s, various political and liberation theologies have intensified the effort to unmask and decenter this subject, to rethink and to transform, from the bottom up, the world that he created.[13] These theologies turned the spotlight on God's invisible human creatures: the exploited, despised, marginalized, poor masses whom Fanon, so lovingly, called "*les damnés de la terre*," the wretched of the Earth. These children, women, and men constitute the majority of humanity. They comprise the one billion who live in absolute poverty, the 660 million who are undernourished, the more than one billion who live with disability (the world's largest minoritized group),[14] the millions sick and dying with HIV/AIDS, COVID-19, malaria, smallpox, and diarrheal diseases.[15] These children, women, and men are the millions sold or forced into wage slavery, prostitution, and murdered—simply because their embodiment, their difference is rejected as gift and offends. These children, women, and men, too, so beloved by God, are human subjects.

From the outset these liberation theologies looked for God in history; this meant a "rediscovery of the indissoluble unity of [the human] and God."[16] The incarnation of God in Jesus of Nazareth set the parameters. Chapter 3 laid out how Jesus understood and revealed himself to be sent to those who were sick, outcast, downtrodden, and poor. These were children, women, and men without choice, without hope, without a future. To them, Jesus announced the coming of the reign of God and promised that beatitude which is God's intention for us all.

For these exploited and suffering poor, the prophet from Nazareth was the incarnation of divine compassion. His life and ministry exemplify what it means to take sides with the oppressed and poor in the struggle for life—no matter the cost. In Jesus of Nazareth, the messianic Son of God endures the shameful spectacle of death by crucifixion. He himself is to be counted among the multitude of history's victims. But as the messianic prophet, the sufferings of the crucified Christ are not merely or only his alone. In his own body, Jesus, in solidarity, shares in the suffering of the poor and weak.[17] Because God was in Christ, "through his passion Christ brings into the passion history of this world the eternal [compassion] of God, and the divine justice that creates life."[18] Through his death on the cross, Christ "identifies God with the victims of violence" and identifies "the victims of violence with God, so that they are put under God's protection and given the rights of which they have been deprived by human beings."[19]

With this critical reading of Scripture, these theologies could not but be directed toward the broken condition of the masses of marginalized poor. Yet it soon became evident that in their demand for a new relationship to history and society, in spite of a christologically directed solidarity and careful social analysis, these theologies had covered over the angular condition of women.[20] Political and liberation theologies had exposed those master narratives that had deformed not only our basic human living but also our religious, moral, and intellectual praxis. But, in order to make good on their claim to be critical, to face head-on their own contradictions, they had to place self-criticism in the forefront alongside collaborative praxis. These theologies had to take into account the humanity and realities of poor Red, Brown, Yellow, White, and Black women. Moreover, they had to grapple with the deep psychic wounds of despised, marginalized poor human beings—internalized oppression, self-abuse, violence, nihilism, self-contempt.[21]

Once the humanity and realities of poor women, particularly poor women of color, are moved to the foreground, a new question orients Christian reflection on anthropology: What might it mean for poor women of color to grasp themselves as human subjects, to grapple with the meaning of liberation and freedom? This new anthropological question seeks to understand and articulate authentic meanings of human flourishing and liberation, progress and salvation. Moreover, this question holds foundational, even universal, relevance for the faith of a global church seeking to mediate the gospel in what, quickly and ambiguously, has become a global culture.

My thesis here is quite basic: the Enlightenment "turn to the subject" coincided with the dynamics of domination. From that period forward, *human being-in-the-world* literally has been identical with White male bourgeois European being-in-the-world. His embodied presence "usurped the position of God" in an anthropological "no" to life for all others.[22] This rampant presence is met only by the church's praxial affirmation of the anthropological "yes" begun in the ministry and sacrificial love of Jesus of Nazareth, whose solidarity with the outcast and poor revealed God's preferential love. That revelation directs us to a new anthropological subject of Christian theological reflection—exploited, despised, poor women of color.[23]

Three sections elaborate the thesis of this chapter. The first assumes the new subject of theological anthropology, drawing on the work done in critical theologies for human liberation. Since Valerie Saiving first interrogated the position of women nearly half a century ago,[24] feminist, womanist, *mujerista, mestiza, minjung* theologians, ethicists, and biblical scholars have challenged the anthropological displacement of human being with bourgeois European White male being. The work of these scholars made analysis of human and social experience—embodiment, sexuality, and eros; identity, otherness, and difference; self-criticism; ecology and peace—thematic in Christian theology. In this process, they retrieved, analyzed, and reinterpreted key insights in biblical studies, Christian doctrine (the Trinity, Christology, ecclesiology), and ethics.[25] Their project stands as another phase in which Christian theology reaffirms the need for authentic solidarity in word and in deed. To presume this project is to presume a new anthropological subject for the *whole* of Christian theology.

The second section probes the implications of solidarity in light of this new subject, whose presence reorients notions of personhood and praxis. If personhood is now understood to flow from formative living in community rather than individualism, from the embrace of difference and interdependence rather than their exclusion, then we can realize our personhood only in solidarity with the exploited, despised, poor "other." In this praxis of solidarity, the "other" retains all her (and his) "otherness"—her (and his) particularity, her (and his) self; she (and he) is neither reduced to some projection, nor forced to reproduce a mirror image. Likewise, we retain particularity and self; we are not reduced by *ressentiment*[26] to projection or caricature. Rather, perhaps, a new and authentic human "we" emerges in this encounter; yet, that new "we" can only be realized in the gift of grace.

The realization of that gift is the healing of a "body of broken bones"[27] unto the mystical body of Christ. This third section makes explicit the eschatological meaning of Christian solidarity on the side of exploited, despised, poor women of color. The doctrine of the mystical body of Christ focuses attention on the metaphysical and historical relations of our communion with one another and the concrete and mystical relations of our union with the Triune God. It accentuates the meaning of hope, which includes an acceptance of uncertainty and of suffering love.

Finally, this thesis involves not only a critique but also a judgment. This judgment discloses something *not* only or exclusively about the White male bourgeois European subject, but about *all* of us—White and non-White, men and women. This judgment exposes the way in which we *all* have betrayed the very meaning of humanity—our own, the humanity of exploited, despised poor women of color, and the humanity of our God.

A NEW ANTHROPOLOGICAL SUBJECT

What does it mean to recognize a new anthropological subject of Christian theological reflection, to identify exploited, despised, poor women of color as that subject? First, this recognition neither satisfies the demands of a numerical majority nor enacts a kind of turnaround, as if now an anthropological "baton" is passed to poor women of color. If this were the case, then the subject of Christian anthropology would be subordinate to so-called liberal political correctness on the one side, or to a classicist reactionariness on the other. Identity politics can never determine the content of theological anthropology. Second, recognizing a new anthropological subject is no mere calculation, as if the previously overlooked experience of poor women of color now simply could be added on. If these women's stories and social suffering were retrieved in this way, theology would resume an alignment with those master narratives, which have run roughshod over the subjectivity and agency of the oppressed. Third, thinking about the subject in this way implies critique and involves judgment, but that critique and judgment neither intend to nor need alienate those who are White (European) or powerful or privileged or male. If this were the case, then theology's very articulation would be little more than ideology or crude justification or a new desecration of the *humanum* (to borrow a term developed by Edward Schillebeeckx).[28] Fourth, taking poor women of color as an anthropological subject admits the risk of self-righteousness, of manipulating (White and male) guilt, and, more importantly, of romanticizing or idealizing, thus depersonalizing, human persons. Finitude and sin are not alien to poor women of color. But this risk may place us in the path of grace: To take oppression as a point of departure for theological reflection brings about encounter with the purifying powers of God in history "even before we are completely liberated."[29] Finally, taking poor women of color as the subject ensures that we are in no way attempting to reinstate any of the earlier and contested anthropological models (androgyny, unisex, and complementarity).[30] Mary Aquin O'Neill's caution is worth repeating:

> Androgyny advocates a development of the individual such that she or he includes within the self all that has been traditionally divided between male and female; the unisex approach takes one or the other sex as the ideal and sets about to accommodate the self to it, no matter what is given in nature; and the theology of complementarity has been based on the image of an individual body in which the male is the head and the female the lower part to be ruled over [by] the head, seat of reason and intelligence.[31]

The first and second of these models remain bound to the European Enlightenment notion of human being as autonomous, isolated, individualistic, and acquisitive; the third is tied to confusions in understanding that are related to the absence of what Bernard Lonergan called "differentiation of consciousness."[32]

Our search for the *humanum* is oriented by the radical demands of the incarnation of God; it reaches its term in the dynamic realization of human personhood. Thus, to be a human person is to be (i) a creature made by God; (ii) person-in-community, living in flexible, resilient, just relationships with others; (iii) an incarnate spirit, that is, embodied in race, gender, sex and sexuality, culture; (iv) capable of working out essential freedom through personal responsibility in time and space; (v) a social being; (vi) unafraid of difference and interdependence; and (vii) willing daily to struggle against "bad faith" and *ressentiment* for the survival, creation, and future of all life.[33] The realization of humanity in this notion of personhood is a dynamic deed rooted in religious, intellectual, and moral conversion. Taken together, the various theologies for human liberation push us in self-giving love to work for this realization and its flourishing in disregarded subjects—exploited, despised poor women of color. Only in and through solidarity with them, the very least of this world, shall humanity come to fruition.

SOLIDARITY

Love of neighbor was the hallmark of early Christianity. ("See how they love one another.") This apprehension of the "other" as neighbor startled and provoked admiration, for that love was expressed through spiritual and corporal works of mercy. Almsgiving, in particular, was the work and duty of charity, the remedy for injustice and inequity in the human community. However, there was little attempt to probe the social or cultural reasoning for the tenacious and cruel poverty of the majority of human persons. This was the state of affairs up until the late nineteenth century, when "Rerum Novarum" responded to the moral breakdown caused by the abuses of the Industrial Revolution. But the notion of charity could not meet the level of demand by the new structures and problems in society. In the effort to redefine the meaning of the common good, Leo XIII drew on the newer notion of social justice.[34]

The nineteenth-century notion of linear progress has not only collapsed but also decayed. The cynical retreat of the nation-state, regressive programs of structural adjustment, repressive taxation, rising oil prices, gross inflation, market manipulation, food shortages, pandemics, drought, and wars have trapped not only the peoples of the two-thirds world but also most of the rest of us in "a vicious cycle of increasing immigration, decreasing formal employment, falling wages, and collapsing revenues."[35] We need thorough-going, practical, genuine systemic change in the present global order. At the same time, we sense a need for something deeper and beyond the moral attention that social justice accords to the distribution of the material and cultural conditions for human living. That something deeper and beyond, I suggest, is solidarity.[36]

Solidarity has secular roots in the European labor-union movements of the mid-nineteenth century and entered only recently into Christian vocabulary. In his 1917 Taylor Lectures at Yale, Walter Rauschenbusch clarified his notion of the social gospel, orienting it around solidarity as relationship with

God and human persons, as service to and for others for the kingdom of God.[37] René Coste has located papal use of the term in the encyclicals, texts, and allocutions of popes Pius XII, John XXIII, Paul VI, and John Paul II.[38] Although Benedict XVI did not address the topic directly, compassionate love of neighbor formed a *leitmotiv* in his early papal writing, but Francis has substantively elaborated and integrated solidarity in his encyclicals and speeches.[39] Increasingly, solidarity has become a category in Christian theology and, as such, denotes the empathetic incarnation of Christian love.[40]

As a category in theological anthropology, solidarity stands as a crucial test in theology's analysis of personal, social, and historical action—intelligent, active, compassionate love for the other in "a situation in which authenticity cannot be taken for granted."[41] The criterion for theology's judgment is located in that most resonant, inexhaustible, gratuitous act of love—the Father's donation of the Son for the world and the Son's embrace of the Father and the world. The solidaristic life praxis of Jesus of Nazareth grounds theological anthropology's application of both a hermeneutic of suspicion and a hermeneutic of recovery, its understanding and judgment, decision and evaluation of acts as authentic or inauthentic.[42]

Solidarity presents a discernible structure with cognitive, affective, effective, constitutive, and communicative dimensions. Through a praxis of solidarity, we not only apprehend and are moved by the suffering of the other, we confront and address its oppressive cause and shoulder the other's suffering. Orienting ourselves before the cross of the crucified Christ, we not only attempt to realize ourselves as the mystical body, but intersubjectively, linguistically, practically, prayerfully to communicate who we are, and for what and for whom we struggle.[43] Solidarity sets the dynamics of love against the dynamics of domination.

From the perspective of the new anthropological subject—exploited, despised, poor women of color—solidarity is basic to the realization of *humanum*. Inasmuch as solidarity involves an attitude or disposition, it entails the recognition of the humanity of the "other" as human, along with regard for the "other" in her (and his) own otherness. The principle of openness flows from this recognition and regard. Openness implies receptivity, that is, a willingness to receive the other and to be received by the other in mutual relationship, to take on obligation with and to the other.

Although recognition and regard, mutual openness and obligation form crucial constitutive elements, solidarity is more than a sum total of these basic gestures. Solidarity is a task, a praxis through which responsible relationships between and among persons (between and among groups) may be created and expressed, mended and renewed. As we shall see, in the discussion below, the fundamental obligations that arise in the context of these relationships stem not from identity politics or from the erasure of difference, but rather from basic human creatureliness and love.

The Transgression of Humanum

On February 12, 1992, the *Times* of London reported the following story:

> The plight of a Somali woman who gave birth unassisted beside a road in Southern Italy as a crowd stood by and jeered prompted telephone calls yesterday of solidarity and job offers.
>
> The indifference shown by Italians to Fatima Yusif, aged 28, when she went into labor on the outskirts of Castel-volturno, near Naples . . . provoked condemnation across the political spectrum and calls for the authorities to introduce legislation to curb the burgeoning racism against immigrants.
>
> "I will remember those faces as long as I live," Ms. Yusif, who was born in Mogadishu, told *Corriere della Sera* as she recovered in hospital. "They were passing by, they would stop and linger as if they were at the cinema careful not to miss any of the show." There was a boy who, sniggering, said, 'Look what the negress is doing.'"
>
> [Help came] to the immigrant mother when a passing police car stopped half an hour after her baby boy Davide, weighing 5lb, was born. Television reports of the incident brought telephone calls to the hospital to which mother and child were taken, expressing solidarity with Ms. Yusif and offering her work. The Vatican newspaper, *L'Osservatore Romano*, said the bystanders were not "worthy of the word man."
>
> Livia Turco, for the Democratic party of the Left, the former Communist party, said that the episode "throws an obscure and disturbing light on the real level of humanity and civilisation of our country."[44]

This report embarrasses. Of course, there is much we do not know about Fatima Yusif or about the crowd of Italians who gathered to watch and mock: Was Ms. Yusif abandoned by a husband or lover? Had she been raped or seduced, then left to carry the child to term alone? Was the father of the child dead or alive? What are her moral values and what is her character like? How long had she been in Italy? Why was she in this rural town? Was she a resident or working there or merely passing through? Was she looking for the father of her child? Was he too Somali or was he Italian? Why was the crowd so cruel? Were women standing in the crowd, and if so, did one of them come forward to help? What we do know is that this story points up transgression of *humanum*; as such, it is a dramatic "anthropological signifier."[45]

The story of Fatima Yusif enfleshes the interlocking and conditioning oppressions of racism and sexism, social and human exploitation, as well as the impact of border crossings, immigration, *ressentiment*, and bad faith. It captures graphically in our contemporary world what it means to *be* an exploited, despised, poor women of color: to be vulnerable and visible, to suffer and endure shame, to live with little, or no, regard and consolation, to be a spectacle.

On the side of a road, in childbirth, lies the body of one of the human fragments of the colonial legacy of Italy in Africa and the neocolonial ruin of Somalia.[46] Fatima Yusif is an immigrant because social oppression in Somalia so limited her exercise of human freedom, she could no longer meet the most basic human needs—adequate food, clean water, shelter, medicine, work. Long-standing patriarchal rights left her culturally undefended against wife-beating and marital rape. Had Davide been born in Somalia, it is likely he would die of malnutrition and disease before his first birthday; should he live, illiteracy, poverty, and war would be his lot.[47]

Fatima Yusif is an immigrant. Once she crossed the border into Italy, she stepped out of a web of cultural, linguistic, personal, and moral support. Once again social oppression (racism, sexism, and exploitation of the guest-worker) circumscribes the exercise of her human freedom and personal responsibility. On this side of the border, her struggle to survive is met with suspicion and *ressentiment*.

As a Black, female human being, Fatima Yusif is *thrown* into a White world. This White world makes her race and her body visible, but it does so to despise and render her humanity invisible in order to peer, to gaze ("Look at what the negress is doing!"). In this White world, Fatima Yusif's identity is defined for her. In this White world, her identity comes, not from membership in an ethnic-linguistic group or from relationship to family and clan, but from race. On the grounds of naive racist empiricism, she is, can only be, the Black, "the negress." Racial representation so overdetermines her being that she is anonymous—"the negress" and, thus, every Black female human being.

She is not a person, she is not even herself, she is "the negress." Fatima Yusif's personhood is trampled. Her defiant cry "to remember those faces" both discloses her shame and risks the spoiling of her spirit through *ressentiment*.

The story of Fatima Yusif throws light on the way in which exploited, despised, poor women of color are forced to meet the ordinary every day, *lo cotidiano*.[48] These women bear and face the burden of history (*her-stories*); for the ordinary every day brings with it the choice of how to live in relation to oppression, whether to be consumed by it or to resist it.

On the side of a road, (White) Italian men, women, and children watch Fatima Yusif (a poor Black woman) in childbirth. A pornographic gaze forms what they *see*: there is no human being, no human person, no mother, only an exotic body, an object to be watched. A most private human moment now constitutes a spectacle for public consumption. Men, women, and children "linger as if at the cinema," looking at "what the negress is doing!"

Is this *Schadenfreude*, smug self-satisfaction at Fatima Yusif's plight? Is it fear? Perhaps the coarse remarks of members of the crowd are fueled by anxiety, insecurity, and loss. In the global economy, "first-world" rural towns also find it difficult to make ends meet. These women and men sometimes are enflamed by leaders to fear the difference that poor people of color and immigrants represent. They do so, in part, because the humiliation and material poverty that Fatima Yusif suffers could so easily circumscribe their own lives. The frustration and anger that they cannot express directly to venture capitalists, oil barons, and the affluent is spewed out on a poor immigrant Black woman. In the global economy, corporate downsizing and disemployment leave a remainder—dirty jobs and scapegoats. Immigrants—especially women (and men) of color—serve these purposes. After all, *who* will collect garbage, sweep streets, scrub floors, scour toilets, pick grapes, clean fish for canning? And, *who* is said to threaten job security, dilute culture, spoil government, tempt sexual appetites, "breed like rabbits"? Fatima Yusif enfleshes the contradictory inflections of immigration—need and antipathy.

The headline of the *Times*'s article roars: "Racists jeer at roadside birth." No human being is born a racist or a sexist, but every human being is born into the "pathological distortion of human existence," that Bernard Lonergan terms "bias."[49] Racist and sexist behaviors are rooted in bias—the more-or-less conscious choice to suppress the directives of intelligence, to repress conscience, to act in bad faith, that is, to lie to ourselves "in an effort to escape freedom, responsibility, and human being."[50] The racism and sexism displayed by the crowd derive not only from each one's biased behavior, but are promoted by societal legitimation.[51]

It is not surprising that the bystanders are condemned as "unworthy" of being called human or are accused of having betrayed the self-image of their nation. To some degree, these responses approximate basic gestures of solidarity. However, at least by what is reported, these rebukes appear blind to the legacy of European colonialism and fail to grapple with the depth of psychic suffering caused by social exploitation. These comments denounce the inhumanity of the crowd, but overlook the (possibly) bleak social situatedness of the crowd. Moreover, legislation against racism stands little chance in effecting a change of mind and heart. These remarks witness to the assault against *humanum*, but they cannot account for it; and while necessary in the repair of social justice, offers of employment can never (re)constitute it. Only an authentic solidarity that neither apathetically resigns itself to the plight of Fatima Yusif nor self-righteously reproaches the crowd can address the injury done that day in 1992 to the human whole.

The Praxis of Solidarity

Between Fatima Yusif and the crowd lies the potential for an authentic praxis of solidarity—the cross of the crucified Jesus of Nazareth. Through incarnate love and self-sacrifice, Christ makes Fatima Yusif's despised body his own. In solidarity, he shares her suffering and anguish. In his body, in his flesh, Christ, too, has known derision and shame; his broken and exposed body is the consolation of her being. At the same time, his love is available for the women, men, and children in the crowd; his body absorbs their anxiety and sin, their failure to honor *humanum*. ("Father forgive them.")

The cross of Christ exposes our pretense to historical and personal innocence, to social and personal neutrality. It uncovers the limitation of all human efforts and solutions to meet the problem of evil. Thus, the praxis of solidarity is made possible by the loving self-donation of the crucified Christ whose cross is its origin, standard, and judge. Solidarity can never be severed from this self-giving love. Only those who follow the example of the Crucified and struggle on the side of the exploited, despised, and poor "will discover him at their side."[52]

Clearly, then, solidarity is no mere commonsense identification among members of the same group (e.g., nation, class, gender, race), although that identification may be beneficial, sometimes, even necessary. Nor is solidarity to be confused with identity politics, although it does involve recognition of identity and of difference. As a category in theological anthropology's appeal to social praxis, solidarity is an intentional, moral, and ethical task.

Solidarity begins in *anamnesis*—the intentional remembering of the dead, exploited, despised victims of history. This memory cannot be a pietistic or romantic memorial, for always intentional recovery and engagement of the histories of suffering are fraught with ambiguity and paradox. The victims of history are lost, but we are alive. We owe all that we have to our exploitation and enslavement, removal and extermination of despised others. Helmut Peukert recognizes our anxiety when he writes, our "own existence becomes a self-contradiction by means of the solidarity to which it is indebted."[53] Our recognition and regard for the victims of history and our shouldering responsibility for that history form the moral basis of Christian solidarity.

Solidarity calls for the recognition and regard for exploited, despised poor women of color as who they are—God's own creation. Solidarity preserves the universality of love, without renouncing preference for these women of color.[54] In solidarity, the Creator is worshipped, *humanum* honored, particularity engaged, difference appreciated. Solidarity affirms the interconnectedness of human being in common creatureliness. Humanity is no mere aggregate of autonomous, isolated individuals. Humanity is one intelligible reality—multiple, diverse, varied, and concrete, yet one.[55] Whether White or Red or Yellow or Brown or Black, whether male or female, whether Iranian or Mexican, Australian or Chinese, Irish or Kenyan, human beings are intrinsically, metaphysically, ineluctably connected.

Oppression assaults (materially rather than formally) our connectedness to one another by setting up dominative structural relations between social and cultural groups as well as between persons.[56] Oppression is both a reality of the present and a fact of history. Solidarity mandates us to shoulder our responsibility to the past in the here and now in memory of the crucified Christ and all the victims of history.

This shouldering of responsibility obliges us in the here and now to stand between poor women of color and the powers of oppression in society, to do all that we can to end their marginalization, exploitation, abuse, and murder. In memory of the cross of Jesus, we accept this obligation, even if it means we must endure rejection or loss. Moreover, this "shouldering" summons us to take intentional, intelligent, practical steps against "the socially or technically avoidable sufferings of others."[57] For, Christian solidarity repudiates every form of masochism and any assent to suffering for its own sake. Solidarity affirms life—even in the face of sin and death.[58]

This shouldering of responsibility struggles for justice in the concrete and admits of particular tasks for each of us by virtue of our differing social locations. It always requires us to be on guard against any form of self-deceit or self-delusion, any attempt to deny freedom and obligation or to act as if the world were devoid of the bodies of poor despised women of color.

Such shouldering cannot be done by a man or a woman alone; agapic praxis characterizes Christian community. In remembrance of the Body of Christ broken for the world, the followers of Jesus, in solidarity with one another, stand shoulder-to-shoulder, beside and on the side of exploited, despised, poor women of color. This praxis of Christian solidarity in the here and now anticipates the eschatological healing and building up of "the body of broken bones."

ESCHATOLOGICAL HEALING OF "THE BODY OF BROKEN BONES"

If the cries of the victims are the voice of God, the faces of the victims are the face of God, the bodies of the victims are the body of God. The anguish of the victims of history and the demands of authentic solidarity plead for the presence of the supernatural in the concrete. The history of human suffering and oppression, of failure and progress are transformed only in light of the supernatural. And, if humanity is not an abstraction, but a concrete reality that embraces the billions of human beings who ever have lived, are living or will live, and, if each and every human person is a part of the whole of interpersonal relationships that constitute human history, then we, too—each one of us—shall be transformed.

In a meditation on the mystical body of Christ, Lonergan brings its Trinitarian character forward. Formally, the "mystical body of Christ refers to a concrete [perichoretic] union of the divine Persons with one another and with [humanity] and, [humanity's] union with one another and with the divine Persons."[59] Metaphorically, the mystical body of Christ is a compact way of speaking about the role of the supernatural in healing, unifying, and transforming of our body of broken bones. The mystical body is a rich and multivalent way of signifying the concrete oneness of humanity, Christ's identification with the one human race in his own body, New Testament language about the body, and the sacrament of the Eucharist.[60]

For some readers, the phrase "mystical body of Christ" may insinuate a backward, even regressive, step. For others, the phrase may arouse suspicion; for others still, it may edge furtively toward nostalgia. Certainly, the phrase "mystical body of Christ" calls to mind Pius XII's encyclical, "Mystici Corporis Christi."[61] For nearly twenty years, the topic commanded theological interest, only to decline in the 1960s.[62] Since that time scarcely a half-dozen monographs or dissertations have been written on the topic.

With the expression, *mystical body of Christ*, I want to reaffirm salvation in human liberation as an opaque work, that is, a work which resists both the reduction of human praxis to social transformation and the identification of the gospel with even the most just ordering of society. I am looking for a point of vantage that is pertinent to human development, relevant to human change in society, refuses to foreclose human history, and is concrete and comprehensive enough to be compatible with the human *telos* in the divine economy. Further, as I noted earlier, my thesis contains not only a critique but also a judgment—and the judgment indicts us *all*. To think of our human being in the world as the mystical body of Christ retunes our being to the eschatological at the core of the concrete, reminds us of our inalienable relation to one another in God, and steadies our efforts on that absolute future that only God can give.

To bring to light the complexity of the mystical body of Christ, "its manifold differentiations, its comprehensive network of relations," Lonergan traces a fivefold dynamics of love.[63] Love originates in the mutual love of the Three Divine Persons one for another: "First, then, there is the love of the eternal Father for the eternal Son, the love of God for God, love [which] is God the Holy Ghost, who is the infinite love proceeding from the infinite loveableness of God. . . . Second, there is the love of the eternal Father for [the] Son as [human]. . . . Because love is for a person, when the Word became flesh, divine love broke the confines of divinity to love a created humanity in the manner in that God the Father loves God the Son." Third, as human Christ loves other human beings with a human love.[64] The love with which Christ loves us, Lonergan stresses

is the love of a human will, motivated by a human mind, operating through human senses, resonating through human emotions and feelings and sentiment, implemented by a human body with it structure of bones and muscles, flesh, its mobile features, its terrible capacities for pleasure and pain, for joy and sorrow, for rapture and agony.[65]

The human love of Christ is for us irrevocable and fulfills our innermost longing.

Fourth, "there is the love of the Eternal Father for us."[66] This love is as deep, generative, intimate, and encompassing as the love with which the Eternal Father loves the Eternal Son. To capture the dazzling beauty, joy, and humility of this truth, Lonergan quotes the prayer of the Johannine Jesus: "May they all be one. As you, Father, are in me and I am in you, may they also be in us, so that the world may believe that you have sent me and you have loved them even as you have loved me" (John 17:20–23).

The Father embraces us human creatures as daughters and sons. This deepens the already real relations between us as creatures and the God of Jesus, whom we may now call Father. We are daughters and sons of the God and Father of Jesus, and therefore share real relations with one another not only through our creatureliness, but through our new relatedness as sisters and brothers in Christ. And, fifth, because of God's love for God, because we are the children and friends of God, the Spirit is sent to us.[67]

Humanity in its diversity is a reflection of the community of the Three Divine Persons. Their divine love constitutes our unity in and realization of the mystical body of Christ. In this body, each member has her and his own distinct existence; each remains herself and himself. But, even as "we remain ourselves, we do not remain on our own."[68] In the mystical body, we belong to God and we are for one another. Through the animation of the Spirit we are knitted and joined together, we find authentic identity in union with the Three Divine Persons and with one another.

The mystical body of Christ is a "way of being in the world with one another [through the Spirit] and with Christ because of who God is."[69] It is an eschatological reality, anticipated concretely in the here and now through our response to the gift of grace, our engagement in a praxis of solidarity. The mystical body of Christ is a "divine solidarity in grace,"[70] and, as such, makes a claim not only on theological anthropology but also on each of us as believers. Solidarity obliges theological anthropology to acknowledge and repent of its complicity in the transgression of *humanum* in exploited, despised, poor women of color. Further, solidarity summons each of us to a social praxis in the here and now, which contests sin's destructive deformation of ourselves and thus of the society we constitute.

This chapter directed theological anthropology away from a "camou-flaged" subject, toward a "new" subject—exploited, despised, poor women of color. This "new" subject prompts us to rethink the relationship of theology (and theory) to women of color, to poor women, and to Black women, in particular. Here womanist theological and ethical evaluations concur with Marcella Althaus-Reid: we no longer can have "a naïve theology, which attempts to harmonise in a hegemonic and authoritarian way the positive and revolutionary elements of difference and dissent in our communities."[71] When theological anthropology recognizes a "new" subject, it refocuses theology's praxis in a situation in which "human authenticity can no longer be taken for granted."[72] To reiterate: this post-Enlightenment "turning" is in no way identical with erasure or replacement, nor does it demean or dismiss *any other concrete human persons.* Rather, "turning the subject" responds concretely to the dangerous memory of the Body broken and poured out for us *all.* By attending to a "new" subject, we commit ourselves to a praxis of solidarity for human liberation and make the mystical body of Christ vibrantly and publicly visible in our situations. The realization of ourselves as that body of Christ takes place as we reset *our* broken bones through concrete love of God and love of neighbor. We must do so even if the love which summons us and knits us together "brings us suffering by our very contact with one another"[73] as we struggle to enflesh freedom.

CHAPTER 6

Enfleshing Struggle

For Zion's sake I will not be silent,
for Jerusalem's sake I will not rest,
until her vindication shines out like the dawn
and her salvation like a burning torch.[1]

I shall not be moved
Just like a tree planted by the water
I shall not be moved.[2]

Give your hands to struggle.[3]

If slavery persists as an issue in the political life of black America,
it is not because of an antiquarian obsession with bygone days or
the burden of a too-long memory, but because black lives are
still imperiled and devalued by a racial calculus and a
political arithmetic that were entrenched centuries ago.[4]

At the first step of the first forced-march through the bush past markets to musty dark underground cells in forts or warehouses, then onto merchant ships—captured African children, youth, women, and men resisted the theft of their freedom. Packed tight (or loose) in filth, fear, and despair, they resisted with their bodies: refusing to eat or to drink, chancing a leap overboard into the sea, resisting. The Africans scratched and clawed at the chains, planned and prepared, assembled and fought—struggled in hope to enflesh freedom. On board the slave ship *Recovery*, a fifteen-year-old girl, the name her parents gave her unknown to us, enfleshed the struggle for freedom. She refused to dance naked on the deck at the captain's command. He ordered her flogged to death.[5] Resistance. Struggle. Dignity. Death. Life.

We find resonances of this young girl's resistance in the centuries-long commitment of Black people as *a people* to give their minds and hearts, prayers and songs, dreams and desires, feet and hands, blood and tears to enfleshing freedom's struggle. We find resonance of her resistance in the defiance of countless unnamed enslaved Black women; in the audacity of Sojourner Truth, Harriet Tubman, and Ida B. Wells-Barnett; in the resolve of Harriet Jacobs, Maria Stewart, and Anna Julia Cooper; in the valor of Septima Clark, Ella Baker, and Fannie Lou Hamer.[6] These women and thousands like them continue to shoulder the tasks of dreaming, praying, hoping, thinking, imagining, designing, judging, organizing, and fleshing out that future for which Black people yearn, and in which *all* people might flourish.

We may find such commitment to freedom enfleshed in the love, advocacy, solidarity, and action of Alicia Garza, Patrisse Khan-Cullors, and Ayọ (Opal) Tometi, of Kimberlé Crenshaw and Andrea J. Ritchie. In the early decades of the twenty-first century, these women instigated movements to enflesh and further freedom's struggle: #BlackLivesMatter and #SayHerName. These movements form critical incarnate responses to the numerous and ongoing unjust extrajudicial killings of unarmed Black human persons by police or under their authority and aegis (i.e., in police custody under questionable circumstances or by designated or self-designated agents). Quite literally, the very existence of #BlackLivesMatter and #SayHerName affirms Walter Benjamin's assessment: "The tradition of the oppressed teaches us that the 'state of emergency' in which we live is not the exception but the rule."[7] In line with the striking insight of womanist ethicist Angela Sims, we may affirm that, at present, Black people's struggle to enflesh freedom takes place in a *"neo-lynching culture."*[8]

> We may replace the rope and fagot of the late nineteenth and early to mid-twentieth centuries with other killing instruments, the message that not all human life is valued, that black life does not matter, persists. Although persons may not hang from an oak tree on the courthouse lawn or other public spaces for hours, the body of an unarmed teenager lying in the streets for hours conveys to many that lynching is etched into the DNA of this nation.[9]

#BlackLivesMatter and #SayHerName identify and organize and protest the abuse of Black bodies, condemn extrajudicial killings or neo-lynchings, comfort families, resist repression, generate healing, formulate creative life-giving strategies, insist on critically transformative education, agitate for changes in policy and action, and demand dignity. Theologically stated: these movements respond to the dangerous memory of the body broken and poured out for us *all*, the body of Jesus of Nazareth; and they collaborate solidaristically in resetting *our* body of broken bones.

The *explicit* subject at the center of #SayHerName coincides with exploited, despised, poor Black women as theology's new anthropological subject. The *presumed*, although *nonexplicit* subject at the center of the Black Lives Matter movement is the *Black human subject*; however, actual protest performances center the names and stories of the extrajudicial killings of Black *men*. With conspicuous exception (e.g., Sandra Bland and Breonna Taylor), the names and stories of the extrajudicial killings of Black women are overlooked. This omission erases Black women, leaves them unacknowledged. Just when Black intragroup unity and solidarity are so crucial, so necessary, such neglect wounds and provokes disappointment.

This oversight *in* public renders Black women invisible. Sadly, the invisibility of Black women has a much larger history that cannot be addressed fully here; however, through probing the mutual conditioning of race and sex in American society, we may gain some purchase on key features of that larger account and this forms the lengthiest and first of this chapter's three sections. The second section overviews each of these new movements, identifies some differences and dissents, and comments on their reception in church and society; the third offers a theo-poetic interpretation.

THE INVISIBILITY OF BLACK WOMEN

Taking Jesus's parable of the Last Judgment (Matt 25:31–46) as background, pioneer womanist theologian Jacquelyn Grant argues Black women are "the least." This phrase functions "to descriptively locate the condition of Black women. . . . Their tri-dimensional reality renders their particular situation a complex one. One could say that not only are they the oppressed of the oppressed, but their situation represents 'the particular within the particular.'"[10] Black women (and women of color) endure the intensifying marginalization of racism, misogyny, heterosexism, economic exploitation, political powerlessness, cultural suppression, and societal domination. Moreover, these women are confronted by the numbing refracted violence perpetrated against them by marginalized Black men (and men of color). Moreover, from an early age, Black girls and women (*all* girls and women), individually and collectively, medically and physically, spiritually and literally, learn to live daily with the fear of violence—of sexual harassment, assault, abuse, and rape; of bodily physical assault, even death.

It would be a misconception to dismiss the depth of feeling Black women experience during Black Lives Matter demonstrations when the names of Black women and girls are omitted. This is not a case of "oppression Olympics," rather an authentic desire to memorialize publicly and to lament communally the names and stories of Black women cut down in extrajudicial killings—a desire for public recognition, remembrance, reverence, respect, and regard. The inclusion of the names of Black women and girls would send "the powerful message that, indeed, all Black lives do matter."[11] In their response to these omissions, Garza, Cullors, and Tometi, founders of Black Lives Matter, declared:

> As organizers who work with everyday people, BLM members see and understand significant gaps in movement spaces and leadership. Black liberation movements in this country have created room, space, and leadership opportunities for mostly Black heterosexual, cisgender men—leaving women, queer and transgender people, and others either in the background to move the work forward with little or no recognition.[12]

While commending the women for the frankness of their statement, educators Lori Patton and Nadrea Njoku assert that "it is insufficient to primarily focus on cisgender Black men while simultaneously lending minimal or no attention at all to Black women and Black trans and queer communities."[13]

Kimberlé Crenshaw rightly called for "an intersectional, Black feminist perspective. . . . When the lives of marginalized Black women are centered, a clearer picture of structural oppression emerges."[14] Intersectionality is an analytic problem-solving tool or heuristic through which to understand the dynamic interaction among such social variables as race, gender, class, sexuality, age, nationality, debility, and how these often operate together and intensify each other.[15]

Intersectionality has come under sharp criticism by media pundits, politicians, and people who seem intent on stoking chaos and racial resentment. Intersectionality is *neither* a religion *nor* a cult; it is *neither* about being "woke" *nor* about being "politically correct." To the contrary, as Vivian May points out, intersectionality "is contextual, concerned with eradicating inequity, oriented toward unrecognized knowers and overlooked forms of meaning, attentive to experience as a fund of knowledge and interrogative (focused on asking questions, incrementally and continuously)."[16] Quite importantly intersectionality requires a commitment to openness, to listening, to self-correction. Authentic self-correction might begin by listening closely to the centuries-long story of sexual violence perpetrated against the bodies of Black women.

Stereotypes, Race, and Sex

Recall that, in chapter 2, the voices of formerly enslaved Black women, as recorded in slave narratives, disclose the brutality of their sexual, physical, and psychological humiliation and suffering. At the same time, these women do not allow us to forget the courage and cunning that they and other enslaved Black women showed in protecting their children and in defending one another and themselves. We should remember that during enslavement Black women were never "protected by men or by law, and their womanhood [was] totally denied." Even after Emancipation, in the troubled aftermath of Reconstruction, life challenged Black women to a distinctively "different kind of womanhood, nothing like that of white women."[17] Living freedom required of them just as much courage and cunning. Furious or resentful observers of their inner strength and daring derisively caricatured Black women as Sapphire or Jezebel.[18] These figures, concocted from the period of slavocracy, rank and rankle; as *myths-turned-stereotypes*, they were inscribed like hieroglyphs on Black women's flesh. These stereotypes construed Black women as lazy, unreliable, liars; "man-like, overly aggressive and accustomed to violence within their environment";[19] immoral, libidinous, promiscuous and, thus, (un)rape-able. Womanist ethicist Katie Cannon quite pointedly wrote: "Perceived through the lens of hetero-patriarchal imagination, Black women's bodies have been degraded, demeaned, and demonized—locked into an oppressive gaze of beauty created in opposition to us."[20] Poignantly, educator Monique Morris shows that these stereotypes extend into the contemporary and when applied to young Black *girls* adultification results. Morris maintains that "[I]n the public's collective consciousness, latent ideas about Black females as hypersexual, conniving, loud, and sassy predominate . . . [Further] age compression renders Black *girls* just as vulnerable to these aspersive representations."[21]

For centuries, Black women (and men) have tried to debunk racist mythologies and fantasies that depict Black sexuality as depraved, excessive, insatiable. Recall that chapter 1 examined the harrowing case of Sarah Baartman and the way that her body was pejoratively scripted scientifically, aesthetically, and morally by the White male pornographic gaze.[22] The current American socio-cultural context is shaped by the internet, various virtual platforms, advanced technological communication, and easy access to websites and social media content. With this toolset readily at hand, we assume that the American public possesses or has access to accurate (age-appropriate) information about female and male human bodies, sex, psychology, and appropriate (ethical) sexual behavior. But perhaps myth and misbelief prevail: we *all* are caught in over-lapping intricate webs woven long ago by a hypocritical morality that locates proper sexual activity within heterosexual marriage for procreation and that still regards, if not upholds, Victorian codes of respectability. Yet that moral-ity and those codes allow *and* excuse ("boys will be boys") unbridled sexual behavior by some (especially White men), while severely punishing such behavior by others (*all* women). Just recall the Senate Confirmation Hearings of Supreme Court Justices Clarence Thomas (1991) and Brett Kavanaugh (2018). Now recall senatorial and public reactions to the presence and testi-monies of Anita Hill and of Christine Blasey Ford.[23]

Patricia Hill Collins maintains that sexual violence has served as an instrument of social regulation through which White men control African Americans, women, poor people, lesbians, gays, transgender women and men, and others. In *Black Sexual Politics*, she explicates the functions of lynching and rape in maintaining racial subordination and oppression:

> Together, lynching and rape served as gender-specific mechanisms of sexual vio-lence whereby men were victimized by lynching and women by rape. Lynching and rape also reflected the type of binary thinking associated with racial and gender segregation mandating that *either* race *or* gender was primary, but not both. Within this logic of segregation, race and gender constituted separate rather than intersecting forms of oppression that could not be equally impor-tant. One was primary whereas the other was secondary. As targets of lynching as ritualized murder, Black men carried the more important burden of race. In contrast, as rape victims, Black women carried the less important burden of gender.[24]

The results of carrying "the less important burden of gender" have resulted in the marginalization, erasure, and invisibility of Black women and their experiences in both feminist and antiracist movements. The conclusion is pre-dictable: despite their active and committed presence, Black women's voices are silenced, their suffering disregarded or relativized, their bodies invisible.

The sexual violation and abuse of Black women's bodies, Collins concludes, "has historically carried *no* public name, garnered *no* significant public censure, and has been seen as a crosscutting gender issue that diverts Black politics from its real job of fighting racism."[25] In 1977, the Black feminist Combahee River Collective declared: "If black women are free, it would mean that everyone else would have to be free since our freedom would necessitate the destruction of *all* the systems of oppression."[26]

CONTINUING FREEDOM'S STRUGGLE

The struggle of Black people for freedom in the United States did not begin with the civil rights movement of the 1950s and 1960s; rather, that sacred time of struggle was one in a long series of chronic eruptions by Black children, youth, women, and men for public recognition of and respect for their humanity and their legal inclusion in the political, educational, economic, cultural, and societal structures of the nation. While the Reverend Dr. Martin Luther King Jr. struggled for the full inclusion of Black people in the nation, he also repeatedly called for the moral and spiritual transformation of a nation mired in racism, poverty and extreme materialism, violence and militarism. #BlackLivesMatter has been flagged by some as "'not your grandfather's civil-rights movement,' to distinguish its tactics and its philosophy from those of nineteen-sixties-style activism."[27] Yet both #BlackLivesMatter and #SayHerName cannot but draw on strategic, intellectual, cultural, moral, religious, and spiritual resources preserved from previous eruptions of struggle.

#BlackLivesMatter

By now, it is well known that #BlackLivesMatter was founded by Alicia Garza, Patrisse Khan-Cullors, and Ayọ (Opal) Tometi in the weary and angry aftermath of the acquittal of George Zimmerman for the 2013 killing of seventeen-year-old Trayvon Martin. #BlackLivesMatter lifted up Trayvon's name and protested his death, and the crude dismissal of his young life.[28] Originally developed as a "campaign to inspire a new generation of organizers," Garza, Khan-Cullors, and Tometi aimed to use Twitter and Facebook to provoke their thinking and conversation about the state of Black life in the United States.[29] But the extrajudicial murder of eighteen-year-old Michael

Brown on August 9, 2014, in Ferguson, Missouri, impelled the women and their collaborators to act. Garza, Khan-Cullors, and Tometi, along with hundreds of other organizers, traveled to Ferguson to support Brown's family and Ferguson's Black community, and to demonstrate that Black Lives Matter. Their instigation of the movement represents a public option with and for marginalized, dispossessed, despised, and excluded Black human persons. BlackLivesMatter is a fierce political and spiritual cry—a cry of recognition from a position of minoritization, a cry of justice from a site rife with oppression, a cry for freedom in a condition of absurdity.

Garza, Cullors, and Tometi define Black Lives Matter as an "ideological and political intervention in a world where Black lives are systematically and intentionally targeted for demise. It is an affirmation of Black folks' contributions to this society, our humanity, and our resilience in the face of deadly oppression."[30] Almost immediately after Ferguson, the Black Lives Matter movement expanded rapidly, broadly, and globally, with independent but loosely affiliated chapters that insist not only on reforms but for systemic and fundamental change.[31] The movement (BLMM/M4BL) is commonly known as Black Lives Matter, and the Black Lives Matter Global Network (BLMGN) is but one of dozens of organizations within a "larger constellation" of groups that fall under the umbrella Movement for Black Lives movement (BLMM/M4BL).[32]

Black Lives Matter's innovative, decentralized grassroots organizing style builds upon and supports self-empowerment, decision-making, and liberatory action led by Black people and those allied with them against anti-Black racist oppression.[33] Principles of the Black Lives Matter movement constitute a Black humanist platform that commits adherents to work for the freedom, liberation, and flourishing of Black human persons as selves and as subjects of their own lives. Briefly summarized, these principles include: diversity as respect and celebration of differences and commonalities; recognition of a global African-connectedness along with critical sensitivity to the differentiated social locations of Black human beings around the world; commitment to demonstrate actively human regard and respect for all, and intentionally naming and embracing the presence and collaboration of transgender persons, gay and lesbian and queer persons, families, and persons of different ages and different systems of belief or religions; commitment to work to dismantle sexism, heterosexism, cisgender privilege, ageism, ableism; commitment to practices of restorative justice; commitment to embody and practice justice, liberation, and peace, as well as empathy in all dealings with all others; and an "unapologetic" commitment to Black people, their freedom and right to live in justice.[34]

#SayHerName

The year 2014 marked the fatal shooting of Michael Brown by police in Ferguson, Missouri. This incident, coupled with the fact that for at least four hours Brown's body lay in the street after he was shot, ignited local protest and sparked a nationwide, broad-based movement against police violence and anti-Black racism.[35] The year 2014 also marked "the unjust police killings of Black women, including Gabriella Nevarez, Aura Rosser, Michelle Cusseaux, and Tanisha Anderson."[36] Four years earlier, in 2010, seven-year-old African American Aiyana Stanley-Jones was killed, while she slept, by a single shot from the weapon of a member of the Detroit police force's Special Response Team, who were conducting a "no-knock search" for a murder suspect, but at the incorrect address.[37]

"It is hard," Michelle Jacobs maintains, "to educate the public about violence against Black women because it so rarely makes the news."[38] This "erasure" of Black women is not for want of data. For instance, in New York City researchers found a nearly "identical pattern" between Black women and Black men with regard to police stops, frisks, and arrests.

> In 2013, of all men stopped by police in NY: 10.9 percent (White), 55.7 percent (Black), 29.3 percent Latino. In 2013, of all women stopped by police in NY: 13 percent (White), 53.4 percent (Black), and 27.5 percent (Latino).[39]

According to US Census data at the time, Black people were 27 percent of the city's residents. Note that the rates of negative engagement by police with Black women and Black men exceed their percentage of the population. But Crenshaw and her colleagues contend that "media, researchers, and advocates tend to focus only on how profiling impacts Black men."[40]

With this male-centric approach, the names and stories of Black women and girls, as young as seven and as old as ninety-three, of transgender women and of gender-nonconforming people "who [also] are targeted, brutalized, and killed by police are too often excluded from mainstream narratives around police violence."[41] To remedy this oversight, #SayHerName was established in December 2014 by the African American Policy Forum (AAPF) and the Center for Intersectionality and Social Policy Studies (CISPS).

In the report, "SayHerName: Resisting Police Brutality Against Black Women," Crenshaw and Ritchie explain that

> the resurgent racial justice movement in the United States has developed a clear frame to understand the police killings of Black men and boys, theorizing the ways in which they are systematically criminalized and feared across disparate class backgrounds irrespective of circumstances. Yet Black women who are profiled, beaten, sexually assaulted, and killed by law enforcement officials are conspicuously absent from this frame even when their experiences are identical. When their experiences with police violence are distinct—uniquely informed by race, gender, gender identity, and sexual orientation—Black women remain invisible.[42]

To counter the invisibility of Black women and girls, the #SayHerName movement functions as a "multi-dimensional campaign" to hold up and speak aloud the names of Black women and girls lynched by the police and to tell their stories. Further, #SayHerName insists drawing connections between anti-Black violence and *all* members of the Black community exposes systemic realities that often go unnoticed and unanalyzed.[43]

The staff of #SayHerName have developed a user-friendly website that allows access to information provided through various media—text, short YouTube videos, podcasts, and so on. The home page of the website incorporates a multimedia approach: an animated video of figures of women and men carrying placards announcing the names of women concurrently with their photos and the recitation of their name. The speakers who say and chant the names include Crenshaw, Nikole Hannah-Jones, Janelle Monáe, Alicia Keys, Zoë Kravits, and Beyoncé, among others. The speakers are backed by a chorus of mixed voices chanting "Hell You Talmbout" (the phonetic spelling in African American vernacular English of "you talking about").

- The *demands* of #SayHerName include investments in forms of community safety and security that do not rely on law enforcement officers, reallocation of funds from police budgets into resources for mental health services, the end of no-knock warrants, respect by law enforcement of gender identity and expression during police interactions, searches, and placements in police custody.[44]
- *In Memoriam*: this tab opens on nearly two hundred black rectangular boxes or memorial plaques, each bearing the name of the woman

or girl, her age, the date that she was lynched. Double-clicking on the box opens a short summary of the circumstances surrounding her lethal encounter with police. These memorial plaques begin with the most recent (at this writing from 2021 to 1975).

- The *Mothers Network* reaches out to mothers and family members of Black women and girls killed by police. Opening this tab introduces us to this group, which met officially for the first time in November 2016 under the auspices of the African American Policy Forum (AAPF). Members may participate in lobbying for policy changes on Capitol Hill, in strategy sessions or focus groups evaluating and responding to policy, in ascertaining the needs of family members of those newly cut down in extrajudicial killings, in organizing memorial and vigils for murdered Black women and girls.

  #SayHerName Mothers Network recorded a message for the next mother whose daughter was lynched at the hands of police.

- *The Mothers of the Movement* met June 11–18, 2018, under the auspices of AAPF along with BYP100 (Black Youth Project) and numerous other groups and individuals who advocate racial justice and gender justice. This tab allows mothers and other family members and groups to hold up and honor the names and stories of their loved ones. Short films and podcasts bring the viewer into the ordinary lives of these women and girls.

- The #SayHerName *Mothers Network in Memoriam* honors the deaths of the mothers and close family members of the murdered women.

- *Her Dream Deferred*: Each year, at the end of March, in honor of Women's History Month and the UN's International Decade for People of African Descent, AAPF hosts a weeklong series of workshops, presentations, and activities that identify the harm that Black women and girls have endured, but that also provide strategies and tools to dismantle structural barriers.

Controversy and Accountability

African American studies scholar Frank Leon Roberts maintains that "BlackLivesMatter's focus has been less about changing specific laws and more about fighting for a fundamental reordering of society wherein Black lives are free from systematic dehumanization. Still, the movement's measurable impact on the political and legal landscape is undeniable."[45] Historian Barbara Ransby observes: "The breadth and impact of *Black Lives Matter* the term has been extraordinary. It has penetrated our consciousness and our lexicon. . . . The powerful phrase has resonated as a moral challenge, and as a slap in the face, to the distorting and deceptive language of colorblindness and postracialism."[46]

In 2016, three years after the founding of the movement, the Pew Research Center conducted a survey that concluded roughly 43 percent of *all* Americans polled favored the Black Lives Matter movement;[47] after the 2020 murder of George Floyd, support for the movement soared to 61 percent.[48] More recent surveys report a shift in attitude toward the movement, particularly in response to mob-fueled looting and destruction of property after large demonstrations—even if, these actions were neither sponsored nor endorsed by Black Lives Matter.

Criticism comes from Christian congregants, jurisdictional leaders, administrators, pastors, clerics, and administrators. In *The Color of Compromise: The Truth about the American Church's Complicity in Racism*, Jemar Tisby, an Evangelical writer and podcaster, presents results from a survey conducted by the Barna Research Group on attitudes about racial justice among White evangelicals. When it came to Black Lives Matter, "just 13 percent of evangelicals supported the 'message' compared to 27 percent of adults over all and 45 percent of millennials."[49] In *White Evangelical Racism: The Politics of Morality in America*, religious studies scholar Anthea Butler cites comments about police violence posted on Facebook in March 2015 by Franklin Graham: "Listen up—Blacks, Whites, Latinos, and everybody else. Most police shootings can be avoided. It comes down to respect for authority and obedience. . . . It's as simple as that. Even if you think the police officer is wrong—YOU OBEY."[50]

Bishop Thomas Daly declared that Black Lives Matter "is in conflict with Church teaching regarding marriage, family and the sanctity of life."[51] Bishop Mark Seitz knelt in solidarity with protesters for Black liberation and stated plainly: "To say that Black lives matter is just another way of repeating something we in the United States seem to so often forget, that God has a special love for the forgotten and oppressed."[52] One Catholic priest called Black Lives Matter members and demonstrators "maggots and parasites";[53] another Catholic priest defended the movement as highly compatible with the Catholic tradition of finding the universal within the particular.[54]

Sociologists Robert Putnam and David Campbell indict believers of every religion: "Just as religious Americans have *not* been in the vanguard of concern over income equality, they have *not* led the way in racial tolerance. Social connections across class and racial lines do not necessarily inspire action to increase social justice."[55] We must put forward an adequately complex and comprehensive analysis of the structure of White racist supremacy—a critical analysis that accounts for its shape-shifting in economic or political or cultural routines or procedures to foster pseudo-equality, to deprecate the humanity of others, to warp the vivid life of the mystical body of Christ.

ENFLESHING FREEDOM'S STRUGGLE:
FLESHLY PERFORMATIVE THEO-POETICS IN A NEO-LYNCHING CULTURE

Taken together, #BlackLivesMatter and #SayHerName may be appreciated as performative theo-poetics. These movements affirm and testify to freedom's struggle, that is, the survival and lived lives, dignity and resistance, flourishing and beauty of Black children, youth, women, and men. In their nonviolent action and unswerving commitment to human and social transformation, in their solidarity with *all* who are poor, excluded, and dispossessed, these movements collaborate in resetting *our* body of broken bones.

With the word *poetics*, I refer to "exploration of the human powers to make (*poiesis*) a world in which we may poetically dwell."[56] With the word poetics, I signal a social imaginary that makes and remakes the Black lifeworld as beautiful, that discloses Black human potential and its realization of Black lives of truth and justice. Thus, by reaching out and bringing together, unifying a humanly rich and complexly diverse "public" through education and research, observation and critique, advocacy, organizing, and protest, these movements enflesh the struggle of Black women and men for freedom; they enact and perform a *poetics of imagining*. These movements imagine (and form) a new public space for bodily (fleshly) and embodied (enfleshed) holy connecting and touching, speaking and listening, conversation and interchange—for a range of necessary and desired healing and creative human actions.

By imagining, envisioning, and performing a new social imaginary, #SayHerName and #BlackLivesMatter reinterpret the very notion and meaning of *public*. Bringing together children, youth, women, men, elders—of every racial, cultural-ethnic, socioeconomic group—who affiliate with and accept their principles and priorities—composes a new public. These children, youth, women, men, and elders are not rendered abstract, homogeneous, or deracinated. This new public as reinterpreted through these movements is not circumscribed or hemmed in by citizenship or immigration status, by sexual orientation or gender conformity, by debility or health, by socioeconomic or political or religious or cultural or racial allegiance. Rather, #SayHerName and #BlackLivesMatter imagine and facilitate new *public* spaces into which all participants step—and within which they too may imagine, embody (enflesh), perform, and enact what is required for the survival, quality of life, and human flourishing of each and every human life. And, what is required? Namely, the face, presence, and selfless affirmation of an-*other* through fiercely loving compassionate solidarity. By locating the meaning of humanness, the meaning of human life in the affirmation and protection of the bodies of Black children, youth, women, and men, these movements "repoliticize [US] public life."[57] They restore us to a meaning of politics as that inclusive horizon within which we comport and realize ourselves as *human beings* within history. This promotes a politics of inclusion and initiates groundwork for generating a potentially authentic common good (participatory democracy).

Within this inclusive horizon differences matter. No participant is required to discard or conceal their particular and differing experiences, perspectives, and affiliations. *No one is colorblind*: Within this space children, youth, women, men, elders encounter one another as human beings. In more explicit theological terms: each one sees the other as *ikon* of the Divine Transcendent One, as another human person made in the image and likeness of God.

Such repoliticization calls not only for conscientization but also critical formation of (moral) conscience that is so necessary in sustaining a new "social imaginary." As is well known, the term "conscientization" and its critical practice originate in the work of Brazilian educator Paulo Freire. Conscientization refers to the process of raising and attuning our awareness or consciousness to an issue or problem; to the process of coming to deeper, more complex understanding of how cultural, social (i.e., political, economic, technological), societal, and religious structures and institutions intersect and reinforce one another in order to organize and sustain the cultural and societal reality within which we live. Conscientization occurs through questioning that reality and its construction, through probing and reflecting on answers discovered and uncovered. Moreover, it is vital to study, critique, dialogue, and debate those answers in order to unmask the ideologies that sustain those structures and institutions and enable them to appear to us as natural, as the logical conclusions of historical development, and as the way things have been, are, ought to be, and shall be for all eternity. Yet study and critique, dialogue and debate are not enough: the protracted persistence of any iniquitous system of living and the ideologies that support and defend it rely upon our inertia, our anxiety at questioning the "norms, habits, symbols [and] assumptions underlying institutional rules and the collective consequences of following those rules."[58] These spurious ideologies thrive on our fear and nervousness to act, our anxiety at seizing the possibilities of personal and communal transformation. But, we must act together; we must engage in praxis together—take up ongoing action and reflection and action.[59]

Conscientization requires critical self-reflection; such self-reflection leads inevitably to the moral dimension of human consciousness—conscience.[60] Conscience concerns our conduct, intentions, and character regarding our sense of obligation to do what is right. In order to perceive the directives of conscience, we must be "sufficiently present" to ourselves; hence, cultivation of our interiority.[61] Interiority regards our exploration of the innermost depths of mind and heart. Interiority asks the question of conscience, "Who am I?" The answer is decisional action or performance—or not. We ask and answer the question "Who am I?" with our very being, our very lives at pivotal moments of understanding, of judging, of valuing, of deciding, and of acting in accord with what we know, judge, value, and love. In this way, each of us embodies (enfleshes) at any given moment who and what we are. To stand with, to participate with, to affirm, to support #SayHerName and #BlackLivesMatter is a decision about "who each of us is" and "who each of us is for."

We may appreciate these movements as reimaging public discourse as a poetics of testimony characterized by three features: *truth-telling, memory and mourning*, and *eliciting an ethical summons*. A poetics of testimony critiques the ideology of dominant cultural practices and contests how that ideological reality is both represented and created through public discourse.[62] A *first* characteristic of a poetics of testimony is *truth-telling*. One of poet Mari Evans's most famous poems importunes us to "speak truth . . . talk sense to the people." Free them with "Love and Courage / and Care for their Being."[63] These movements insist that if we are to experience and authentically engage freedom, then we must give testimony with and for the most marginalized Black human persons—women, trans women, women with debilities.

"In a society where many voices sound yet public speech that is honest and empowering is rare," contends New Testament scholar Thomas Hoyt, "people sorely need testimony."[64] The idea of testimony draws from judicial and religious domains: in courtrooms, witnesses are expected under pain of severe penalty, even imprisonment, to speak truth when questioned. In some Black and in some free-church traditions, testimony is part of the fabric of worship, part of the fabric of religious experience. Here is how Hoyt describes the pattern of testimony in the Black Church: "A believer describes what God has done in her life, in words both biblical and personal, and the hands of her friends clap in affirmation. Her individual speech thus becomes part of an affirmation that is shared."[65]

Testimony coalesces as a rich, robust tradition among African-descended peoples, well prior to our marginalization and commodification during the time of enslavement in the United States. Indeed, during that period enslaved people could not give legal testimony, and certainly not against any Whites. Black people had no standing under nearly all federal and state law—except as merchandise or property to be bought, sold, bartered, or mortgaged. Thus, the enslaved people told the *truth* of their experience to the Divine Transcendent One, to God and to one another in prayer, storytelling, song, shout, and preaching.[66] In their testimony and prayer, the people chronicled their suffering as they experienced and endured it and lit the fire of hope as their sorrow-psalms rose like incense to the Absolute Compassionate and Merciful One.

Through a *poetics of testimony*, these movements witness, testify to the *truly true*—the truth of the contemporary Black human condition. Through a poetics of testimony, these movements contest those cover stories that conceal or excuse the neo-lynchings and "unexplained deaths" of Black (and Brown) women and men in police custody. #SayHerName and #BlackLivesMatter give an account of the social suffering of Black human children, youth, men, and women.

Second, a poetics of testimony *holds* families, communities, and marchers in mourning and memory. During protest marches, speaking and chanting the names of the dead supports families and communities in their loss of loved ones in the ongoing Black struggle to enflesh freedom. This chanting or speaking the names of the dead *enfolds* them in that great cloud of witnesses who compose the "Martyrology of Black Freedom." The recitation of the litany of their names *re-members* and *holds* their persons and stories in public mourning and memory. Testimony's public speech of truth enfleshes *anamnetic solidarity*.

The litany of the murdered dead honors and speaks the names of wives and husbands, mothers and fathers, daughters and sons, sisters and brothers, aunts and uncles, nieces and nephews, cousins and fictive kin, lovers and friends. This litany gives back to wounded and grieving Black families, friends, and communities memories—old and bittersweet, joyful and tender. Publicly speaking the names of the murdered dead brings together concrete historical events and recognition of the power of transcendence. Through incarnating mourning and memory, a poetics of testimony pours a healing balm and binds up psychic and spiritual wounds inflicted by structural violence, even as this mourning and memory evokes and demands the seemingly impossible: the *unity* of the differing and differentiated peoples of the nation confronting the insidious "monster" of our time.[67]

Third, a poetics of testimony invokes an ethical summons to attend to the other in responsive and responsible ways, an ethical summons to love.[68] #SayHerName and #BlackLivesMatter impose on our moral consciousness and evoke our social responsibility.[69] And, how difficult, how arduous it is to live against pliant and seductive collusion with White racist supremacy. Black self-love must neither be smug with self-satisfaction nor be simplistic with unqualified appeal to racial community. Black self-love calls for disciplined resistance to the lure of both the dominant culture and the appeal of the politics of respectability. Black self-love calls for the hard work of wholeness, of personal integrity or authenticity. White self-love must neither be indulgent with naive justification nor be glib with self-congratulations.

These movements assert what earlier movements for the freedom of Black people asserted: we are responsible to and for one another. If we as a nation are to have any future at all, we must speak and act with and for one another. "To keep silent when one should have spoken out is to refuse to acknowledge the humanity of others, of those in pain."[70] We must love one another: Love expresses itself concretely in option and action. Love calls for the radical disposal of ourselves for, on behalf of, and with all those children, youth, women, and men whom society deems poor, marginalized, and despised. Further, these new movements assert that we are responsible for the reality in which we live. They provide emotional and existential, intellectual and cultural space in which those who seek their own human integrity and who are committed to preserve and protect the human integrity of others may strategically engage in networks of thinking and planning, healing and creating, sharing in loving solidarity the bread and wine of experience, work, and sacrifice for life to enflesh the struggle for freedom. For this struggle makes visible the mystical body of Christ and this visibility, to borrow a notion from William Cavanaugh, must be "ordered by the Eucharist."[71]

CHAPTER 7

Eucharist, Racism, and Some Bodies

Unless you eat the flesh of the Son of Man and drink his blood,
you have no life in you, for my flesh is true food and my blood is true drink.[1]

Slavery was the worst days that ever seed in the world.
They was things past tellin',
but I got the scars on my old body to show to this day.[2]

The Eucharistic gift consists in the fact
that in it love forms one body with our body.[3]

The mere linguistic convergence of *Eucharist* and *racism* disturbs. It makes us queasy, uncomfortable. It should. Bringing these realities together defies all religious, theological, and moral logic, for they signify opposing horizons of meaning. Eucharist and racism implicate bodies—raced and gendered bodies, the body of Christ. The meaning of Eucharist not only lies beyond the immediacy of corporeality, it also joins the body's ultimate transformation and the supernatural destiny of the human person. ("In my flesh I shall see God," Job 19:26.) Eucharist relies upon resurrection faith and eschatological imagination. Racism focuses on and interprets the body through an aesthetic scale that hypostatizes phenotype; it rests on the separation of humanness from body.

Eucharist radiates from the trajectory set by the dangerous memory of the audacious rabbi from Nazareth, who asserted "unless you eat the flesh of the Son of Man and drink his blood, you have no life in you . . . for my flesh is food indeed, and my blood is drink indeed" (John 6:53, 54). These words evoke Jesus's great nourishing sacrificial gift of his own life in the struggle to bring about his Father's dream of love, mercy, joy, and peace.

In Christian worship, Eucharist commemorates the meal that Jesus ate with his friends on Passover only hours before he died. Like millions of Jews before him and millions of Jews after him, in this ritual meal Jesus acknowledged, blessed, and praised God, who, through mighty acts, chose, liberated, guided, protected, nourished, sustained, and ennobled a people. The words and gestures of Jesus at that Passover meal and its bloody aftermath embody the etymology of the Greek verb *eucharistein*, that is, "proper conduct of one who is the object of a gift."[4]

The fullest meaning of Eucharist goes well beyond a mere attitude of thankfulness and presses with eager yearning for concrete outward evidence of gratitude that indicates the gift is "effective and present."[5] Eucharist is that inalienable gift, which anchors believers in time, connects them one to another as well as to their origin, intimates their future, and "concentrate[s] the greatest imaginary power and, as a consequence, the greatest symbolic value."[6] Eucharist is of inestimable value: no rate of exchange, no price can be set on the gracious, gratuitous, unmerited gift Eucharist is. No medium of exchange can calibrate the meaning of Christ as God's gift or the meaning of Christ's self-gift in bread and wine.

The sacramental meal of the Christian church grows from these notions of thanksgiving and gift. In this meal, the community of the faithful acknowledges, blesses, and praises the gratuitous gift of Jesus Christ. His ministry and his being effect for us the very conditions of the possibility to claim the gift of his body, person, and spirit; to dwell within the horizon of the *magnalia Dei*. Thus, we embrace his Father as our own and seal our pledge to incarnate the Triune love of God through acts of concrete compassion and solidarity in the here and now.

But, above all, Eucharist denotes the great mystery of the very presence of Christ in the sacrament. Through the compassionate love of the Father and the power of the Holy Spirit, the body and blood of Jesus Christ are present with us and to us. In sacramental reception, his self-gift nourishes, strengthens, and orders us as we make visible his body through a praxis of solidarity, which counters the disorder of this world. Eucharist signifies and makes visible the body raised up by Christ for himself within the body of humanity, the "mystical body" through which the domain of Jesus's body is extended, a counter-sign to the encroaching reign of sin.

Racism opposes the order of Eucharist. Racism insinuates the reign of sin; it is intrinsic evil. As structural or systemic, racism goes beyond prejudice or even bigotry by binding negative or vicious feelings or attitudes to the exercise of putatively legitimate power. Racism is both an ideology and a set of practices. It does not rely on the choices or actions of a few individuals; rather, racism infiltrates, permeates, and deforms the institutions of politics, economy, culture, even religion.[7] Racism exploits the interdependence of individuals in and upon society through the formulation of ideology. Ideology as a mental construction may be defined as a biased way of thinking, which justifies and maintains an iniquitous way of living.[8] Not only does racism ignite pseudo-rationality, incite vicious practices and violent acts, it poisons the racist—crippling a woman's or a man's potential for authentic religious, cultural, social, moral, psychological, and spiritual growth.

As intrinsic evil, racism is lethal to bodies, to Black bodies, to the body of Christ, to Eucharist. Racism spoils the spirit and insults the holy; it is idolatry. Racism coerces religion's transcendent orientation to surrender the absolute to what is finite, empirical, and arbitrary, and contradicts the very nature of a religion. Racism displaces the Transcendent Other, selects and enthrones its own deity.

For more than 450 years on the North American continent, religion, greed, law, labor, myth, and violence consumed the bodies of Black women and men. If, since the first Eucharist, a "hurting body has been the symbol of solidarity for Christians,"[9] how are we to grasp the relation of Eucharist to hurting Black bodies? In a context of White racist supremacy, what is the position and condition of Black bodies? If the Eucharistic meal is that ritual which celebrates the redemption of the body, then how does the sign and reality (*res et sacramentum*) of Eucharist contest the marginal position and condition of Black bodies?

In the following pages, the first section regards the wounding of the Black body through "the trade"—captivity, storage, commodification, abuse, and sale. The second section parallels the gruesome and sadistic spectacle of crucifixion with spectacles of lynching and neo-lynching, with attention to the lynching of Black women. Calling attention to the lynching of Black women does not dismiss or demean the brutal lynchings of Black men. Calling attention to the lynching of Black women may widen and deepen our theoretical understanding of White racist supremacy. Taking Black women, Evelyn Simien argues, "as symbolic representatives of lynching challenges often taken-for-granted assumptions about lynching and its victims."[10]

The questions raised above about the relation of Eucharist and Black bodies can admit no idealized or bloodless evaluation of Eucharist or its doctrinal articulation, for the Eucharist memorializes the death of Jesus as a "first-century lynching."[11] By this dangerous memory, "we are formed into a body which transfigures the world's violence through self-sacrifice and reconciliation."[12] But, since our formation takes place in "a situation in which authenticity cannot be taken for granted,"[13] notions and speech about self-sacrifice and reconciliation are suspect. The church which *holds* the body of the Lynched One is always in need of conversion. Finally, the third section weighs what it might mean, through practices of Eucharistic solidarity, to em-body Christ in a social context shaped by "violent normalcy."[14]

WOUNDING THE BODY OF A PEOPLE

The Atlantic slave trade wounded the very body of Africa. Human loss reverberated in personal and communal life. Before the continent became a hunting ground, before "Africans"[15] were commodities, they were social subjects. As such, women and men held place and standing in their communities, supported dependents and upheld obligations, nurtured hopes and dreams. Kidnap and seizure, whether by force or by deception, required not only that the captive redefine her or his personal and social identity but also that those left behind do so as well. The disappearance of a spouse or parent could translate into deprivation; the loss of a child or sibling could cause depression, perhaps even madness. However, as historian Stephanie Smallwood suggests, "The indelible bonds of kinship meant that once out of sight, [the] departed could never be out of mind."[16]

Sociologist Orlando Patterson has argued that slavery was social death.[17] But this death was quite unlike death as understood by precolonial West African peoples. For these cultural groups, the dead remained intimately connected to the living. The honored dead, the Ancestors, were capable of intervening in daily affairs, bestowing blessing, or meting out punishment. And, if one had lived a good life, he or she could expect to cross the *kalunga* line, that separated the world of the dead from the land of the living, and to reemerge recognizable in the bodies of grandchildren or future generations.[18] But, the captive African disappeared into a kind of netherworld—physically severed from kin and community, ritually removed from cultural ceremonies of honorable death, metaphysically cut off from the ancestral realm. The captured were now among the dead who still lived; the Atlantic became the *kalunga* line and their bodies were carried beyond a point of no return.

However, Smallwood suggests that some Atlantic African communities believed that persons who were sold into slavery did return. But they did so

transmuted as wine and gunpowder, on the material plane of commodities—an idea suggesting that the special violence of commodification produced not only social death, but more ominous still a kind of total annihilation of the human subject.[19]

Commodification wounded the captive body, mocking its marginality, its "loss of natality as well as honor and power."[20] The Atlantic market for slaves consumed those bodies and "through its language, its categories, its logic," made it impossible for the Africans to return to their communities, to take up being human without wound.[21]

Scholars estimate that roughly ten to twelve million human beings, "fifty or sixty thousand a year in the peak decades between 1700 and 1850,"[22] were drawn through the "door of no return."[23] Abolitionist agitation may have brought about an end to the importation of captured Africans into England and the United States after 1808, but the close of international trade did not bring about the end of chattel slavery.

In the seven decades between the Constitution (1789) and the Civil War, approximately one million enslaved people were relocated from the upper South to the lower South according to the dictates of the slaveholders' economy, two thirds of these through a pattern of commerce that soon became institutionalized as the domestic slave trade.[24]

Buyers and sellers mingled in auction houses and slave pens. Potential buyers examined Black bodies for signs of illness or injury or scars from beatings. They inspected teeth, prodded and manipulated muscle and joints. But Black bodies could also be disguised, "disciplined into order and decorated for market . . . packaged for sale."[25] Hired out to a Missouri slave trader by the name of James Walker, William Wells Brown recalled in his narrative how he was instructed to shave the grizzled facial hair of men and pull out or darken grey strands to hide age.[26] Slaveholders were literally looking for sound, "likely"[27] bodies, predictive of not only skill, physical stamina, and prowess but also the growth and stability of plantation wealth.

James Martin gave this description of an auction to an interviewer:

Slaves [were] put in stalls like the pens they use for cattle—a man and his wife with a child on each arm. And, there's a curtain, sometimes just a sheet over the front of the stall, so the bidders can't see the "stock" too soon. The overseer's standin' just outside with a big blacksnake whip and a pepperbox pistol in his belt. Across the square a little piece, there's a big platform with steps leading to it. Then . . . the overseer drives the slaves out to the platform, and he tells the ages of the slaves and what they can do. . . . When the slaves is on the platform—what they calls the "block"—the overseers . . . makes 'em hop, he makes 'em trot, he makes 'em jump.[28]

W. L. Bost said that he would "hear [the auctioneer's] voice as long as [he lived]."[29] Willis Coffer recalled that, after being herded into the pens, Black people were put on scales and weighed, but generally their value was assessed by skill. Young women of childbearing age and skilled workers, for example, carpenters or masons or smiths, often were priced from two thousand to five thousand dollars, respectively. Male and female field hands sold for a few hundred dollars.[30] "At these auction-stands," Brown wrote, "bones, muscles, sinews, blood and nerves, of human beings, are sold with as much indifference as a farmer in the north sells a horse or sheep."[31] Slavery blurred "the line between things and persons."[32] The subjection of Black bodies to exchange rates and the logic of the market wounded Black being. Moreover, slavery conformed those bodies to the "ideological imperatives of slaveholding culture—whiteness, independence, rationality, necessity, patriarchy, paternalism, and fancy."[33]

Slavery was a moral fiction riddled with contradictions. Enslaved women and men may have been deemed valuable, but they were nonetheless subordinated to the overweening power of the slaveholder. Moreover, as Patterson states, "no society took the position that the slave, being a thing, could not be held responsible for [his] actions."[34] What was the extent and scope of the slaveholder's or his/her delegate's disciplinary action? "The conch shell blowed afore daylight," Mary Reynolds said, "and all hands had better git out for roll call or Solomon [the overseer] bust down the door and git them out. It was hard work, git beatin's and half-fed."[35] Enslaved people judged too slow or inexact in performance of their duties could expect harsh punishment. Charlie Moses recounted beatings, whippings, even shootings when "slaves done something to displease [Master Rankin]."[36] According to Fannie Griffin, slaveholder Joe Beard treated the enslaved people fairly, but his wife Grace did not: "She whip us a heap of times. When she go to whip me, she tie my wrists together with a rope and put that rope through a big staple in the ceiling and draw me off the floor and give me a hundred lashes."[37] Richard Carruthers described the cruelty of an overseer by the name of Tom Hill.

Hill used to whip me and the other [slaves] if we don't jump quick enough when he holler and he stake us out like you stake out a hide and whip till we bleed. Sometime he take salt and rub on the [slave] so he smart and burn and suffer misery.[38]

Thomas Cole sympathized with other enslaved people on plantations where "the owners shore was bad." One nearby planter, Cole said, beat the people frequently and he described this common punishment:

After strippin' 'em off plum naked, [the slaveholder] would have dem tied hand and foot, and bends dem ovah, and runs a pole 'tween de bend in de arms at the elbow and under de legs at de knees, and whip dem wid a cat-o'-nine tails till he bust de hide in lots of places 'cross deir backs, and blood would run offen dem on de groun'. Den he would put salt in dose raw places, specially iffen dey makes out lak dey wants ter fight or sasses him.[39]

"What I hated most was when they'd beat me," Reynolds said, "and I didn't know what they beat me for, and I hated them strippin' me naked." There was more that could be said about life on the Kilpatrick plantation, Reynolds insinuated, but chose not to do so. During slavery, she said, "they was things past tellin', but I got the scars on my old body to show to this day."[40] The bodies of enslaved women (and men) were torn open, lacerated, and punctured at the whim or rage of sadistic power. Yet these marks of oppression also signal the enslaved people's consciousness of their condition and their willingness to assert themselves.

Lavinia Bell was stolen as an infant from freeborn parents in Washington, DC, and held in bondage in Texas. From the age of fourteen, she repeatedly tried to escape but, lacking knowledge of the geographic terrain, each time she was overtaken and returned to Master Whirl. The mistress of the plantation took pity on Bell and explained the directional location as well as symbolic and political meaning of the North Star (freedom) and its goal (Canada). Reportedly, Bell started out on foot and reached Mississippi; there she gave birth to twins, one of whom was stillborn. Again, Whirl overtook and reclaimed her. Upon return to Texas, Whirl "slit both [Lavinia Bell's] ears, then branded her on the back of her left hand with a hot iron, cut off with an axe the little finger of her right hand, searing the wound with hot iron, and also branded her on her stomach."[41] When the slaveholder learned that Bell had urged other enslaved people on his plantation to escape, he tortured her to force her to inform on the person who had told her about Canada.

> She with the spirit of a martyr, refused to give any information, whereupon he had her fixed in what is there technically termed a "buck." This was doubling her in two, until her legs were passed over her head, where they were kept by a stick passed across the back of her neck. . . . While in this position she was whipped. The wounds caused by the lash were rubbed with salt and water, and pepper.[42]

Despite repeated whippings, branding, and a severed finger, Lavinia Bell refused to surrender to slavery. During previous escape attempts, Bell had carried her child with her into what she surely must have hoped would be a new life. But, when she was arrested in Zanesville, Ohio, under the Fugitive Slave Law, her little son was taken from her. When Lavinia Bell told her story in Montreal, Canada, it was as an appeal to raise funds to purchase the freedom of her child.

The Christian reader, perhaps, will best grasp the import of these excerpts, if they are understood as passages from a "Martyrology of Black Freedom." These accounts bear poignant comparison not only to the persecution of Christians but also to the torture and crucifixion of Jesus of Nazareth. The humiliation of women and men and children on the auction block; the whipping, staking, and salting; the scars, lacerations, and lesions on the bodies of Fannie Griffin, Richard Carruthers, Mary Reynolds, Lavinia Bell, and countless others encode immeasurable and unnecessary suffering. Their wounds constitute another stigmata. These "hieroglyphics of the flesh"[43] not only expose human cruelty but also disclose the enslaved people's moral grasp of the inalienable sacredness, dignity, and worth of their humanity.[44]

Mary Reynolds directs us obliquely to her scarred body, which evokes memory of the scarred body of the Risen Christ. Standing before Thomas, the Lord of Life seals his identity with the crucified Jesus of Nazareth by displaying his wounds. The apostle does not touch him, but surely traces the wounds with his eyes, retrieving his relationship with the rabbi he came to love (John 20:19–23). We cannot trace with our fingers or eyes the scars on the bodies of Mary Reynolds or Lavinia Bell. If we could do so, their bodies might disclose wounds, which, perhaps, might scald our eyes and fingers, our minds and hearts. Lavinia Bell's broken body communicates the risk of enfleshing freedom. The marks on her flesh identify her, tell us who she is, and bear witness to her desire and agency. Defying a universe in which she had been rendered *no-thing*, Lavinia Bell achieved God's gracious gift of her humanity.

Slavery was social sin: it was moral and physical evil acted out on Black bodies. Sin is a personal and individual act, yet affects social or public institutions and structures. Moreover, through direct and voluntary participation, approbation, silence, and protection, ordinary women and men participate in, even benefit from, that sin. Slavery was a national social sin. But with its legal demise, the practices and attitudes that had sustained it were extended through various means, but none more horrific than lynching.

THE TREE OF GOLGOTHA AND THE LYNCHING TREE

More than 2000 years separate the tree of Golgotha and the lynching tree: the crucifixion of the Jew Jesus of Nazareth was a *first-century lynching* and the neo-lynching of unarmed Black youth, women, and men in the United States is *modern-day crucifixion*. The cross of Jesus of Nazareth and the lynching tree are ineluctably entwined. This has been the case ever since enslaved Africans poured out his pain and theirs in sorrow-songs or Spirituals:

Were you there when they crucified my lord?
Were you there when they nailed Him to the tree?
Were you there when they pierced him in the side?
Oh! Sometimes it causes me to tremble, tremble, tremble.[45]

The enslaved people struggled through time and space, through their own tragic suffering with insistent hope to reach Jesus—to walk with him, to be with him, to comfort him, to remember and to testify to the injustice of his suffering on Golgotha. Rejecting the sacrilegious claim that their enslavement was decreed by God, these bruised and battered *images of God in black* recognized their own oppression in the injustice, cruelty, and torture that Jesus suffered at the hands of the powerful. They trembled, but they resisted; they would not surrender to slavocracy's "necropower."[46]

Crucifixion, Lynching, and Neo-Lynching

The word "crucifixion" derives from the Latin *cruciare*, meaning to torture. In the ancient world, for the Persians, Greeks, Romans, Jews, and many other peoples, the cross was utterly offensive, obscene.[47] Roman statesman, philosopher, and writer Cicero called crucifixion "the most extreme form of punishment" and Jewish historian Josephus called it "the most pitiable of deaths."[48] For the Romans crucifixion was typically a means by which to punish slaves, dangerous and violent criminals, and traitors, and to "pacify" already subjugated peoples who dared to persist in rebellion.[49]

Crucifixion called for the display of a naked victim at a prominent public place—a thoroughfare, highway, crossroad, outside the walls of a city, or high ground. The victim first was flogged, tortured, and humiliated; then, often, made to carry the cross-beam through the city streets to the place of execution. There, the victim's "arms were attached to a crosspiece of wood, usually with nails, sometimes by rope. Finally, the victim was hoisted by way of the crosspiece (*crux* in Latin) onto a pole, and the crosspiece was attached to the pole so that [the] feet did not touch the ground."[50] If the victim survived this torment, death would come by way of suffocation: unable to support the weight of the body with torn hands or wrists, the diaphragm would slowly be crushed.[51] The most insulting and derisive aspect of crucifixion was leaving the corpse unburied to rot or to be eaten by wild beasts or birds. And, the Roman historian Tacitus reports that sometimes "when daylight faded, [some crucified victims] were burned to serve as lamps by night."[52] As a spectacle of punishment, crucifixion was not directed merely at the individual victim. It was a deterrent aimed to silence and intimidate, terrify and terrorize anyone who might share ideas similar to those of the crucified.

The term lynching denotes "murder by mob action."[53] Lynching refers to extrajudicial intentional lethal (or near-lethal) racial murder, assault and/ or injury inflicted under the aegis of White racist supremacy. Like crucifixion, lynching functions as a spectacle of warning, terror, and death; like crucifixion, lynching neither focused exclusively on the individual, often random victim, but aimed to deter, to intimidate, to silence others. Lynching was deployed to maintain supremacy, to manage and control boundaries of status, class, gender, sex, sexuality, and racial caste.[54] The *act* of lynching concerned and concerns illegal lethal or near-lethal assault for *alleged* charges of homicide, assault, theft, insult to Whites, rape and/or attempted and/or alleged rape of White females.

"The form of crucifixion," writes Martin Hengel, "could vary considerably: crucifixion was a punishment in which the caprice and sadism of the executioners were given full rein."[55] The Roman writer Seneca records the ferocity of crucifixion: "I see crosses there, not just of one kind but made in many different ways: some have their victims with head down to the ground; some impale their private parts; others stretch out their arms on the gibbet."[56] The Romans made widespread use of crucifixion throughout conquered provinces, at times executing hundreds or thousands *en masse*. Jewish people living in first-century Palestine would have witnessed frequent crucifixions since many Jewish revolutionaries suffered this fate.[57]

The form of lynching varied and, like crucifixion, allowed the mob to fully indulge capriciousness and sadism. The reports of Ida B. Wells rival those of Seneca: lynching was accompanied by such tortures as skinning, emasculation of males and cutting open pregnant females, mutilation, shooting, burning, and collection of body parts for souvenirs.[58] The largest documented mass lynching in American history occurred in Los Angeles, California, on October 24, 1871, when a mob of around five hundred White and Hispanic persons attacked, robbed, murdered, then hung seventeen Chinese immigrants, putatively in retaliation for the shooting of two White men caught in a dispute between rival Chinese factions.[59]

Lynching was a capricious instrument of terror that Southern as well as Northern Whites used to deconstruct the new order of political and economic relations that the Union victory achieved and the amended US Constitution affirmed. Between the end of the Civil War and 1968, ordinary White men and women (the majority of whom were Christians) tacitly or actively legitimated the lynching of more than five thousand Black men and women. The alleged reasons for lynching Blacks included homicide, assault, robbery, and theft, but the grounding reasons for lynching were insult to Whites, rape, and attempted rape.[60] But most basically, lynching sought to restore and maintain White dominance or supremacy, to monitor and control the boundaries of racial caste and class.[61]

The spectacle of a castrated, mutilated, lynched, and burnt Black man or woman aimed to intimidate and pacify purportedly restive Blacks. And, as James McGovern argues, it also put Whites on notice that anyone "who balked at the caste system and attempted to initiate personal as against caste relationships with blacks ran the risk of severe social ostracism, especially in the small towns and rural areas."[62] Northerners deemed lynching revolting, but as George Frederickson points out, their "opposition to it was a limited and ineffectual phenomenon."[63]

In Nashville, Tennessee, in March 1901, a mob surrounded the home of Ballie Crutchfield, took her to a bridge, tied her hands behind her, shot her, and lynched her because they *suspected* her of colluding in a theft.[64] Members of a White mob reportedly broke into the jail in Okemah, Oklahoma, dragged out Laura Nelson, *accused* of murdering a sheriff, raped her, then hung her along with her teenage son from a bridge.[65] In Plaquemines, Louisiana, in March 1906, thirty masked men *accused* William Carr of Nashville, Tennessee, of stealing a White man's cow, then lynched him.[66] In 1921, a man in Jonesboro, Arkansas, was lynched because he *organized* young men to refuse to work for White planters at starvation wages.[67] In Jackson, Tennessee, "a colored woman *accused* of poisoning a white one was taken from the county jail and stripped naked and hung up in the courthouse yard and her body riddled with bullets and left exposed to view."[68]

On April 28, 1899, in Georgia, Sam Hose, a Black farm laborer, was charged with killing his White employer in a quarrel over wages.[69] In the presence of a crowd of more than two thousand people, Hose was first tortured before being doused with oil and burned. *The Springfield (Massachusetts) Weekly Republican* recorded these events:

> Before the torch was applied to the pyre, the [N]egro was deprived of his ears, fingers and genital parts of his body. He pleaded pitifully for his life while the mutilation was going on, but stood the ordeal of fire with surprising fortitude. Before the body was cool, it was cut to pieces, the bones crushed into small bits, and even the tree upon which the wretch met his fate was torn up and disposed of as "souvenirs." The Negro's heart was cut into several pieces, as was also his liver. Those unable to obtain the ghastly relics direct paid their more fortunate possessors extravagant sums for them. Small pieces of bones went for 25 cents, and a bit of liver crisply cooked sold for 10 cents.[70]

Lynching was "celebrated as a spectacular event and drew large crowds of people. . . . Mothers held their babies in tow, standing next to the corpse of a dead body and smiling for a photo opportunity."[71] In *Without Sanctuary, Lynching Photographs in America*, James Allen has collected, displayed, and published portions of his extensive collections of picture cards and photographs depicting lynching.[72] This collection evinces social sin. With seeming nonchalance, the "celebrants" sent these grim souvenirs as postcards to friends and relatives, parents and siblings through the US Mail. These photographs reveal as much about the racist orgiastic behavior of a White mob bent on consuming Black bodies as they do about the fear, pain, and anguish of lynched men and women. The images bend credulity; the viewer does not know where to direct the eye. A flood of feeling rises: pity, sorrow, anger at the burnt body; horror, shame, anger at human arrogance, at the furious glee on the faces of those who preside over what sociologist Orlando Patterson names a "feast of blood."[73]

Lynching victims were fungible or replaceable: once a mob actualized itself, it did not seem to matter precisely who the putatively offending party actually was. After a barn was burned near Columbus, Mississippi, the son of Cordelia Stevenson surfaced as the prime suspect. Unable to find the son, the mob seized the mother, "tortured her, left her naked body hanging to the limb of a tree for public viewing."[74]

In Helena, Arkansas, in 1921, nineteen-year-old William Turner was alleged to have assaulted a White telephone operator, but he was never brought to trial. William Turner was lynched, not once, but twice: after one mob of Whites lynched him, a second mob cut down his body and burned it in a bonfire in front of city hall. The *St. Louis Argus* reported that Turner's body

> was hauled through Helena to provide a moving target for white men armed with pistols who lined the principal streets of this town.... Turner's corpse was roped to the rear end of an automobile and driven up and down the main streets of Helena at various speeds as white men hooted, yelled, and perfected their marksmanship by shooting at the almost disintegrating remains. No colored folks were allowed on the streets. When the celebrants had had their fill, the body was burned.[75]

To further demonstrate their supremacy, these White men forced August Turner, William Turner's father, to remove the battered and charred remains of the body of his son.

In *Gender and Lynching*, literary scholar Julie Buckner Armstrong draws a horrifying connection between "several Barbie dolls painted black and hung in a tree" outside the main entrance of Lowndes County High School in Lowndes County, Georgia, in 2002 and the 1918 lynching of Mary Turner. For several weeks, Armstrong reports, public opinion in newspapers and community meetings wavered as to whether the nooses signaled a "hate crime or a harmless prank." But, Armstrong points out, "twenty miles from the high school, Mary Turner's body remains buried where she was lynched with her fetus in May 1918."[76] When Turner, eight months pregnant, learned that her husband Hayes has been lynched, she vowed to find those responsible, to have them punished by the law. But a mob of several hundred men and women determined that they would "teach her a lesson."[77] Members of the mob tied Turner's ankles together, hung her upside down from a tree, doused her clothes with gasoline, set her on fire, shot her. Someone took a knife, cut open her abdomen, the fetus fell out and cried. A man from the mob came forward and crushed its head with his heavy boots.[78] "Both Turner and her child were buried about ten feet from the tree, the grave marked by a whisky bottle with a cigar in the neck."[79] Armstrong poignantly observes: "For almost 90 years this incident remained a taboo subject."[80] No one was ever convicted of this crime, no one ever held accountable.

Organized protest to lynching dates to the turn-of-the-century campaigns led by journalist Ida B. Wells, W. E. B. Du Bois, and the National Association for the Advancement of Colored People (NAACP).[81] Their work attracted the support of the Black community, as well as some influential White political allies. However, "with the upsurge of mass movements during the thirties," Angela Davis contends, "white people began to take a more active role in antilynching efforts."[82] In December 1951, famed artist, cultural leader, and human rights advocate Paul Robeson, along with a small group of Black lawyers, municipal officials, scholars, and family members of lynch victims, appealed to the United Nations, charging the US government with the crime of genocide against its Black citizens.[83]

"This protest gained little attention outside the Black press. But four years later in 1955, Mrs. Mamie Till Bradley, the mother of murdered fourteen-year-old Emmett Louis Till, challenged the nation to confront its legacy of social sin in racial hatred. Mrs. Bradley sent her son from Chicago to visit relatives near Money, Mississippi. Till, unfamiliar with the codes and constraints of Southern segregation, took up a dare to speak to White female shopkeeper Carolyn Bryant. What precisely young Till said to Bryant as he made a purchase in her husband's store may never be known, but she accused him of an impertinent remark and whistling at her. Three days later, Emmett Till was dead. His mother insisted upon an open coffin for her son in order to show the world the ravages of lynchlike violence and mutilation.[84] The men charged and tried for Till's murder, Carolyn Bryant's husband Roy Bryant and J. W. Milam, were acquitted by an all-White, all-male jury.[85]

Lynching was a potent weapon of spatial and social control. Lynching regulated Black motion and movement—restricting not only where Blacks were to sit or eat or walk or recreate or shop, but also how they were to comport themselves during these activities. It policed *all* relations between Blacks and Whites, demanding the protection of White women. From Reconstruction until well into the twentieth century, lynching reasserted and secured White power and authority over Black bodies. During slavery, power and authority over those bodies rested with slaveholders; that power and authority could be extended to other Whites with tacit or active permission. But not all Whites were slaveholders and not all Black bodies were enslaved. Lynching salvaged and resituated the overweening power of the slaveholder in "whiteness" and assuaged Southern defeat with its privilege. Functionally, lynching purged Blacks from the (White) body politic and usurped those legal rights and duties accorded to them by the Thirteenth Amendment, the Civil Rights Act of 1866, and the Fourteenth Amendment to the US Constitution.[86] Lynching as "the violent sacrifice of black bodies," writes literary scholar Walton Muyumba, "protects psychologically and politically the economic and social coherency of the [white] nation."[87]

"There is a preponderance of sociological evidence," argues Angela Sims, to confirm "that actions designed to manufacture a fear of death are tantamount to perpetuating a culture of lynching" or neo-lynching.[88] Neo-lynching rises from a culture of terror, one in which Black people live in fear of random, violent death. Further, Sims declares: "In this age of neo-lynching, an individual's credentials and accomplishments, accepted forms of compliance, and prescribed modes of orderly engagement are no guarantees that black lives matter."[89]

In April 2001, a White police officer chased and fatally shot nineteen-year-old Timothy Thomas in an Over-the-Rhine alleyway in Cincinnati, Ohio. In the six years prior to Thomas's death, fourteen Black men were killed by Cincinnati police under controversial circumstances.[90] Seventy-seven years after a mob sadistically dragged William Turner's body through the streets of Helena, Arkansas, on June 7, 1998, in Jasper, Texas, three White men chained James Byrd by his feet to the back of a pick-up truck and dragged him for nearly three miles until he died, his body partially dismembered.[91] Emmett Till's murder had been sanctioned culturally and legally by nearly all sectors of White society, but Byrd's murder elicited from Blacks and many Whites revulsion, horror, shame, sorrow, and "Christian forgiveness."[92]

Neo-lynching materializes in senseless extrajudicial killings of hundreds of Black women and men, including Eric Garner, whom police held in chokehold and whose last words were "I can't breathe"; Renisha McBride, who approached a house, knocked on door for help, and was killed with a shotgun blast through the closed door; Walter Scott, who was stopped by police for a nonfunctioning brake-light, ran, and was shot in the back; Reika Boyd, who was shot in the head as she stood partying with friends in a park; Sandra Bland, who was found hanged in a jail cell three days after she was arrested for a traffic violation; Sharonda Coleman-Singleton, Cynthia Hurd, Susie Jackson, Ethel Lance, Tywanza Sanders, and Myra Thompson, all of whom were participating in Bible study at Mother Emanuel African Methodist Episcopal Church; Ahmaud Arbery, who was hunted as he jogged, then killed as he tried to defend himself; Breonna Taylor, who was struck down by six bullets when police forced their way into her apartment with a "no-knock" warrant; George Floyd, who died of asphyxia gasping "I can't breathe," calling out "Mama" as a police officer pressed his knee on Floyd's neck; Tyree Nichols, who was stopped by police, then chased, tasered, beaten, pepper-sprayed, and punched, who called out to his mother before he lost consciousness.

The theological anthropology developed here centers the experience of poor, despised, and excluded Black women, "the least of the least." At the same time, the compassionate solidaristic embrace of suffering, stigmatized and marginalized others lies squarely within this theology's circumference. For Black women, like the Good Samaritan, will not pass by the murder of lesbian, gay, and transgender women and men in Orlando, Florida's Pulse Night Club. Black women will not pass by the murder of eleven Jewish women and men in Pittsburgh, Pennsylvania's Tree of Life Synagogue. Black women will not pass by the murder of twenty-three women and men of Hispanic and Latinx descent in El Paso, Texas. Black women will not pass by the murder of six women of Asian descent in metropolitan Atlanta, Georgia, or the murder of Asian women and men in Half Moon Bay, California. Black women will not pass by the murders in school shootings all across the nation. Indeed, Fannie Lou Hamer once declared:

My whole fight is for the liberation of all people because no man [sic] is an island to himself: when a white child is dying, is being shot, there's a little bit of America being destroyed. When it's a Black child shot in America, it's a little bit of America being destroyed. If they keep this up, a little of this going, and a little of that going, one day this country will crumble. But we have to try to see to it that not only the lives of young and adult Blacks are saved in this country but also the whites.[93]

Lynching and neo-lynching objectified Black bodies, rendered those bodies—indeed, *all* Black bodies—hyper-visible and vulnerable. These Black women and men, along with countless others who shared their fate, claim a place in the "Martyrology of Black Freedom." Their torture and death by hanging on a tree or shooting and suffocation mirrors the torture and death by crucifixion of another dark man on Golgotha.

Christianity, the Cross, and the Lynching Tree

"Strange Fruit," as sung by blues legend Billie Holiday, offers a haunting image of the mangled, battered Black body:

> Southern trees bear a strange fruit, Blood on the leaves and blood at the root,
> Black body swinging in the Southern breeze, Strange fruit hanging from the poplar trees.
> Pastoral scene of the gallant South, The bulging eyes and the twisted mouth,
> Scent of magnolia sweet and fresh, And the sudden smell of burning flesh!
> Here is a fruit for the crows to pluck, For the rain to gather, for the wind to suck,
> For the sun to rot, for a tree to drop. Here is a strange and bitter crop.[94]

Billie Holiday called "Strange Fruit" her "personal protest" not only against lynching but also against the myriad physical and psychic humiliations inflicted daily on Black bodies.[95] While "Strange Fruit" emerged from particular historical and social circumstances, the song evokes resonance with a most potent and sacred symbol of Christianity—the cross.

Black literary artists discerned the relation between the crucifixion of Jesus of Nazareth and the lynching of Black men and women. Among others, Countee Cullen, Langston Hughes, Claude McKay, and W. E. B. Du Bois have portrayed the symbolic meaning of the "tree of the cross" in the lynching tree.[96] But, as James Cone has remarked, "The crucifixion of Jesus by the Romans in Jerusalem and the lynching of blacks by whites in the United States are so amazingly similar that one wonders what blocks the American Christian imagination from seeing the connection."[97] Black theologians and preachers do not evade Cone's critique: most have failed to make explicit connection between the cross and the lynching tree.

The collusion of Christianity and Christian theology in human oppression is unquestionable. What remains shocking is "the reality of significant Christian participation in, if not instigation of, a crime as odious as lynching."[98] What made lynching possible, acceptable? Why did so many devout Christian men and women embrace ritual cross burning and invest it with such power? How could "good" Christians twist the tree of the cross into the lynching tree?

Patterson disentangles an ugly web of psychological, religious, and social meanings: In the aftermath of the Civil War, White Southerners were forced to rethink their conceptions both of themselves and of the former enslaved people. They responded in two ways: on the one hand, Whites constructed a paternalistic fantasy of the humble, childlike, uncomplaining, faithful slave, who could not survive outside slavery.[99] On the other hand, Whites recoiled from the nascent success of Blacks and viewed the newly freed people as a threat to their superiority. Blacks—males in particular—were deemed menacing to the sexual purity of White women. In fear and loathing, propped up by a version of fundamentalist Christianity, Southern Whites conflated Blacks with a "satanic presence" that must be eliminated.[100] Lynching was the instrument by which Black bodies were to be purged from the (White) body politic. Then, in a mental leap of "profound theological inconsistency,"[101] Whites deliberately associated the scapegoat sacrifice of Blacks with the mocked, tortured, crucified Christ. "The cross—Christianity's central symbol of Christ's sacrificial death—became identified with the crucifixion of the Negro, the dominant symbol of the Southern Euro-American supremacist's civil religion."[102]

To reiterate: from the nineteenth through the mid-twentieth centuries, the Christian church wavered in response to the wanton lynching of Black women and men; even in contemporary neo-lynching culture, the church arrives, if at all, either breathless and late or patronizing and indifferent. Leon Litwack registers the comment of one White Mississippian in the early twentieth century: "The only way to keep the pro-lynching element in church is to say nothing which would tend to make them uncomfortable as church members."[103] In the conclusion of *A Red Record*, Ida B. Wells-Barnett writes that

The very frequent inquiry made after my lectures by interested friends is, "What can I do to help the cause?" The answer always is, "Tell the world the facts." When the Christian world knows the alarming growth and extent of outlawry in our land, some means will be found to stop it.[104]

Regrettably, the "Christian world" did know, but either was impotent or ineffectual in marshalling that knowledge for widespread solidarity and action on behalf of suffering Black people. Only recently have Christian churches, their congregants, and scholars begun to approach the challenge laid down by James Hal Cone "to see the cross and the lynching tree together . . . to identify Christ with a 'recrucified' black body."[105]

Tracing the philosophical and theological roots of an "heretical tradition" of oppressive Christianity, Kelly Brown Douglas makes explicit the connection between the crucifixion of Jesus and the lynching of Black bodies. While not the focal point of her argument, lynching, she states, "reveals the utter evil of white terror against Black bodies [and] brings the gravity of Christianity's connection to Black oppression into sharp focus."[106] Douglas traces Christianity's disdain for matter, for the body (some bodies more than others), as well as its uneasiness with nonprocreative sex to uncritical absorption of Platonic and Stoic ideals. "The integration of these two philosophies into Christian thought," she contends, "produced a tradition driven by dualistic thinking and ascetic sentiments."[107] This heretical tradition accounts for Christian persecution of the Jews, Christian participation in the oppression and persecution of others including Indigenous peoples and women, as well as Christian alliance with dubious political power.[108] Moreover, a version of this tradition was assimilated into Southern evangelical Protestantism and, during and after Reconstruction, shaped the cultural and social, moral and "theological consciousness of those whites who were party to black lynchings."[109]

Douglas exposes as well the poignant "paradox" of Black people's confession and affirmation of Christianity, "the very religion others use to justify their shameful treatment."[110] To live with and within such paradox requires enormous psychological strength and a "powerful imagination to see both tragedy and beauty, futility and redemption in the cross."[111] To live with and within such paradox requires absolute belief that Jesus Christ, the Incarnate Compassion of the Triune God, denounces this heretical distortion.

The cross and the lynching tree interpret each other. Both were public spectacles, shameful events, instruments of punishment reserved for the most despised people in society. . . . [T]he lynching tree frees the cross from the false pieties of well-meaning Christians. . . . [T]he lynching tree reveals the true religious meaning of the cross for American Christians today. The cross needs the lynching tree to remind Americans of the reality of suffering—to keep the cross from becoming a symbol of abstract, sentimental piety. . . . Yet the lynching tree also needs the cross, without which it becomes simply an abomination. It is the cross that points in the direction of hope, the confidence that there is a dimension to life beyond the reach of the oppressor.[112]

The cross of Jesus of Nazareth demonstrates, at once, the redemptive potential of love and the power of evil and hatred. On the cross, Jesus overcame evil with great love; his resurrection disclosed the limits of evil. But the cross can never be reduced to a cheap or simplistic solution to the problem of evil. The cross and the lynching tree represent unmeasured suffering and anguish. To place maimed lynched and neo-lynched bodies beside the maimed body of Jesus of Nazareth is the condition for a theological anthropology that reinforces the sacramentality of the body, contests objectification of the body, and honors the body as the self-manifestation and self-expression of the free human subject. Slavery, lynching, neo-lynching, and their extension in White racist supremacy aimed to de-create Black bodies and desecrate Black humanity. As intrinsic moral social evil, these vicious practices waged a frontal challenge to (Black) bodies as mediators of divine revelation, as signifiers of the sacred reality being human is.[113]

In chapter 5, I sketched out a meaning of solidarity as commitment to exploited, despised, poor women of color as basic to the realization of our humanness. Examples in this chapter reinforce that commitment. Solidarity begins in an *anamnesis*, which intentionally remembers and invokes the Black victims of history, martyrs for freedom. Theologically considered, their suffering, like the suffering of Jesus, seeds a new life for the future of all humanity. Their suffering, like the suffering of Jesus, anticipates an enfleshment of freedom and life to which Eucharist is linked ineluctably. Eucharist, then, is counter-sign to the devaluation and violence directed toward the Black body.

EUCHARISTIC SOLIDARITY: EMBODYING CHRIST

The idolatrous practices of slavery, lynching, neo-lynching, and White racist supremacy violate Black bodies, blaspheme against God, defame the body of Christ. Such intrinsic evil threatens the communion (*communio*) which is the mediation and the fruit of Eucharist. On more than one occasion, Augustine

reminded us that the Eucharist is "the symbol of what we are."[114] He identified sacrament (*sacramentum*) with "revealing sign" (*sacrum signum*), that
which discloses something (*res*) or Someone hidden or concealed. Sacraments
disclose, mediate, and express, writes David Power, the "abiding presence of
Christ's mystery in the world wherein the Church is united with Christ as his
Body through the gift and action of the Spirit."[115] Sacraments form and orient
us to creation, to human persons, and, above all, to the Three Divine Persons.
Sacraments pose an order, a counter-imagination not only to society but also
to any ecclesial instantiation that would substitute itself for the body of Christ.

Sacramentality signifies the real symbolic unity between what we are as
humans, even as the de-creation of Black bodies clarifies the cost of daring
to em-body Christ in a morally degraded context of White racist supremacy.
What might it mean to em-body Christ? What might it mean, in the *here and
now*, to reveal his abiding but hidden presence in our world, to *be* the body of
Christ? What might it mean to invest exploited, despised Black bodies with
eschatological meaning?

In chapter 5, I proposed that solidarity has a discernible structure with
cognitive, affective, effective, constitutive, and communicative dimensions.
A praxis of solidarity arises from apprehension and heartfelt response to
accounts of historic and contemporary abuse and violence directed against
Black bodies. Protests against slavery and agitation for abolition rightly may
be read as forms of solidarity throughout the eighteenth and nineteenth centuries. Women and men, Black and White, including David Walker, Maria
Stewart, William Wilberforce, Frederick Douglass, Prudence Crandall,
Harriet Beecher Stowe, and William Lloyd Garrison incarnated such solidarity. In her reflection on the intentionality behind the lyrics and style of
performance of "Strange Fruit," philosopher Angela Davis makes a compelling
nontheological case for human openness and solidarity:

> If those touched by "Strange Fruit" were left feeling pity for black victims of
> racism instead of compassion and solidarity, this pity would have recapitulated
> rather than contested the dynamics of racism. It would have affirmed rather
> than disputed the superior position of whiteness. But unless one is an incurable
> racist, it is difficult to listen to Billie Holiday singing "Strange Fruit" without
> recognizing the plea for human solidarity, and thus for the racial equality of
> black and white people in the process of challenging racist horrors and indig-
> nities. Her song appeals to listeners of all ethnic backgrounds to identify the
> "black bodies swinging in the southern breeze" as human beings with the right
> to live and love.[116]

Davis recognizes that cognitive and affective dimensions alone remain inadequate; awareness and pity merely nod toward solidarity. Awareness and pity must be strengthened, extended, and enriched through personal encounter, responsible intellectual preparation, and healing and creative action for change in society. We shoulder suffering and oppression, take up a position beside exploited and despised Black bodies. Further, solidarity involves critique of self, of society, of church. This critique takes on and includes existential reflection, historical scrutiny, presence to memory, social analysis, acknowledgment and confession of sin, authentic repentance—change of heart, change of life, change of living.

A Christian praxis of solidarity denotes the humble and complete orientation of ourselves before the lynched Jesus, whose shadow falls across the table of our sacramental meal. In his raised body, a compassionate God interrupts the structures of death and sin, of violation and oppression. A divine praxis of solidarity sets the dynamics of love against the dynamics of domination—recreating and regenerating the world, offering us a new way of being in relation to God, to others, to self.

Eucharistic Solidarity

Our daily living out, and out of, the dangerous memory of the torture and abuse, death and resurrection of Jesus Christ constitute us as his own body raised up and made visible in the world. As *his body*, we embrace with love and hope those who, in their bodies, are despised and marginalized even as we embrace with love and forgiveness those whose sins spawn the conditions for the suffering and oppression of others. As *his body*, we pulse with new life for Eucharist is the heart of Christian community. We know in our bodies that eating the bread and drinking the wine involve something much deeper and far more extensive than consuming elements of the ritual meal. Eucharistic solidarity is a virtue, a practice of cognitive and bodily commitments oriented to meet the social consequences of Eucharist. We women and men strive to become what we have received and to do what we are being made.

Eucharist is counter-sign to the devaluation and violence directed toward the exploited, despised Black body. The liturgical narrative for Eucharistic celebration does not "directly expose a tortured body, but points implicitly to it, a body that carries the marks of violence."[117] Yet such implicit pointing requires explicit resistance to the antiliturgy which racism performs.

Eucharistic solidarity opposes all intentionally divisive segregation of bodies on the specious grounds of preference for race or gender or sexual orientation or culture. Eucharistic solidarity contests any performance of community as "an atomized aggregate of mutually suspicious individuals"[118] or as self-righteously self-sustaining or as historically innocent or as morally superior or as monopoly on truth. In spatial inclusion, authentic recognition, and humble embrace of different bodies, Eucharistic celebration forms our social imagination, transvalues our values, and transforms the meaning of our being human, of embodying Christ. For "to participate in the Eucharist is to live inside God's imagination."[119]

To put it compactly, embodying Christ is discipleship, and discipleship is embodied praxis. This praxis is the embodied realization of religious, cognitive, and moral conversion.[120] Commitment to intentional and conscious Eucharistic living initiates a change of direction in the personal and social living of an individual, as well as the living of many. Eucharistic solidarity challenges us in living out the implications and demands of discipleship. Prerogatives rooted in socially constructed disparities are deconstructed. We become aware of ourselves as striving to realize concretely the fruitful insights of practical intelligence and rectitude. Eucharistic solidarity orients us to the cross of the lynched Jesus of Nazareth, where we grasp the enormity of suffering, affliction, and oppression, as well as apprehend our complicity in the suffering, affliction, and oppression of others.

Eucharistic solidarity sustains our praxis of discipleship as we stand the ground of justice in the face of White racist supremacy, injustice, and domination; take up simplicity in the lure of affluence and comfort; hold on to integrity in the teeth of collusion; contest the gravitational pull of the glamour of power and evil. Yet, in our agitation for social justice, whether in church or in society, we cannot surrender to the temptation to secure "gains" only for "our" specific group. Too often this approach has deflected attention away from our suffering sisters and brothers and "concealed the [fact] that a lasting transformation of society can never rest on a movement based on the ideology of getting more—no matter how just these demands may be."[121] Eucharistic solidarity teaches us to imagine, to hope for, and to create new possibilities. Because that solidarity enfolds us, rather than dismiss "others," we act in love; rather than refuse "others," we respond in acts of self-sacrifice—committing ourselves to the long labor of creation, to the enfleshment of freedom.

Yet the crucial social consequences of Eucharist may never overtake the real presence Eucharist effects. At the table that Jesus prepares, *all* may assemble: In his body we are made anew, a community of faith—the living and the dead. In our presence, the Son of Man gathers up the remnants of our memories, the broken fragments of our histories, judges, blesses, and transforms them. His Eucharistic banquet re-orders us, re-members us, restores us, and makes us one.

Epilogue

I want Jesus to walk with me.
All along my pilgrim journey,
I want Jesus to walk with me.[1]

The task of the philosopher-rhetorician
is to out-narrate domination.[2]

The body of the text does not belong to the text,
but to the One who is embodied in it.[3]

The primary subjects and the subject of my theologizing in this work are the dead, the "Many Thousand Gone." Through attending critically to the bodies of Black women, I have expressed in the particular the universal claim of the inviolability and sacredness of Black humanity and reaffirmed Black dignity and worth. These broken Black bodies lie beside the body of the crucified Jewish Jesus on the altar of my heart. This suffering—*his* and *theirs*—demands from me as a theologian a "praxis and a theory, a text for living and for dying,"[4] a text that honors their enfleshing freedom.

For us, the living, their wounds can only evoke reverence and a firm purpose of amendment: these wounds reveal Black women's moral and ethical, intellectual and spiritual courage, and disclose the grave evil and spiritual disease of White racist supremacy. Confession of sin for the wrongs committed against her body is a condition for the possibility of engaging the humanizing and reconciling work of Christ on behalf of our redemption. Moreover, to place her Black broken body beside his crucified broken body is a condition for a theological anthropology that grasps the sacramentality of the body in the concrete as an expression of the freedom of the human subject.

This work may be read on several levels: Certainly, it is a constructive exercise in theological anthropology. As such, it mediates between a cultural matrix and the significance and role of religion in that matrix. On Lonergan's account of eight functional specialties in the theological task, communications, the last of the specialties, must be involved in each of the other seven. In writing about body, race, and being, I have tried to work dialectically, but with an eye toward foundations.

This book is as much an articulation of womanist theology as it is of Catholic theology as it is of political theology. As a *womanist* theological reflection, *Enfleshing Freedom* emerges from religious faith's critical reasoned consideration of the ultimate meaning of Black women's experience: here the term "experience" denotes the differentiated range and complex interconnections of Black women's religious, historical, racial, cultural, sexual, social, political, economic experience. In striving for religious coherence, intellectual adequacy, and authentic relevance, this effort participates in redressing the deformation of God's image in Black women's bodies. As a *Catholic* theological reflection, this work demonstrates faith seeking understanding in a context hostile to the aims of God and to the sacredness of God's Black human creatures (and surely the idol of White racist supremacy can be nothing but hostile).

As a *catholic* theological reflection, this work focuses the experience of "the least of the least" to assure *all* God's human creatures of divine love and compassionate solidarity, and to welcome *all* within the wide circumference of that body of broken bones seeking healing and liberation in the One Lynched and Risen, who walked and continues to walk with *all* humanity by the grace and power of the Spirit. Theology becomes *political* when it questions, reasons, interprets, critiques, and challenges religion *and* church (or synagogue or temple or mosque), culture *and* society on behalf of and alongside those children, youth, women, and men whom we as a society impoverish and exclude, marginalize and render powerless, brutalize and murder—simply because *they may be different and exist*.[5] Political theology as a Christian formulation does this in remembrance of the first-century crucified Jewish rabbi Jesus of Nazareth. At the same time, political theology clarifies for all people of good will what it means to act in freedom through love and responsibility for the common human good.

Enfleshing Freedom also may be read as a meditation on Toni Morrison's great novel *Beloved*; hence, it gestures concretely toward a theology of remembering and of remembrance. This work also may serve as a meditation on the blues: "The blues," Ralph Ellison wrote, "is an impulse to keep the painful details and episodes of a brutal experience alive in one's aching consciousness, to finger its jagged grain, and to transcend it, not by the consolation of philosophy but by squeezing from it a near-tragic, near-comic lyricism."[6] What but enslavement could evoke such sorrow! What but the struggle to enflesh freedom could invoke such admiration! What but living Black could produce such tragicomic blue joy! Jean-Luc Marion writes, "that theology, of all writing . . . causes the greatest pleasure."[7] For the theologian of the Black experience, writing theology may also evoke the deepest sorrow, the deepest gratitude, the deepest love.

Acknowledgments (2023)

For more than a decade, *Enfleshing Freedom* has had a life well beyond anything that I ever could have imagined. This is due to generous, curious readers with open minds and hearts. Thank you to the seminary, divinity school, college, and university professors in the United States, Australia, Canada, and the United Kingdom who required or recommended this book in their courses and shared it with colleagues and friends. Thank you to readers, especially students, who found solidarity in the pages of *Enfleshing Freedom* as they too wrestled with unjust and unholy restrictions on human flourishing and who discerned here encouragement to appropriate their own existential, religious, moral, and intellectual freedom.

Thank you to all the "church-folk," parishioners, congregants who read and discussed this book. Thank you to all, especially students, who wrote to me by email and old-fashioned long-hand. Your messages did my heart good, cheered my spirits, brought me joy, and gave me much to ponder.

Thank you to the faculty and to all my students of the Department of Theology, Boston College, for collegiality and support, questions and challenges; and to the faculty of the Theologicum, l'Institut Catholique de Paris, France, who offered space and time to think, engage, and lecture, in particular Philippe Bordeyne, Sylvain Brison, and especially Isabelle de Vendeuvre of École Normale Supérieure.

Thank you to all who contributed to *Enfleshing Theology*: Michele Saracino and Robert Rivera, Susan Abraham, Katie Geneva Cannon,[†] Laurie Cassidy, Shawnee Daniels-Sykes,[†] Dierdre Dempsey, Roberto Goizueta, Susan L. Gray, Mary Ann Hinsdale, Christine Firer Hinze, Willie James Jennings, Bryan Massingale, Maureen O'Connell, Nancy Pineda-Madrid, Stephen T. Ray Jr., Karen Teel, Eboni Marshall Turman, and Kathleen M. Williams.

This revision of *Enfleshing Freedom* would not have been possible without the encouragement of my editor Ryan Hemmer (and now editor-in-chief) at Fortress Press. From the start of his involvement in this project, Ryan championed this book; he coaxed, pushed, encouraged, challenged, and always advocated.

I am very appreciative of the patient, experienced, and gifted editorial support of Lisa Eaton and Louise Spencely. I thank Ronald Brooks, Barbara Bzura, Carolyn Caveny, and Jeffrey Krieble for assistance with proofreading.

I am deeply grateful for the love and encouragement of my mother, Geraldine Williams, and my family. I am immensely grateful to Barbara Bzura, who has heard too many variations of my original blues tune "almost done" for far too long, yet has never wavered in interest, questions, encouragement, homemade chocolate chip cookies, travel, and love.

Acknowledgments (2010)

This book, like those of so many academics, traces its origins to the classroom. More years ago than I care to admit, I taught a seminar at Yale Divinity School on the body in religion and society. Learning from that teaching experience was poured into a course at Marquette University on theological anthropology that reframed the nature-grace paradigm around issues of embodiment, in particular, race and gender. These classroom experiences, along with ongoing research, laid the foundation for the several lectures and articles in which many of the ideas developed here initially were expressed. I am grateful for the many opportunities I have had to teach and to learn and for the many lecture invitations I have received to present and test some of the ideas in this book. I am immensely grateful to Michael West, editor-in-chief of Fortress Press, who encouraged this project, understood it, respected it, and sustained it with enormous intelligence, generosity, and patience.

Writing about the body has been, for me, a bodily challenge. Three major surgeries in four years, along with intensive therapies left me questioning not only *the* body but, *my* body. I could not have encountered surgeons with sharper skills, more openness, and more sympathy than Dr. R. John Wright and Dr. E. Brandon Earp. My therapists, especially Sarah Bresnick-Zocchi, Jackie Pommeroll, Rick Grubb, and Mary T. O'Brien, were always demanding, always helpful, and always caring.

During periods of recovery, and just as importantly before and after, a host of friends made my daily life not only practically possible, but lovely, and whimsical. Nancy Richardson and Elaine Huber, Chris and Brad Hinze, Deirdre Dempsey, Nancy Pineda-Madrid, and Larry Gordon are among the most giving and gracious persons I know, and Lisa Fitzgerald is among the most uncompromising. Cheryl A. Giles, Mary Rose D'Angelo, Mary Ann Hinsdale, IHM, Joan Martin, Claudia Highbaugh, Pat Rathbone, Kwok Pui-lan, Lisa Sowle Cahill, Gail Yee, and Valerie Dixon nourished my body with delicious meals and good wine, and when my spirits flagged offered good books, good conversation, and bracing walks. Belva Brown Jordan helped me feel much better about my hair and Maryanne Confoy, RSC, gave me the companionship of music. From time to time, Katie G. Cannon, Emile Townes, Matt Ouellette, Nancy Ramsay, and Anne Patrick, SNJM, "looked" in on me. Pat De Leeuw was always in my corner. I am appreciative of the kindness and concern of my colleagues and staff in the Department of Theology at my university, especially Kenneth Himes, Gloria Rufo, and Toni Ross.

At a crucial stage of this project, the tendons in my left hand ruptured. Clarissa Atkinson typed for me and with me and encouraged me. My teaching assistant Bienvenu Mayemba, SJ, did more than drive me to and from classes in the long, bleak New England winter that crept ever so reluctantly into spring: his goodness, enthusiasm, and concern, along with our analyses of the long 2008 presidential campaign, kept the embers of my spirits glowing.

But, without the devoted friendship of Ann Johnston, RSCJ, and Francine Cardman, I would never have made it through those four years. Ann is the embodiment of compassionate care, Francine the embodiment of compassionate skepticism.

Jamie T. Phelps, OP, and Kathleen M. Williams, RSM, stood with me every day across space and time. Jamie's keen theological perception and friendship are inestimable. Kathleen read every word of this manuscript; her generous and mindful engagement with my work, her thoughtful questions and incisive insights are invaluable; her friendship has made this a better book and me a better theologian.

Notes

PREFACE TO THE SECOND EDITION

1   Johnetta Elzie's sentence was printed in stark white capital letters against a black background that covered Sunday's edition (May 10, 2019) of the *New York Times Magazine*.

INTRODUCTION

1   After Jeremiah 8:21–23. All biblical quotations are taken from *The New Oxford Annotated Bible*, New Revised Standard Version, 3rd ed., augmented (Oxford: Oxford University Press, 2007).

2   Negro Spiritual.

3   Sven Lindqvist, *"Exterminate All the Brutes": One Man's Odyssey into the Heart of Darkness and the Origins of European Genocide*, trans. Joan Tate (New York: The New Press, 1992), 2.

4   As an exercise in systematic theology, this book explicitly treats *one* doctrine—the doctrine of the human person or theological anthropology. Implicitly, however, this work relates to and implicates other Christian doctrines: *creation* (that all human beings share in the *imago Dei*); *incarnation* (that God in the Jew Jesus of Nazareth took on flesh for us and entered into human history); and *church* (that the common confession through the power of the Holy Spirit that Jesus is Lord produces a new communion or community of women and men, and that communion or community transgresses gender, race, culture, sexual orientation, socioeconomic status). This book also addresses *ethics* (the inseparability of love of God and neighbor) and *Eucharist* (that the body of Jesus is for flourishing life in the here-and-now and life in an eschatological future).

5   Johann Baptist Metz, *Faith in History and Society: Toward a Practical Fundamental Theology*, trans. J. Matthew Ashley (1992; New York: Crossroad Publishing Company, 2007), 75.

6   See Oliver Davies, *A Theology of Compassion: Metaphysics of Difference and the Renewal of Tradition* (Grand Rapids, MI, and Cambridge: William B. Eerdmans, 2001), 10, and Toni Morrison, *Playing in the Dark: Whiteness and the Literary Imagination* (Cambridge, MA, and London: Harvard University Press, 1992), 7.

7   Nell Irvin Painter, "Soul Murder and Slavery: Toward a Fully Loaded Cost Accounting," in *US History as Women's History: New Feminist Essays*, ed. Linda K. Kerber, Alice Kessler-Harris, and Kathryn Kish Sklar (Chapel Hill and London: University of North Carolina Press, 1995), 127, 129. Page duBois in *Slaves and Other Objects* (Chicago and London: University of Chicago Press, 2003) exposes the nineteenth-century "troubled connections between the foundation of classical studies as a professional discipline in the United States and the history of slave-holding in the southern states" (13). She cites the influence of Basil Lanneau Gildersleeve, who served in the Confederate cavalry during the Civil War and who devoted his life to classical studies. Gildersleeve taught at the University of Virginia and held the chair of Greek at Johns Hopkins University. DuBois concludes: "Participants in the debates concerning slavery mined the histories of ancient Greece and Rome and set them up as examples of political excellence, sometimes defending freedom as a concept possible only in the context of slave-holding societies" (18).

8   Wendy Warren, *New England Bound: Slavery and Colonization in Early America* (New York: Liveright Publishing Corporation, 2016), loc. 16 of 429, Kindle.

9   For some examples of the relation of universities to slavery, see Craig Steven Wilder, *Ebony and Ivy: Race, Slavery and the Troubled History of America's Universities* (New York: Bloomsbury, 2014), Adam Rothman and Elsa Barraza, ed., *Facing Georgetown's History: A Reader on Slavery, Memory, and Reconciliation* (Washington, DC: Georgetown University Press, 2021), Leslie M. Harris, James T. Campbell, and Alfred L. Brophy, eds., *Slavery and the University: Histories and Legacies* (Athens: University of Georgia Press, 2019).

10 Neither the enslavement of Africans nor anti-Black racism is unique to the United States. Belgium, the United Kingdom, France, Germany, Portugal, Spain, and several countries in Latin America—all have participated in or contributed to the slave trade and to the extension of White or Eurocentric supremacy and the circumscription of Black people or people of African descent by inferiority.

11 Metz, *Faith in History and Society*, 101.

12 Only since about 2010 have plantation tours made reference to slave quarters or attempted to exhibit them. A suitable memorial honoring the contributions of African American people to the nation was first conceived in 1915, but came to realization in 2016 as the National Museum of African American History and Culture, a Smithsonian Institution, in Washington, DC.

13 *The Sunday New York Times*, Opinion, June 28, 2020, 4.

14 I have for several years used the phrase "structural embarrassment," attributing it to Dr. Charles H. Long, the brilliant historian of religions, whose work continues to have enormous impact on the ongoing development of Black and African American theologies. After a diligent search of Long's material available to me, I could not find the phrase. I asked for the assistance of two scholars who are intimately engaged with Long's scholarship, Dr. Juan Floyd-Thomas of Vanderbilt Divinity School and Dr. Raymond Carr, Director, Codex Charles H. Long Papers Project, Visiting Professor and Scholar, Harvard Divinity School, Research Associate Harvard University. Carr accessed Long's computer but could not locate the exact phrasing. The closest reference Carr found was Long's critique of sociologists who failed to address the religious presence of Blacks in America, see *The Collected Writings of Charles H. Long: Ellipsis* (London: Bloomsbury Academic, 2018), loc. 62 of 425, Kindle. In this same work, Long uses the phrase "structural presence" to speak of the "three races"

that inhabit the United States (loc. 16 of 425). I only encountered Long's phrase "structural presence" in reading *Ellipsis* over the past two years.

I do not want to attribute to myself what is not mine, but it is possible that I came up with the phrase after reading and teaching for many years Long's "Structural Similarities and Dissimilarities in Black and African Theologies," *Journal of Religious Thought* 32, no. 2 (January 1975): 9–24, and "Perspectives for a Study of Afro-American Religion in the United States," in *Significations: Signs, Symbols, and Images in the Interpretation of Religion* (1986; Aurora, CO: The Davies Group Publishers, 1999), 187–98. The phrase would have been my response to the emphasis Long gives to "the involuntary presence of the Black community in America" (190). Given America's persistently ahistorical and thoughtless revelry in freedom, the presence of enslaved people and their descendants constitutes a structural embarrassment.

15 I mean here what Metz means—a practical fundamental theology, a political theology.

16 Metz, *Faith in History and Society*, 105.

17 Katie G. Cannon, "Sexing Black Women: Liberation from the Prisonhouse of Anatomical Authority," in *Loving the Body: Black Religious Studies and the Erotic*, ed. Anthony B. Pinn and Dwight N. Hopkins (New York: Palgrave/Macmillan, 2004), 17.

18 Saidiya V. Hartman, *Scenes of Subjection: Terror, Slavery, and Self-Making in Nineteenth-Century America* (New York: Oxford University Press, 1997), 3.

19 Any move toward solidarity should never be confused with sentiment and its tendency to persuade us to forget the cruelty and conflict that domination causes. "A ruling class," James Bowman writes, "is always subject to sentimentalism, since it helps it to close its eyes to the brutality on which its domination ultimately rests. . . . We are sentimental about the historical sufferings of all kinds of 'minorities' in a way that our grandfathers never used to be precisely because the time when those minorities could constitute any threat to our wealth and power and privilege is long past. Having bought long-term security, we grow almost immediately sentimental about those at whose expense we bought it just so long as it doesn't cost us anything," "Sorry about That," *The New Criterion* 16, no. 9 (May 1998): 54.

20 Toni Morrison, *What Moves at the Margin: Selected Nonfiction*, ed. Carolyn C. Denard (Jackson: University Press of Mississippi, 2008), 70.

21 *Beloved* concludes with this injunction: "This is not a story to pass on"; Toni Morrison, *Beloved* (New York: Alfred A. Knopf, 1987), 27.

22 "Many Thousand Gone" is the title of a Negro Spiritual. Verses: 1. No more peck o' corn for me, No more, no more; No more peck o' corn for me, Many Thousand Gone. 2. No more driver's lash for me . . . 3. No more pint o' salt for me . . . 4. No more hundred lash for me . . . 5. No more mistress' call for me . . .

23 Jenny Sharpe, *Ghosts of Slavery: A Literary Archaeology of Black Women's Lives* (Minneapolis: University of Minnesota Press, 2003), xxiii.

24 Michel de Certeau, *The Practice of Everyday Life*, trans. Steven Rendall (Berkeley: University of California Press, 1984), xiii.

25 Metz, *Faith in History and Society*, 104.

26 Davies, *A Theology of Compassion*, 3.

27 Rachel Holmes, *African Queen: The Real Life of the Hottentot Venus* (New York: Random House, 2007), 28.

28 Cornel West, *Prophesy Deliverance! An Afro-American Revolutionary Christianity* (1982; Louisville, KY: Westminster John Knox Press, 2002), 53.

29 Toni Morrison, *Beloved* (New York: Alfred A. Knopf, 1987).

30 Tertullian, *De res.* 8, 2:PL 2, 852, quoted in *The Catechism of the Catholic Church* (Ligouri, MO: Ligouri Publications, 1994), 265.

31 See Katie G. Cannon, *Black Womanist Ethics* (Atlanta, GA: Scholars Press, 1988); Katie G. Cannon, "Sexing Black Women," in Pinn and Hopkins, eds., *Loving the Body*, 11–30; also see M. Shawn Copeland, "'Wading through Many Sorrows': Towards a Theology of Suffering in Womanist Perspective," in *A Troubling in My Soul: Womanist Reflections on Evil and Suffering*, ed. Emilie M. Townes (Maryknoll, NY: Orbis Books, 1993), 109–29.

32 James H. Cone, *The Cross and the Lynching Tree* (Maryknoll, NY: Orbis Books, 2011), Anthony B. Pinn, *The Terror and the Triumph: The Nature of Black Religion* (Minneapolis: Fortress Press, 2003); Kelly Brown Douglas, *What's Faith Got to Do with It? Black Bodies/Christian Souls* (Maryknoll, NY: Orbis Books, 2005); see *Enfleshing Freedom*, 1st ed. (Minneapolis: Fortress Press, 2010), chap. 5, and Angela D. Sims, *Lynched: The Power of Memory in a Culture of Terror* (Waco, TX: Baylor University Press, 2016).

 The more than 4,400 African American children, women, and men who were lynched are memorialized in the National Memorial for Peace and Justice (also known as the National Lynching Memorial). The memorial opened on April 26, 2018, and was founded by the nonprofit Equal Justice Initiative which was founded by attorney Bryan Stevenson. The memorial preserves this brutal legacy in order to summon our nation to face up to the grotesque past that informs our present and shapes our future, and to invite us to conversion, confession, repentance, and transformation. This project, and the associated Legacy Museum: From Enslavement to Mass Incarceration in Montgomery, Alabama, were developed under the leadership of attorney and human rights defender Bryan Stevenson; see his, *Just Mercy: A Story of Justice and Redemption* (New York: Spiegel & Grau, 2015), and Equal Justice Initiative, Just Mercy, https://tinyurl.com/yjyy8ab6 (accessed May 9, 2023).

33 Womanist, *mujerista*, feminist theologians and exegetes—most notably Delores S. Williams, Kelly Brown Douglas, Elisabeth Schüssler Fiorenza, Rosemary Radford Ruether, Ada Maria Isasi-Diaz, Kwok Pui-lan, Nancy Pineda Madrid—have underscored the impact of the distorted preaching and theologizing about the cross and suffering on the bodies and psyches of women.

34 Perhaps, we may say that this Negro Spiritual attests to "hope against hope," a glimpse of God's *hesed* or steadfast, unwavering love of our God in Jesus.

CHAPTER 1

1 Genesis 1:31.

2 Franz Fanon, *Black Skin, White Masks* (New York: Grove, 1967), 232.

3 Elizabeth Alexander, "Body of Life," in *Body of Life* (Los Angeles: Tia Chucha, 2009), 74.

4   Jörg Splett, "Body," in *Encyclopedia of Theology: The Concise Sacramentum Mundi*, ed. Karl Rahner (New York: Crossroad Publishing, 1984), 157.

5   Splett, "Body," 157.

6   Yves Cattin, "Human Beings Cross Frontiers," in *Frontier Violations: The Beginnings of New Identities, Concilium*, vol. 2, ed. Felix Wilfred and Oscar Beozzo (London and Maryknoll, NY: SCM Press/Orbis Books, 1999), 3–4.

7   Cattin, "Human Beings Cross Frontiers," 4.

8   Michael Scanlon, "Postmodernism and Theology," *The Ecumenist* 37, no. 2 (Spring 2000): 18.

9   Mary Douglas, *Natural Symbols: Explorations in Cosmology*, 2nd ed (London and New York: Routledge, 1996), 73.

10 See Bernard Lonergan, *Collected Works of Bernard Lonergan* (hereafter *Collected Works*), vol. 3, *Insight, A Study of Human Understanding*, ed. Frederick E. Crowe and Robert M. Doran (Toronto: University of Toronto Press, 1988), chaps. 6 and 7.

11 Natasha Gordon-Chipembere, *Representation and Black Womanhood, The Legacy of Sarah Baartman* (New York: Palgrave Macmillan, 2011), loc. 8 of 208, Kindle. This collection interrogates the development of the White racist, misogynist gaze from the nineteenth-century construction of Sarah Baartman's body to the contemptuous treatments of the bodies of Black African and diasporic women. Nothing was more hurtful to Black women than the "dissection" of Michelle Obama by media pundits and popular press, see Gordon-Chipembere, "Under Cuvier's Microscope: The Dissection of Michelle Obama in the Twenty-First Century," in *Representation and Black Womanhood*, loc. 165–79 of 208, Kindle.

12 Janell Hobson, *Venus in the Dark: Blackness and Beauty in Popular Culture* (New York: Routledge, 2005), loc. 45 of 226, Kindle.

13 Paul Anthony Farley, "The Black Body as Fetish Object," *Oregon Law Review* 26 (1977): 531; cf. Michel Foucault, who writes: "The critical ontology of ourselves has to be considered ... as an attitude, an ethos, a philosophical life in which the critique of what we are is at one and the same time the historical analysis of the limits that are imposed on us and an experiment with the possibility of going beyond them," in Michel Foucault, "What Is Enlightenment?" ("*Qu'est-ce que les Lumières ?*"), in *The Foucault Reader*, ed. Paul Rabinow (New York: Pantheon, 1984), 32–50, and the website Michel Foucault Info, https://tinyurl.com/3tdv3c5a (accessed May 9, 2023).

14 Emmanuel Chukwudi Eze, ed., "Introduction," in *Race and the Enlightenment: A Reader* (Oxford: Blackwell, 1997), 5; see also Cornel West, *Prophesy Deliverance! An Afro-American Revolutionary Christianity* (1982; Philadelphia: Westminster, 2002), 47–65.

15 Eze, "Introduction," *Race and the Enlightenment*, 5.

16 Susan Buck-Morss, in *Hegel, Haiti, and Universal History* (Pittsburgh: University of Pittsburgh Press, 2009), queries Hegel's incapacity to notice the discrepancy between Enlightenment notions of freedom and colonial enslavement. See also Michelle M. Wright, *Becoming Black: Creating Identity in the African Diaspora* (Durham, NC: Duke University Press, 2004), especially chap. 1; and Berel Lang, in *Heidegger's Silence* (Ithaca, NY: Cornell University Press, 1996), questions Heidegger's political stance during the Nazi occupation of Germany in relation to his philosophical thought.

17 Hume continues: "On the other hand, the most rude and barbarous of the Whites, such as the ancient Germans, the present Tartars, have still something eminent about

them, in their valour, form of government, or some other particular. Such a uniform and constant difference could not happen, in so many countries and ages, if nature had not made an original distinction between these breeds of men. Not to mention our colonies, there are Negro slaves dispersed all over Europe, of whom none ever discovered any symptoms of ingenuity; though low people, without education, will start up amongst us, and distinguish themselves in every profession. In Jamaica, indeed, they talk of one Negro as a man of parts and learning; but it is likely he is admired for slender accomplishments, like a parrot who speaks a few words plainly," *Essays and Treatises on Several Subjects*, 2 vols. (Edinburgh, 1825), I: 521–22.

18   Immanuel Kant, *Observations on the Feeling of the Beautiful and Sublime* (orig. pub. 1764, *Beobachtungen über das Gefühl des Schönen und Erhabenen*), trans. John T. Goldthwait (Berkeley: University of California Press, 1960), 111.

19   Georg Wilhelm Friedrich Hegel, "Geographical Basis of World History," in Eze, ed., *Race and the Enlightenment*, 124.

20   In "The God-Given Order of Nature," Carl von Linné states: "The American [is] copper-coloured, regulated by customs. The European [is] fair, governed by laws. The Mongolian [is] sooty, governed by opinions. The Black, governed by caprice," in Eze, ed., *Race and the Enlightenment*, 13.

21   Stephen Jay Gould, "The Geometer of Race," *Discover Magazine* 15, no. 11 (November 1994): 64–69, at 68.

22   Johann Friedrich Blumenbach, "Degeneration of the Species," in Eze, ed., *Race and the Enlightenment*, 90, 79.

23   Gould, "The Geometer of Race," 68.

24   Cited in Rachel Holmes, *African Queen: The Real Life of the Hottentot Venus* (New York: Random House, 2007), 112.

25   Philosophically, these arguments were grounded through eliding the juncture between observation and judgment, thus bypassing the cognitional operations of questioning, understanding, and verification. Lonergan's analysis of cognition pursues the question, "What am I doing when I am knowing?" He recovers and isolates distinct operations of experience-understanding-judging-deciding. The full statement of Lonergan's cognitional theory is found in *Insight*; two summaries of that theory may be found in "Cognitional Structure," in *Collected Works*, vol. 4, *Collection*, ed. Frederick E. Crowe and Robert M. Doran (Toronto: University of Toronto Press, 1998), 205–21; and *Collected Works*, vol. 14, *Method in Theology*, ed. Robert M. Doran and John D. Dadosky (Toronto: University of Toronto Press, 1988), 7–27. Lonergan's cognitional proposals oppose not only the contemporary appeal to interactive linguistic behavior in philosophy favored by Richard Rorty (*Philosophy and the Mirror of Nature* (Princeton, NJ: Princeton University Press, 1979) and *The Consequences of Pragmatism* (Minneapolis: University of Minnesota Press, 1982)), but also the neglect of judgment in the epistemological emphases of Immanuel Kant, see *Critique of Pure Reason*, trans. N. Kemp-Smith (1781; London: Macmillan, 1929).

26   J. Yolande Daniels in "Exhibit A: Private Life without a Narrative" explores the liminal physiological and psychological space that was constructed to contain Baartman as an "aberration—as an othered 'other,'" in *Black Venus 2010: They Called Her "Hottentot,"* ed. Deborah Willis (Philadelphia: Temple University Press, 2010), 62. Sheila Smith McKoy, in "Placing and Replacing 'The Venus Hottentot':

An Archeology of Pornography, Race, and Power," argues that the actual fact of Baartman's "coercion is absent from the legal proceedings. . . . Instead court records suggest that Baartman came to London of her own free will to exhibit herself for profit" in *Representation and Black Womanhood: The Legacy of Sarah Baartman*, ed. Natasha Gordon-Chipembere (New York: Palgrave Macmillan, 2011), loc. 85 of 208, Kindle.

27 Deborah Willis, in her "Introduction: The Notion of Venus," explains the confusion around Sarah Baartman's name: it has been variously rendered "Sartjee, Saartje, Saat-je, Saartji, Saat-Jee, and Saartjie (all derived from the Afrikaans pronunciation, diminutive forms of Sara) as well as the Anglicized Sara or Sarah. Saartjie, with its Afrikaans diminutive "-tjie" is now generally regarded as patronizing. . . . Her surname, presumably given to her upon her baptism in Manchester, England, in 1811, has been represented as Baartman, Bartman, Baartman, or Bartmann." Moreover, the prevailing scholarly consensus considers the attribution of Baartman as Hottentot to be "erroneous, and the term contentious" (Willis, *Black Venus 2010*, 4–5).

28 Holmes, *African Queen*, 8–24.

29 Holmes, 28.

30 Holmes, 28, 39, 33–70.

31 Willis, "Introduction: The Notion of Venus," 4.

32 The 1893 World's Columbian Exposition held in Chicago, Illinois, displayed and stereotyped "living exhibitions" of Dahomeans, Algerians, Tunisians, Bedouins, Egyptians, Samoan Islanders, and Eskimos, among others. Journalist and anti-lynching activist Ida B. Wells-Barnett and abolitionist Frederick Douglass objected to these displays and the distribution of photographs, particularly of nude or semi-nude Black women; see Barbara J. Ballard, "A People without a Nation," *Chicago History* (Summer 1999): 27–43, at 31, https://tinyurl.com/3k5vv3f6. At the same time, Douglass and Wells-Barnett were pleased to view the Haitian pavilion at the 1893 exhibition, "the only structure erected by a black nation and the only autonomous representation of people of African descent" located in the main area of the fairgrounds called the "White City" "due to the color of its buildings and its pristine environment," 31; for another discussion of the 1893 fair, see Deborah Willis and Carla Williams, *The Black Female Body: A Photographic History* (Philadelphia: Temple University Press, 2002), 73–76; see also Michele Wallace, "The Imperial Gaze: Venus Hottentot, Human Display, and World Fairs," in *Black Venus 2010*, 149–54.

33 George Yancy, *Black Bodies, White Gazes: The Continuing Significance of Race* (Lanham, MD: Rowman & Littlefield, 2008), 91.

34 Holmes, *African Queen*, 82–93.

35 Holmes, 99. During the course research in Paris, Gould reported that in 1982 he accidentally noticed three jars labeled "*une négresse*," "*une péruvienne*," and "*la Vénus Hottentote*." These jars contained the relics of Sarah Baartman. Twelve years later, Nelson Mandela requested the return of Sarah Baartman's remains for proper burial; Thabo Mbeki oversaw her interment in 2002.

36 Lorraine O'Grady, "Olympia's Maid: Reclaiming Black Female Subjectivity," in *New Feminist Criticism*, ed. Joanna Freuh, Cassandra L. Langer, and Arlene Raven (New York: HarperCollins, 1994), 152, author's emphasis, cited in Willis and Williams, ed., *The Black Female Body*.

37   See Evelynn M. Hammonds and Rebecca M. Herzig, eds., *The Nature of Difference: Sciences of Race in the United States from Jefferson to Genomics* (Cambridge, MA, and London: MIT Press, 2008).

38   James H. Sweet, "The Idea of Race: Its Changing Meanings and Constructions," in *Schomburg Studies on the Black Experience*, ed. Colin A. Palmer and Howard Dodson (Ann Arbor, MI: Pro Quest, 2005) (electronic edition). Our understandings of gender, sexuality, and class also result from such historical and social construction and replication.

39   Pierre Bourdieu, *Outline of A Theory of Practice*, trans. Richard Nice (1972; Cambridge: Cambridge University Press, 1977), 72, 78.

40   Sweet, "The Idea of Race"; see Eduardo Bonilla-Silva, *Racism without Racists: Color-Blind Racism and the Persistence of Racial Inequality in the United States*, 5th ed. (Lanham, MD: Rowman & Littlefield, 2018). Bonilla-Silva defines *White habitus* as "a racialized, uninterrupted socialization process that *conditions and creates* Whites' racial taste, perceptions, feelings, and emotions and their views on racial matters," loc. 121 of 254, Kindle.

41   Lonergan, "Metaphysics as Horizon," in *Collection*, ed. Crowe and Doran, 198. In "The Subject," Lonergan explains: "There is a sense in which it may be said that each of us lives in a world of his own. That world is usually a bounded world, and its boundary is fixed by the range of our interests and our knowledge.... So the extent of our knowledge and the reach of our interests fix a horizon. Within that horizon we are confined.... Such confinement may result from the historical tradition within which we are born, from the limitations of the social milieu in which we were brought up, from our individual psychological aptitudes, efforts, misadventures. But besides specifically historical, social, and psychological determinants of subjects and their horizons, there are also philosophic factors" (in *Collected Works*, vol. 13, *A Second Collection*, ed. Robert M. Doran and John D. Dadosky (Toronto: University of Toronto Press, 2016), 60. The classic literary narrative of Black invisibility remains Ralph W. Ellison's *Invisible Man* (1947; New York: Vintage, 1995).

42   See Lonergan, *Insight*, chaps. 6, 7.

43   Lonergan, *Insight*, 191.

44   Lewis Carroll presents a wonderful example of the malleability of meaning in the conversation between Humpty Dumpty and Alice in *Alice's Adventures in Wonderland and Through the Looking-Glass* (1865; 1871; London and New York: Penguin, 1997): "When I use a word," Humpty Dumpty said in a rather scornful tone, "it means just what I choose it to mean—neither more nor less." "The question is," said Alice, "whether you can make words mean different things." "The question is," said Humpty Dumpty, "which is to be master—that's all" (237).

45   Evelyn Brooks Higginbotham, "African-American Women's History and the Metalanguage of Race," *Signs* 17, no. 2 (Winter 1992): 255, 253.

46   Paul Gilroy, "Race Ends Here," *Ethnic and Racial Studies* 21, no. 5 (September 1998): 847.

47   Bonilla-Silva argues heuristically rather than definitively that with the explosion of the US Latino population a "reshuffling [of] the biracial order typical of the United States ... is evolving into a complex and loosely organized triracial stratification system similar to that of many Latin American and Caribbean nations. Specifically ... that the emerging triracial system will be comprised of 'whites' at

the top, an intermediary group of 'honorary whites' . . . and a nonwhite group or the 'collective black' at the bottom," *Racism without Racists*, loc. 183 of 254, Kindle.

48 Consider that professional golfer Tiger Woods, the son of a Black father and a Thai mother, has identified himself as Cablinasian, i.e., a mixture of Caucasian, Black, and (American) Indian, and Asian.

49 Consider that Barack Hussein Obama, former president of the United States (2009–17), refers to himself as the son of a Black man from Kenya and a White woman from Kansas.

50 Lonergan, *Insight*, 8.

51 Nigel C. Gibson uses the phrase "crushing objecthood," in his *Fanon: The Postcolonial Imagination* (Cambridge: Polity Press, 2003), 22.

52 Lewis R. Gordon, "Existential Dynamics of Theorizing Black Invisibility," in *Existence in Black: An Anthology of Black Existential Philosophy*, ed. Lewis R. Gordon (New York: Routledge, 1997), 70.

53 Fanon, *Black Skin, White Masks*, 113–14. I have substituted the word "Negro" in brackets so as not keep alive the abomination and disparagement intended in the word "nigger" that Fanon appropriately used.

54 Gordon, "Existential Dynamics of Theorizing Black Invisibility," 71.

55 W. E. B. Du Bois, *The Souls of Black Folk* (1903, 1996; New York: Modern Library, 2003), 3.

56 The term "agent intellect" (Latin: *intellectus agens*) is employed by Aristotle to explain human cognition (see *On the Soul* (*De Anima*), Book III, 3–5). Aristotle uses the analogy of light making potential colors into actual colors to illustrate the distinction of active and passive intellect: Passive intellect receives intelligible forms of things, whereas active intellect abstracts from those forms to make potential knowledge into actual knowledge. See Norman Kretzmann and Elenore Stump, "Thomas Aquinas: Theory of Knowledge," in *Routledge Encyclopedia of Philosophy*, https://doi.org/10.4324/9780415249126-B007-1. Lonergan notes, "Aquinas found [agent intellect] immanent within us because, he argued, the light of intelligence in each of us performs the functions Aristotle ascribed to agent intellect," in *Insight*, 394. Aquinas is to be credited with giving this theory of human knowledge its currency in theological anthropology because he situates the powers or faculties of intellect in the soul. Through the light of created intellect (understanding) humans participate in the light of Divine Uncreated Light (infinite understanding).

57 Gordon, "Existential Dynamics of Theorizing Black Invisibility," 73, 74, 75; see also Cheryl Harris, "Whiteness as Property," in *Critical Race Theory: The Key Writings That Formed the Movement*, ed. Kimberlé Crenshaw, Neil Gotanda, Gary Peller, and Kendall Thomas (New York: New Press, 1995), 276–91, and Stephanie M. Wildman, with contributions by Margalynne Armstrong, Adrienne D. Davis, and Trina Grillo, *Privilege Revealed: How Invisible Preference Undermines America* (New York and London: New York University Press, 1996).

58 Gordon, "Existential Dynamics of Theorizing Black Invisibility," 76.

59 Gordon, 76.

60 Farley is both accurate and poignant, when he writes: "Acts of racialization separate black people from their humanity. They are both expressions of disgust and invitations to self-loathing," "The Black Body as Fetish Object," 500, 529–30.

61 Robert Birt, "Existence, Identity, and Liberation," in *Existence in Black: An Anthology of Black Existential Philosophy*, 208.

62 James Baldwin, *The Fire Next Time* (New York: Dial, 1963), 39.

63 Lonergan, *Insight*, 497–500.

64 Elaine Scarry, *On Beauty and Being Just* (Princeton, NJ: Princeton University Press, 1999), 22–23, 46, 47. I do not quote Scarry in order to argue against her, but rather to present some commonly recognized notions of beauty.

65 Paget Henry, *Caliban's Reason: Introducing Afro-Caribbean Philosophy* (New York: Routledge, 2000), 5.

66 Farley, "The Black Body as Fetish Object," 527.

67 Henry, *Caliban's Reason*, 149.

68 Song of Solomon 1:5.

69 Victor Anderson, *Beyond Ontological Blackness* (New York: Continuum, 1995), 104. Anderson is critical of the subordination of Black identity to the "totality of racial ideology and the black heroic genius . . . each of which is determined by black masculinity" (119). I am thinking here of Lonergan's notion of the "truncated subject," that is, "the subject that does not know himself [sic] and so unduly impoverishes his [sic] account of human knowledge," in "The Subject," in *A Second Collection*, 65. In the case of the Black subject this human knowledge is a critical form of self-knowledge, which includes knowledge of one's people's history, culture, and social life. At the same time, even as the Black human subject lives in an oppositional (i.e., anti-Black) cultural and social matrix, the subject is *totally determined* neither by a racially bias-induced horizon and its negative assessments of Black identity nor by Black racial ideology that romanticizes or reifies blackness.

70 Anderson, *Beyond Ontological Blackness*, 14.

71 Anthony Appiah, "The Uncompleted Argument: Du Bois and the Illusion of Race," in *"Race," Writing, and Difference*, ed. Henry Louis Gates Jr. (Chicago: University of Chicago Press, 1985), 35.

72 Lonergan, "The Subject," in *A Second Collection*, 64–65; see also Frederick G. Lawrence, *The Fragility of Consciousness: Faith, Reason, and the Human Good*, ed. Randall S. Rosenberg and Kevin M. Vander Schel (Toronto: University of Toronto Press, 2017), 229–77.

73 Herbert Marcuse, *One Dimensional Man: Studies in the Ideology of Advanced Industrial Society* (Boston: Beacon Press, 1964), 11.

74 Farley, "The Black Body as Fetish Object," 514.

75 Cultural critic Peter Brooker distinguishes the uses of the terms "postmodernity," "postmodernism," "postmodern theory." Postmodernity refers to the "historical dimensions of postmodernism as something which emerges following the Second World War, that is, after or post-modern." Postmodernity highlights the shift from Fordism (the efficiency and monotony of the assembly line that Frederick Winslow Taylor developed for Henry Ford) to post-Fordism or the new high-tech industries. Postmodernism denotes "the cultural condition" linked to this industrial and social change and manifests itself in "eclectic" styles of art and architecture, of media-saturation, and everyday living. Postmodern theory refers to the philosophical debates of French ex-Marxist intellectuals Jean-François Lyotard (rejection of grand narratives in history or religion), Jean Baudrillard (the *simulacra*, the hyperreal), and the North American Marxist Fredric Jameson (the dominance of image and consumption), as well as the French thinkers Jacques Derrida, Michel Foucault, and

Jacques Lacan. Cited in James Procter, *Stuart Hall* (London: Routledge, 2004), 108. The literature on postmodernism is extensive: some works consulted here include Albert Borgmann, *Crossing the Postmodern Divide* (Chicago: University of Chicago Press, 1992), Jean-François Lyotard, *The Postmodern Condition: A Report on Knowledge* (Minneapolis: University of Minneapolis Press, 1984), Barry Smart, *Postmodernity* (London and New York: Routledge, 1993); Anthony Giddens, *Modernity and Self-Identity: Self and Society in the Late Modern Age* (Stanford, CA: Stanford University Press, 1991).

76 bell hooks, "Postmodern Blackness," in *A Postmodern Reader*, ed. Joseph Natoli and Linda Hutcheon (Albany: State University of New York Press, 1993), 512.

77 Stuart Hall, "On Postmodernism and Articulation: An Interview with Stuart Hall," in *Stuart Hall: Critical Dialogues in Cultural Studies*, ed. David Morley and Kuan-Hsing Chen (London: Routledge, 1996), 133, 137.

78 See Emmanuel Eze, *Achieving Our Humanity: The Idea of a Postracial Future* (New York and London: Routledge, 2001), and West, *Prophesy Deliverance!*

79 bell hooks, "Postmodern Blackness," 516.

80 bell hooks, 516.

81 See bell hooks and Cornell West, *Breaking Bread: Insurgent Black Intellectual Life* (Boston: South End Press, 1991) and Cornell West, *Keeping Faith: Philosophy and Race in America* (New York and London: Routledge, 1993), especially 82–85.

82 Lonergan, *Insight*, 475–78. Whatever else the notion of identity means, it discloses the self-affirmation of consciousness that is at once empirical, intellectual, and rational. Personal identity denotes the condition of me being myself and not another and remaining myself under varying conditions and circumstances. Thus, identity implies a unity, a whole, stability, while never precluding development and loss, growth and transformation, limitation and transcendence expressed as "the concrete unity-in-tension that is [the person]," *Insight*, 385.

83 For all their criticality and (de)constructive creativity, postmodern formulations of Christian theological anthropology have accorded scant attention to the Black body or its conditions. For example, see James B. Nelson, *Embodiment: An Approach to Sexuality and Christian Theology* (Minneapolis: Augsburg Press, 1978), Lisa Isherwood and Elizabeth Stuart, *Introducing Body Theology* (Sheffield: Sheffield Academic Press, 1998), Marcella Althaus-Reid and Lisa Isherwood, eds., *Controversies in Body Theology* (London: SCM Press, 2008), Michael Scanlon, "Postmodernism and Theology."

84 For some examples, see Delores S. Williams, *Sisters in the Wilderness: The Challenge of Womanist God-Talk* (Maryknoll, NY: Orbis Books, 1993); Katie G. Cannon, *Black Womanist Ethics* (Atlanta, GA: Scholars Press, 1988); Katie G. Cannon, *Katie's Canon: Womanism and the Soul of the Black Community* (New York: Continuum, 2002); Linda Thomas, "Womanist Theology, Epistemology, and a New Anthropological Paradigm," *Cross Currents: The Journal of the Association for Religion and Intellectual Life* 48, no. 4 (Winter 1998/99): 488–99; Kelly Brown Douglas, *Sexuality and the Black Church: A Womanist Perspective* (Maryknoll, NY: Orbis Books, 1999); Kelly Brown Douglas, *What's Faith Got to Do with It? Black Bodies/Christian Souls* (Maryknoll, NY: Orbis Books, 2005); Emilie M. Townes, *Womanist Ethics and the Cultural Production of Evil* (New York: Palgrave Macmillan, 2006); and Pinn and Hopkins, eds., *Loving the Body*, particularly chapters by Katie G. Cannon, Irene Monroe, Karen Baker-Fletcher, and Kelly Brown Douglas.

85 See Charles H. Long, "Structural Similarities and Dissimilarities in Black and African Theologies," *The Journal of Religious Thought* 32, no. 2 (Fall/Winter 1975): 9–24.

CHAPTER 2

1 Genesis 1:27.

2 Negro Spiritual.

3 Gregory of Nyssa, "Homily IV on Ecclesiastes," in *Homilies on Ecclesiastes: An English Version with Supporting Studies: Proceedings of the Seventh International Colloquium on Gregory of Nyssa*, ed. Stuart George Hall (Berlin and New York: W. de Gruyter, 1993), 74.

4 Deborah Gray White, *Ar'n't I a Woman? Female Slaves in the Plantation South* (New York: W. W. Norton, 1985), 27.

5 Karmen MacKendrick employs the word *somatophobic* in her *Word Made Skin: Figuring Language at the Surface of Flesh* (New York: Fordham University Press, 2004), 26.

6 For discussions of the fusion of Christian thought with Neoplatonic and Stoic philosophies, see Douglas, *What's Faith Got to Do with It?*, 3–38, and MacKendrick, *Word Made Skin*, 25–47.

7 Michael Scanlon, "Postmodernism and Theology," *The Ecumenist* 37, no. 2 (Spring 2000): 18.

8 For one of the major collections, see George P. Rawick, ed., *The American Slave: A Composite Autobiography*, 19 vols. (1941; Westport, CT: Greenwood, 1972). This collection of interviews with freed Black people was begun under the auspices of the Federal Writers' Project of the Works Project Administration (WPA) from 1936 to 1938. The Slave Narrative Collection consists of more than ten thousand pages of typescript and contains two thousand interviews, approximately 2 percent of the total of emancipated African peoples in the United States in 1937. This collection augmented earlier oral histories undertaken in the first quarter of the twentieth century by Hampton Institute in Virginia, Southern University in Louisiana, and Fisk University in Tennessee.

9 See John W. Blassingame, "Using the Testimony of the Ex-Slaves," in *The Slave's Narrative*, ed. Charles T. Davis and Henry Louis Gates Jr. (New York: Oxford University Press, 1985).

10 James C. Scott, *Domination and the Arts of Resistance* (New Haven, CT: Yale University Press, 1990), 4–5.

11 Scott, *Domination and the Arts of Resistance*, 4–5.

12 Scott, 4–5.

13 Given the link between race and bondage, it was difficult for free Black people to own slaves. In Louisiana, however, the existence of a caste of "free people of color," or *gens de couleur libres* or Creoles, made this possible to some extent. Historians note that the motives for such purchases remain obscure. Certainly, some Black and free people of color had enslaved people work in their homes and businesses, but others "purchased" relatives or friends to extract them from enslavement. At the same time, laws regarding manumitted slaves were quite restrictive. Some states

required that manumitted people leave the area within strict time limits or face reenslavement. Moreover, free Black people would have found it particularly difficult to own slaves after the 1850 passage of the Fugitive Slave Law. This law abrogated the rights of free Black people, putting them at risk of kidnap and sale. In his *Twelve Years a Slave* (1853; Minneola, NY: Dover Publications, 1970), Solomon Northup recounts his own kidnapping and sale.

14 Marcus Rediker, *The Slave Ship: A Human History* (New York: Viking, 2007), 8.

15 See Katie Geneva Cannon, "Christian Imperialism and the Atlantic Slave Trade," *The Journal of Feminist Studies in Religion* 24, no. 1 (2008): 127–34.

16 David Brion Davis, *The Problem of Slavery in Western Culture* (Ithaca, NY: Cornell University Press, 1966), 100–101.

17 Cited in Albert J. Raboteau, *Slave Religion: The "Invisible" Institution in the Antebellum South* (Oxford: Oxford University Press, 2004), 96.

18 Cited in Raboteau, *Slave Religion*, 98.

19 Cited in Raboteau, 98.

20 Cited in Raboteau, 99, author's emphasis.

21 Riggins R. Earl Jr., *Dark Symbols, Obscure Signs: God, Self, & Community in the Slave Mind* (Maryknoll, NY: Orbis Books, 1993), 13.

22 Raboteau, *Slave Religion*, 100.

23 Raboteau, 112, 113.

24 Perhaps the most well-known discussion of the master–slave relation is to be found in Georg Wilhelm Friedrich Hegel's *Phenomenology of Spirit*, trans. A. V. Miller (1807; Oxford: Clarendon Press, 1977), § 178–96.

25 Raboteau, *Slave Religion*, 103.

26 Contemporary biblical scholarship has identified this passage as pseudo-Pauline; however, in the nineteenth century, it was preached with all the authority of Paul. In fact, Howard Thurman refers to this very verse in his autobiography, noting his grandmother's vigorous objection to hearing these words read aloud. See Mary Rose D'Angelo, "Colossians," in *Searching the Scriptures: A Feminist Commentary*, ed. Elisabeth Schüssler Fiorenza (New York: Crossroad Books, 1994), 313–24.

27 Saidiya Hartman, *Lose Your Mother: A Journey along the Atlantic Slave Route* (New York: Farrar, Straus & Giroux, 2007), 133.

28 Johann Baptist Metz, *Faith in History and Society: Toward a Practical Fundamental Theology*, trans. J. Matthew Ashley (New York: Crossroad Books, 2007), 105.

29 My treatment has much in common with Cannon's *Black Womanist Ethics* (Atlanta, GA: Scholars Press, 1988), especially 31–41. However, here I have expanded material taken from slave narratives and, although the very notion of enfleshing freedom intimates moral agency, my aim is to contribute to the systematic theological treatment of theological anthropology.

30 Toni Morrison, *Beloved* (New York: Alfred Knopf, 1987).

31 Hortense J. Spillers, "Mama's Baby, Papa's Maybe: An American Grammar Book," in her *Black, White, and in Color: Essays on American Literature and Culture* (Chicago: University of Chicago Press, 2003), 206, author's emphasis.

32 William Goodell, *The American Slave Code in Theory and Practice: Its Distinctive Features Shown by Its Statutes, Judicial Decisions, and Illustrative Facts* (1853; New York: Negro Universities Press, 1968), 23, author's emphasis.

33 Goodell, *The American Slave Code in Theory and Practice*, author's emphasis.

34 Spillers, "Mama's Baby, Papa's Maybe," 224.

35 George M. Stroud, *A Sketch of the Laws Relating to Slavery in the Several States of the United States of America* (1827, 1857; reprint, New York: Negro Universities Press, 1968).

36 Stroud, *A Sketch of the Laws Relating to Slavery*, xi–xii.

37 Goodell, *The American Slave Code in Theory and Practice*, 24.

38 James Mellon, ed., *Bullwhip Days: The Slaves Remember, An Oral History* (New York: Avon, 1988), 28.

39 Northup, *Twelve Years a Slave*, 52.

40 Norman R. Yetman, ed., *Voices from Slavery* (New York: Holt, Rinehart & Winston, 1970), 133.

41 Mellon, *Bullwhip Days*, 293.

42 Charles Johnson and Patricia Smith, and the WGBH Series Research Team, *Africans in America: America's Journey through Slavery* (New York: Harcourt Brace, 1998), 431.

43 Yetman, *Voices from Slavery*, 252.

44 Frederick Law Olmsted, *The Cotton Kingdom: A Traveller's Observations on Cotton and Slavery in the American Slave States*, ed. David Freeman Hawke (1861; Indianapolis and New York: Bobbs-Merrill, 1971), 63.

45 Yetman, *Voices from Slavery*, 257.

46 Yetman, 227.

47 Yetman, 151.

48 Mellon, *Bullwhip Days*, 24.

49 John W. Blassingame, ed., *Slave Testimony: Two Centuries of Letters, Speeches, Interviews, and Autobiographies* (1977; Baton Rouge: Louisiana State University Press, 1989), 221.

50 Charles Ball, *Slavery in the United States: A Narrative of the Life and Adventures of Charles Ball, A Black Man* (Lewistown, PA: J. W. Shugert, 1836), 150–51, cited in *Black Women in White America: A Documentary History*, ed. Gerder Lerner (New York: Vintage, 1973), 48.

51 Narrative of Martha Jackson, Alabama Narratives, Federal Works Project, WPA for the State of Alabama, 1939, cited in Lerner, *Black Women in White America*, 8–9.

52 Yetman, *Voices from Slavery*, 228.

53 Frances (Fanny) Kemble, *Journal of a Residence on a Georgian Plantation in 1838–1839* (Savannah: Library of Georgia, 1992), 199, 200, 204.

54 Cannon, *Black Womanist Ethics*, 32.

55 Cf. Revelation 12:1–4.

56 Luce Irigaray, *I Love to You: Sketch of a Possible Felicity in History*, trans. Alison Martin (New York: Routledge, 1996), 25.

57 Gray White, *Ar'n't I a Woman?* 32.

58 Edward E. Baptist, "'Cuffy,' 'Fancy Maids,' and 'One-Eyed Men': Rape, Commodification, and the Domestic Slave Trade in the United States," *American Historical Review* 106, no. 5 (December 2001): 1619–50. For enslaved men's experience of sexual abuse, see, for example, Thomas A. Foster, "The Sexual Abuse of Black Men under American Slavery," *Journal of the History of Sexuality* 20, no. 3 (September 2011): 445–64.

59 Blassingame, *Slave Testimony*, 221.

60 Dorothy Sterling, ed., *We Are Your Sisters: Black Women in the Nineteenth Century* (New York: W. W. Norton, 1984), 25.

61 Mellon, *Bullwhip Days*, 297.

62 Blassingame, *Slave Testimony*, 156.
63 Walter Johnson, *Soul by Soul: Life inside the Antebellum Slave Market* (Cambridge, MA: Harvard University Press, 1999), 113.
64 Johnson, *Soul by Soul*, 113.
65 David Brion Davis, "Slavery, Sex, and Dehumanization," in *Sex, Slavery, and Power*, ed. Gwyn Campbell and Elizabeth Elbourne (Athens: Ohio University Press, 2014), 53.
66 Cited in Lerner, *Black Women in White America*, 51–52.
67 Hazel Carby, *Reconstructing Womanhood: The Emergence of the Afro-American Woman Novelist* (New York: Oxford University Press, 1987), 30.
68 Mellon, *Bullwhip Days*, 121.
69 Northup, *Twelve Years a Slave*, 143.
70 Northup, 143.
71 Harriet Jacobs [Linda Brent], *Incidents in the Life of a Slave Girl* (1861; New York: Harcourt Brace Jovanovich, 1983), 79, author's emphasis.
72 Elizabeth Fox-Genovese, *Within the Plantation Household: Black and White Women of the Old South* (Chapel Hill: University of North Carolina Press, 1988), 396; see also Stephanie E. Jones-Rogers, *They Were Her Property: White Women Slave Owners in the American South* (New Haven, CT: Yale University Press, 2019).
73 Mellon, *Bullwhip Days*, 190.
74 Jamie T. Phelps, OP, "Providence and Histories: African American Perspectives with Emphasis on the Perspective of Black Liberation Theology," *CTSA Proceedings* 44 (1989): 14.
75 Northup, *Twelve Years a Slave*, 158.
76 Blassingame, *Slave Testimony*, 152–53.
77 Yetman, *Voices from Slavery*, 149.
78 Yetman, 145.
79 Mellon, *Bullwhip Days*, 191.
80 Joan M. Martin, *More than Chains and Toil: A Christian Work Ethic of Enslaved Women* (Louisville, KY: Westminster John Knox Press, 2000), 23, author's emphasis.
81 Yetman, *Voices from Slavery*, 134.
82 Mellon, *Bullwhip Days*, 23.
83 Mellon, 190.
84 Yetman, *Voices from Slavery*, 263.
85 Cited in Lerner, *Black Women in White America*, 41.
86 Cited in Lerner, 40–41.
87 Cited in Lerner, 37–38.
88 Yetman, *Voices from Slavery*, 227.
89 Lerner, *Black Women in White America*, 35.
90 Sarah M. Grimké in Theodore D. Weld, *American Slavery as It Is: Testimony of a Thousand Witnesses* (American Anti-Slavery Society, 1839), cited in Lerner, *Black Women in White America*, 18.
91 Kerri K. Greenidge, *The Grimkes: The Legacy of Slavery in an American Family* (New York: Liveright, 2022), loc. 21 of 404, Kindle.
92 Fox-Genovese, *Within the Plantation Household*, 308.
93 Nell Irvin Painter, "Soul Murder and Slavery," in Kerber, Kessler-Harris, and Sklar, eds., *US History as Women's History*, 138.
94 Mellon, *Bullwhip Days*, 32.
95 Mellon, 345.

96 Mellon, 348.

97 Mellon, 348.

98 Mellon, 349.

99 Mellon, 376.

100 Mellon, 454.

101 Mellon, 450.

102 Mellon, 456.

103 Mellon, 456.

104 C. Johnson and A. P. Watson, eds., *God Struck Me Dead* (Philadelphia and New York: Pilgrim, 1969), vii.

105 Moses Grandy, *Narrative of the Life of Moses Grandy, Late a Slave in the United States of America* (Boston: O. Johnson, 1844), 11, cited in Lerner, *Black Women in White America*, 8–9.

106 Morrison, *Beloved*, 23.

107 "The History of Mary Prince," in *Six Women's Slave Narratives*, The Schomburg Library of Nineteenth-Century Black Women Writers, gen. ed. Henry Louis Gates Jr. (New York: Oxford University Press, 1988), 12.

108 Hartman, *Scenes of Subjection*, 172.

109 Barbara Omolade, *The Rising Song of African American Women* (New York: Routledge, 1994), 7.

110 Stephanie M. H. Camp, *Closer to Freedom: Enslaved Women and Everyday Resistance in the Plantation South* (Chapel Hill: University of North Carolina Press, 2004), 67.

111 Camp, *Closer to Freedom*, 67.

112 Painter, "Soul Murder and Slavery," 131.

113 Camp, *Closer to Freedom*, 68.

114 Camp, 68.

115 Morrison, *Beloved*, 87.

116 Judylyn S. Ryan, *Spirituality as Ideology in Black Women's Film and Literature* (Charlottesville and London: University of Virginia Press, 2005), 52.

117 Morrison, *Beloved*, 87.

118 Morrison, 88, author's emphasis.

119 Morrison, 89.

120 Ryan, *Spirituality as Ideology in Black Women's Film and Literature*, 54.

121 Cf. Ryan, *Spirituality as Ideology in Black Women's Film and Literature*, 54, and Theophus H. Smith, *Conjuring Culture: Biblical Formations of Black America* (New York: Oxford University, 1994), 56.

122 Anita Durkin, "Object Written, Written Object: Slavery, Scarring, and Complications of Authorship in *Beloved*," *African American Review* (Fall 2007): 11.

123 Ryan, *Spirituality as Ideology in Black Women's Film and Literature*, 55.

124 Morrison, *Beloved*, 88.

125 Michael Hardt and Antonio Negri, *Empire* (Cambridge, MA: Harvard University Press, 2000), 202.

126 bell hooks, *Killing Rage: Ending Racism* (New York: Henry Holt, 1995), 161.

127 Alexander G. Weheliye, *Habeas Viscus: Racializing Assemblages, Biopolitics, and Black Feminist Theories of the Human* (Durham, NC, and London: Duke University Press, 2014), 131.

128 The word comes from Bob Marley's "Babylon System," *Songs of Freedom*, Island Records, 1992.

CHAPTER 3

1 John 1:1, 14.
2 Negro Spiritual.
3 Athanasius, *On the Incarnation* (Crestwood, NY: St. Vladimir's Seminary Press, 1998) [§ 54. 3], 9.
4 Carlo Maria Martini, *On the Body: A Contemporary Theology of the Human Person* (New York: Crossroad Publishing, 2001), 52. Miguel H. Díaz, *On Being Human: US Hispanic and Rahnerian Perspectives* (Maryknoll, NY: Orbis Books, 2001).
5 Karl Rahner, "The Body in the Order of Salvation," in his *Theological Investigations*, vol. XVII (New York: Crossroad Publishing, 1981), 74.
6 Martini, *On the Body*, 3.
7 Cited in Richard A. Horsley, *The Liberation of Christmas: The Infancy Narratives in Social Context* (New York: Continuum, 1993), 29–30.
8 Tertullian, *On the Flesh of Christ*, trans. Peter Holmes, in *Ante-Nicene Fathers*, vol. 3, ed. Alexander Roberts and James Donaldson (Buffalo, NY: Christian Literature Publishing Co., 1885), 525.
9 Amy-Jill Levine, "The Gospel of Matthew," in *Women's Bible Commentary*, 3rd ed., ed. Carol A. Newsome, Sharon H. Ringe, and Jacqueline E. Lapsley (Louisville, KY: Presbyterian, 2012), 643; see also Havlor Moxnes, *Putting Jesus in His Place: A Radical Vision of Household and Kingdom* (Louisville, KY: Westminster John Knox Press, 2003), 36.
  The unequivocal confession and teaching of the Roman Catholic Church on the virginal conception of Jesus is this: "Jesus was conceived solely by the power of the Holy Spirit in the womb of the Virgin Mary, affirming also the corporeal aspect of this event: Jesus was conceived 'by the Holy Spirit without human seed,'" *Catechism of the Catholic Church* (Liguori, MO: Liguori, 1994), #496, #497, and #500; see also *Lumen Gentium* (the Dogmatic Constitution on the Church), chapter 8.
  Why "birth narratives"? On the one hand, given the remarkable and contested aspects of his public life, scholars propose that these "birth narratives" or infancy narratives may have been a way to meet the curiosity of Jesus's followers about his childhood, upbringing, and ancestry. On the other, apologetics may have been a motive to counter skepticism about a messiah who came from Galilee and to quash rumors of illegitimacy with an account of divine intervention. The "infancy narratives" are found in Matthew 1–2 and Luke 1–2; references to Jesus's mother Mary by name, his brothers (James, Joses, Judas, and Simon), and his unnamed sisters appear in Mark 6:1–3. Joseph's name appears in both birth narratives. For the most detailed and comprehensive scholarly study of the infancy narratives in Matthew and Luke, see Raymond E. Brown, *The Birth of the Messiah* (New York: Doubleday, 1993), 534–42 (Appendix V, "The Charge of Illegitimacy"). Feminist, womanist, Latina readings of these narratives have generated an extensive corpus of literature. For some examples, see Elizabeth A. Johnson, *Truly Our Sister: A Theology of Mary in the Communion of Saints* (New York: Continuum, 2003); Beverly Roberts Gaventa and Cynthia L. Rigby, eds., *Blessed One: Protestant Perspectives on Mary* (Louisville, KY: Westminster John Knox Press, 2002); Amy-Jill Levine and Maria Mayo Robbins, eds., *A Feminist Companion to Mariology* (London: T & T Clark, 2005); Elaine M. Wainwright, *Shall We Look for Another? A Feminist Reading of the Matthean Jesus* (Maryknoll, NY: Orbis Books, 1998). The most vilified and

misunderstood of feminist interpretations sadly remains that by Jane Schaberg, *The Illegitimacy of Jesus: A Feminist Theological Interpretation of the Infancy Narratives*, 20th anniversary ed. (Sheffield: Sheffield Phoenix, 2006).

Sharon Jacob draws out a powerful literary connection between the *textual body* of Mary of Nazareth and the *contextual body* of the Indian surrogate woman. Jacob clarifies the differences and draws out similarities between the two. She aims to "(re) produce a Mary who is relevant to the lives of modern Indian women, and bring to light her contradictions and her ambiguity as a 'victimized her.' At the same time, Mary's choice to become a *mother for the other* captures the complexity of living in a globalizing economy, where choice promises a conditional freedom. By highlighting the ambiguities of agency that beset the Indian surrogate mother, living in a postcolonial India and neocolonial world, [she] also highlights the effects of globalization on the bodies of Indian women in general," in *Reading Mary alongside Indian Surrogate Mothers* (New York: Palgrave MacMillan, 2015), loc. 89 of 4550, Kindle.

10   John Dominic Crossan, *God and Empire: Jesus against Rome, Then and Now* (New York: HarperCollins, 2008), 109.

11   Richard A. Horsley, *The Liberation of Christmas: The Infancy Narratives in Social Context* (New York: Continuum, 1993), 72; see also Janice Capel Anderson, "Jesus Was a Refugee: Reception of Matthew 2:13–23," in *Anatomies of the Gospels and Beyond: Essays in Honor of R. Alan Culpepper*, ed. Mikeal C. Parsons, Elizabeth Struthers Malbon, and Paul N. Anderson (Leiden: Brill, 2018), 91–108; Zhodi Angami, *Tribals, Empire and God: A Tribal Reading of the Birth of Jesus in Matthew's Gospel* (London: Bloomsbury, 2017).

12   Horsley, *The Liberation of Christmas*, 72.

13   Crossan, *God and Empire*, 122.

14   Crossan, 122.

15   Günther Bornkam, *Jesus of Nazareth* (New York: Harper & Row, 1960), 42. Virgilio Elizondo, in *Galilean Journey: The Mexican-American Promise*, rev. ed. (Maryknoll, NY: Orbis Books, 2000), theologically appropriates racial-cultural mixture as *mestizaje* to reclaim the flesh of Jesus for Mexican American inclusion in the "body" of church and the "body" of society.

16   Richard A. Horsley, *Archaeology, History, and Society in Galilee: The Social Context of Jesus and the Rabbis* (Valley Forge, PA: Trinity Press, 1996), 15–42, cited in Mark Lewis Taylor, *The Executed God: The Way of the Cross in Lockdown America* (Minneapolis: Fortress Press, 2001), 72. On the significance of Jesus's Galilean origins to his resistance to empire, see Richard A. Horsley, *Galilee: History, Politics, People* (Valley Forge, PA: Trinity Press, 1995); Marianne Sawicki, *Crossing Galilee: Architectures of Contact in the Occupied Land of Jesus* (Valley Forge, PA: Trinity Press, 2000).

17   Richard A. Horsley, *Jesus and Empire: The Kingdom of God and the New World Disorder* (Minneapolis: Fortress Press, 2003), 35, 15.

18   Horsley, *Jesus and Empire*, 48.

19   Maurice Casey, *Jesus of Nazareth* (London and New York: T & T Clark, 2010), 153.

20   Moxnes, *Putting Jesus in His Place*, 150.

21   Moxnes, 150.

22   Moxnes, 150.

23   Johnson, *Truly Our Sister*, 168.

24   Casey, *Jesus of Nazareth*, 152; Johnson, *Truly Our Sister*, 147.

25   Johnson, *Truly Our Sister*, 147.

26   N. T. Wright, *Jesus and the Victory of God, Christian Origins and the Question of God*, vol. 2 (Minneapolis: Fortress Press, 1996), 203; Horsley, *Jesus and Empire*, 35–54.

27   Wright, *Jesus and the Victory of God*, 243, 280.

28   Horsley, *Jesus and Empire*, 78, 79–104.

29   Horsley, 15.

30   John Dominic Crossan, *Jesus, A Revolutionary Biography* (New York: Harper & Row, 1994), 194–95.

31   Luke 4:18, 6:20–22, 7:22, 14:13, 21; Matt 5:3–6, 11, 11:5.

32   John 9:6; Luke 8:54.

33   Marcella Althaus-Reid, *Indecent Theology: Theological Perversions in Sex, Gender and Politics* (London: Routledge, 2000), 113.

34   Horsley, *Jesus and Empire*, 111.

35   Horsley, 105; also 105–28.

36   Horsley, 108, 109.

37   Crossan, *Jesus, A Revolutionary Biography*, 68

38   Crossan, 68, author's emphasis.

39   Crossan, 67–70.

40   See Farley, "The Black Body as Fetish Object," 459, 464.

41   Sharon H. Ringe, *Jesus, Liberation, and the Biblical Jubilee: Images for Ethics and Christology* (Philadelphia: Fortress Press, 1985), 58.

42   Mark Jordan in *Telling Truths in Church: Scandal, Flesh, and Christian Speech* (Boston: Beacon Press, 2003) counsels against using the phrase "sexual orientation" with regard to Jesus. However, Jordan suggests the phrase may be "very useful to undo the heterosexist presumption that Jesus was, of course, heterosexual. . . . As incarnate God, Jesus violated any number of social expectations" (88–89). While I agree with Jordan, I do not assign any sexual orientation to Jesus (the canonical gospels give us no clues whatsoever about his sexual desires) and I do not suggest that he was homosexual. The canonical gospels are silent on the marital state of Jesus and offer no clues as to that of his male disciples except for Simon Peter (Matt 8:14–16) and the marital state of some of the women who traveled with him (Luke 8:3).

43   Nelson, *Embodiment*, 17.

44   James B. Nelson, *Between Two Gardens: Reflections on Sexuality and Religious Experience* (New York: Pilgrim Press, 1983), 5–6.

45   Rowan Williams, "The Body's Grace," in *Our Selves, Our Souls & Bodies*, ed. Charles Hefling (Cambridge, MA: Cowley, 1997), 59.

46   Sandra Schneiders, *Women and the Word* (New York: Paulist Press, 1986), 55. Schneiders writes "in a certain sense, Jesus had to be male in order to reveal effectively the true nature of God and of humanity" (58). To so-called "male virtues," Schneiders opposes Jesus's validation of so-called "stereotypically female virtues" of "meekness and humility of heart, peacemaking, non-violence, silent patience in the face of injustice and suffering, recourse to personal prayer in times of difficulty, purity of heart, and a nurturing concern for all, especially the sick, the oppressed, sinners, women, and children" (58–59). However, following Horsley, I contend that

while these so-called female virtues have much to teach us, these virtues well may serve to depoliticize Jesus and his social praxis.

47 John W. Riggs, *Postmodern Christianity: Doing Theology in the Contemporary World* (New York: Trinity Press, 2003), 121; Albert Nolan, *Jesus before Christianity* (1978; Maryknoll, NY: Orbis Books, 2002), 73–82.

48 Luke 6:27–28, 32, 11:27–28, 12:52–53, cf. Matt 10:34–36.

49 See Schneiders, *Women and the Word*, 60, 68; Mark:14:6–9; John 4:27–30.

50 José Antonio Pagola, *Jesus, An Historical Approximation*, trans. Margaret Wilde (Miami, FL: Convivium Press, 2009), 70.

51 Pagola, *Jesus, An Historical Approximation*, 72.

52 Jorge N. Ferrer, "Embodied Spirituality, Now and Then," *Tikkun* (May/June 2006): 42.

53 Raymond J. Lawrence, *The Poisoning of Eros: Sexual Values in Conflict* (New York: Augustine Moore Press, 1989), 247; also see Peter Black, "The Broken Wings of Eros: Christian Ethics and the Denial of Desire," *Theological Studies* 64, no. 1 (March 2003): 106–26.

54 Audre Lorde, "Uses of the Erotic: The Erotic as Power," in her *Sister Outsider: Essays & Speeches by Audre Lorde* (Trumansburg, NY: Crossing Press, 1985), 54.

55 Lorde, "Uses of the Erotic," 55, 56.

56 Lorde, 56.

57 Lorde, 56; see Marvin Ellison, *Erotic Justice: A Liberating Ethic of Sexuality* (Louisville, KY: Westminster/John Knox Press, 1996).

58 Mark 10:13–16; Matt 19:13–15; Luke 18:15–17/Matt 27:55, 28:5; Mark 15:40–41; Luke 8:2–3, 7:36–50, 10:38–42; John 12:1–11/Matt 19:16–30; Luke 19:1–10; John 3:1–21, 12:20–26, 19:31–39.

59 My free-form rendering of this prayer takes into account my reading and study of the work of Amy-Jill Levine, *The Misunderstood Jew: The Church and the Scandal of the Jewish Jesus* (New York: HarperCollins, 2006), N. T. Wright, *Jesus and the Victory of God, Christian Origins and the Question of God*, vol. 2 (Minneapolis: Fortress Press, 1996), 148–49, 292–94, 649–50, Obery Hendricks Jr., *The Politics of Jesus: Rediscovering the True Revolutionary Nature of the Teachings of Jesus and How They Have Been Corrupted* (New York: Doubleday, 2006), loc. 101–12, Kindle. That said, *none of these authors would "own" my rendering.*

60 Levine, *The Misunderstood Jew*, 42.

61 Levine, 44, 45.

62 Levine, 45.

63 Ringe, *Jesus, Liberation, and the Biblical Jubilee*, 81–84; Wright, *Jesus and the Victory of God*, 293.

64 Richard Kearney, *The Wake of Imagination* (1988; London: Taylor & Francis, 2003), 47. According to Kearney, the Talmud considered the imagination to be a paradoxical faculty—at once, good and evil. Its most positive interpretation deems imagination "to be that most primordial 'drive of [the human]' which, if sublimated and oriented towards the divine way (*Talmud*), can serve as an indispensable power for attaining the goal of creation: the universal embodiment of God's plan in the Messianic Kingdom of justice and peace" (46). The Talmud portends that the messianic treaty between the Lion and the Lamb will result from an "atoned," i.e., integrated imagination.

CHAPTER 4

1 Matt 25:44–45.
2 Negro Spiritual.
3 Rafael Luciani, "The Itinerant Fraternity of Jesus: Christological Discernment of the Migration Drama," in *Living (with)Out Borders: Catholic Theological Ethics on the Migration of Peoples*, ed. Agnes M. Brazal and María Teresa Dávila (New York: Orbis Books, 2016), 157.
4 Michael Hardt and Antonio Negri, *Multitude: War and Democracy in the Age of Empire* (New York: Penguin, 2004), loc. 2 of 359, Kindle.
5 Hardt and Negri, *Empire*; see also Hardt and Negri, "Empire, Twenty Years On," *New Left Review* 120 (November and December 2019): 67–92.
6 Hardt and Negri, "Empire," in *Thinking Globally: A Global Studies Reader*, ed. Mark Juergensmeyer (Berkeley: University of California Press, 2014), 204–5.
7 Hardt and Negri, "Empire," 206.
8 See Brian P. Flanagan, *Stumbling in Holiness: Sin and Sanctity in the Church* (Collegeville, MN: Liturgical Press, 2018).
9 Ivan Petrella, *Beyond Liberation Theology: A Polemic* (London: SCM Press, 2008), loc. 400 of 5216, Kindle.
10 Howard Winant, "The New Imperialism, Globalization, and Racism," in *The New Politics of Race: Globalism, Difference, Justice* (Minneapolis and London: University of Minneapolis Press, 2004), 131.
11 Indeed, the years of Donald Trump's presidential campaign, election, and term of office (January 20, 2017–January 20, 2021) saw a breathtaking increase in visible, public, and punishing racially charged verbal insults, physical assaults, and street demonstrations against non-White US citizens, Jews, and non-White immigrants. One of the earliest of such events was the "Unite the Right" rally in Charlottesville, Virginia, August 12, 2017. Counter-protesters turned out to condemn the White supremacist group.
12 Hardt and Negri, *Empire*, 191, 193.
13 Winant, "The New Imperialism, Globalization, and Racism," 135.
14 Zygmunt Bauman, *Globalization: The Human Condition* (New York: Columbia University Press, 1998), 70.
15 Winant, "The New Imperialism, Globalization, and Racism," 135.
16 Winant, "Teaching Race and Racism," in *The New Politics of Race*, 76.
17 The term "intersectionality" was coined in 1989 by legal scholar Kimberlé Williams Crenshaw as an analytic tool by which to understand how various forms of structural inequality often operate together, compound, and intensify each other; see Crenshaw, "Demarginalizing the Intersection of Race and Sex: A Black Feminist Critique of Antidiscrimination Doctrine, Feminist Theory and Antiracist Politics," *University of Chicago Legal Forum* 1989 (1989): 138–68, and "Mapping the Margins: Intersectionality, Identity Politics, and Violence against Women of Color," *Stanford Law Review* (1991): 1241–99.
18 The Roman Catholic Church teaches that abortion is immoral and a grave sin. Canon 1398 of the 1983 *Code of Canon Law* imposes automatic excommunication on Catholics who procure an abortion. On June 24, 2022, the US Supreme Court ruled in *Dobbs v. Jackson Women's Health Organization* to overturn *Roe v. Wade*

(the 1973 case that legalized abortion in the United States). The Dobbs ruling ended the constitutional right to abortion and eliminated federal standards on abortion access. As a result, at least at this writing, eighteen states have banned or severely restricted abortion—even in cases of rape and incest. I do not condone abortion, but I will not abrogate a woman's freedom to live and act by the dictates of her conscience.

19 Patricia Hill Collins, *Intersectionality as Critical Social Theory* (Durham, NC: Duke University Press, 2019), loc. 240 of 360, Kindle.

20 Collins, *Intersectionality as Critical Social Theory*, loc. 240 of 360, Kindle.

21 Nancy Pineda-Madrid traces the feminicide, the intentional murder of women because they are women, in *Suffering, Salvation and in Ciudad Juárez* (Minneapolis: Fortress Press, 2011).

22 Pei-Chia Len, "Among Women: Migrant Domestics and Their Taiwanese Employers," in *Global Woman: Nannies, Maids, and Sex Workers in the New Economy*, ed. Barbara Ehrenreich and Arlie Russell Hochschild (New York: Henry Holt, 2004), 172.

23 Gemma Tulud Cruz, "Theology and (De)Humanizing Work in the Twenty-First Century," *Proceedings CTSA* 75 (2021): 7–8.

24 Travis Andersen, "Pizza Shop Owner Injured, Exploited Workers, Federal Prosecutors Say," *Boston Globe*, March 17, 2023, A8, B6.

25 United Nations, International Forum on the Eradication of Poverty, Report of the Meeting, November 15–16, 2006, iv.

26 United Nations, Department of Economic and Social Affairs: Inequality, https://tinyurl.com/99zz5nck, my emphasis (accessed May 6, 2023).

27 United Nations, Department of Economic and Social Affairs: Poverty, https://tinyurl.com/ym3bcfjr (accessed May 6, 2023). On October 17, 2022, the United Nations marked the thirty-fifth anniversary of the "World Day to Overcome Extreme Poverty."

28 See Chay Quinn, "Police Release Photo of Man Wanted after a Polish Immigrant Was Savagely Attacked," *Daily Mail*, June 25, 2022, https://tinyurl.com/587xx39w; United Nations, Human Rights, "South Africa 'on the precipice of explosive xenophobic violence,' UN Experts Warn," July 15, 2022, https://tinyurl.com/47h4336m.

29 Petrella, *Beyond Liberation Theology*, loc. 104 of 5216, Kindle.

30 Transcript of interview between PBS reporter Geoff Bennett and *Atlantic* magazine staff writer Caitlin Dickerson, "How a Trump-Era Policy That Separated Thousands of Migrant Families Came About," August 13, 2022, https://tinyurl.com/4fapcv7f; see also Dan Barry, Miriam Jordan, Anne Correal, and Manny Fernandez, "Cleaning Toilets, Following Rules: A Migrant Child's Days in Detention," *New York Times*, July 14, 2018, https://tinyurl.com/4tkvthvt; Refugees International, Report: "The Trump Zero Tolerance Policy: A Cruel Approach with Humane and Viable Alternatives," July 31, 2018, https://tinyurl.com/4x4nwhhz. At this writing, the administration of President Joseph Biden has not acceded to this policy. It has not yet held officials from the previous administration to account, but has tried to reunite as many children and parents as possible.

31 Kristin E. Heyer, "*Familismo* across the Americas: En Route to a Liberating Christian Family Ethic," in *Living (with)Out Borders*, 98.

32 Winant, "The New Imperialism, Globalization, and Racism," 135. Nativism has had a complex history in the United States; contemporarily it refers to policies aimed

to protect the so-called "native" European population from immigrants who will alter or corrupt American cultural and political values and practices. For historical studies of nativism, see John Higham, *Strangers in the Land: Patterns of American Nativism, 1860–1925* (New Brunswick, NJ: Rutgers University Press, 1992); Mae M. Ngai, *Impossible Subjects: Illegal Aliens and the Making of Modern America* (Princeton, NJ: Princeton University Press, 2004); Ronald T. Takaki, *Iron Cages: Race and Culture in 19th Century America* (New York: Oxford University Press, 1990).

33 Winant, "The New Imperialism, Globalization, and Racism," 130.

34 Bonilla-Silva, *Racism without Racists*. Bonilla-Silva interprets data gathered from a structured survey conducted regionally (Midwest, South, and West coast) among Black and White university students, as well as a "probabilistic survey" of four hundred Black and White Detroit metropolitan-area residents (*Racism without Racists*, loc. 12–15 of 254, Kindle); also see Patricia J. Williams, *Seeing a Color-Blind Future: The Paradox of Race* (New York: Farrar, Straus & Giroux, 1997).

35 Bonilla-Silva, *Racism without Racists*, loc. 74 of 254.

36 Bonilla-Silva, loc. 178 of 254.

37 Francisco Bethencourt, *Racisms: From the Crusades to the Twentieth Century* (Princeton, NJ: Princeton University Press, 2013), 6.

38 Yvonne Abraham, "Immigration Hits Home in Lynn; Blacks Voice Fear of a Loss of Jobs," *Boston Globe*, April 16, 2006, Sunday, 3rd edition, Metro/Region Section, A1. The Pew Hispanic Center conducted a study (February 8, 2005, and March 7, 2006) focused nationally as well as on five cities—Chicago metro area, Las Vegas, Phoenix, Raleigh-Durham metro area, and Washington, DC, metro area. The survey, "America's Immigration Quandary," April 4, 2006, reports that Blacks may not be favorably disposed toward immigration. On the other hand, cities with large Black populations did not consider immigration a "big problem"—with 19 percent agreeing that it was in Chicago, 26 percent in Raleigh-Durham, and 19 percent in Washington, DC. Communities with larger White populations identified immigration as a "big problem"—36 percent in Las Vegas and 55 percent in Phoenix, May 9, 2006, https://tinyurl.com/d22k4jth. This survey interviewed Blacks, Whites, and Hispanic/Latinas/os, but their replies are not distinguished from one another on all questions.

39 See Monica Campbell, "Holiday Visit Worth the Risk for Migrants," *Christian Science Monitor*, The World, 4 (December 23, 2005); Martin Kaste, "For Poor Brazilians, a Perilous, Illegal Journey to US," NPR, April 14, 2006, https://tinyurl.com/5fsubcb5, and "Helping to Rebuild New Orleans, Illegally," NPR, April 14, 2006, https://tinyurl.com/mrxuz5yz. See Mike Davis, "Who Is Killing New Orleans?" *The Nation*, April 10, 2006, https://tinyurl.com/9aypsyn4. To be sure, Mexican workers are *not* the ones who are killing New Orleans!

40 Barbara Crossette, "UN Coaxes out the Wheres and Whys of Global Immigration," *New York Times*, section 1, 7 (July 7, 2002), https://tinyurl.com/5y23j227; Cecilia Esterline and Jeanne Batalova, "Frequently Requested Statistics on Immigrants and Immigration in the United States" (Washington, DC: Migration Policy Institute, March 17, 2022), https://tinyurl.com/585s5eh8; Jeanne Batalova, "Top Statistics on Global Migration and Migrants" (Washington, DC: Migration Policy Institute, July 21, 2022), https://tinyurl.com/585s5eh8.

41 Bonilla-Silva, *Racism without Racists*, loc. 188 of 254, Kindle.

42 See John Catalinotto, "Morocco & Spain Kill, Deport African Immigrants," October 21, 2005, *Workers World*, https://tinyurl.com/y9h9j8pb.

43 Raja Mishra, "Study: Many Job Deaths Are Immigrants," *Boston Globe*, City and Region, April 28, 2006, B4.

44 Erik Camayd-Freixas, "Interpreting after the Largest ICE Raid in US History: A Personal Account," June 13, 2008, 12, https://tinyurl.com/4wy5es8t.

45 Julia Preston, "An Interpreter Speaking up for Migrants," *New York Times*, July 11, 2008, https://tinyurl.com/2p98657a.

46 Yvonne Abraham, "Up to 350 in Custody after New Bedford Immigration Raid," *Boston Globe*, March 6, 2007, https://tinyurl.com/yck5edtb (last accessed June 27, 2009).

47 Boston TV Channel 25 news reporter Crystal Hanes interviewed two immigrants who had been caught up in the ICE raid in New Bedford, Massachusetts, who are still feeling the traumatic impact of the raid more than ten years later and are worried about the ongoing separation of children and parents; "Effects of New Bedford ICE Raid Still Being Felt over a Decade Later," Boston 25 News, July 5, 2018, https://tinyurl.com/4f8f7s7f; Maria Murriel, "A Massive ICE Raid in This Town Didn't Stop Undocumented Labor or Illegal Immigration," WGBH, April 24, 2017, https://tinyurl.com/bdsj3pen.

48 Michelle Liu, "Families Search for Answers Following Immigration Raids; 680 People Working at Food Processing Plants Detained," *Mississippi Today*, August 7, 2019, https://tinyurl.com/36rryjnz.

49 Sean D. Hamill, "Mexican's Death Bares a Town's Ethnic Tension," *New York Times*, July 8, 2009, https://tinyurl.com/2p92ey3s.

50 Lori S. Robinson, "Black Like Whom?" *The Crisis* (January/February 2006): 24.

51 Robinson, "Black Like Whom?" 27.

52 Robinson, 27.

53 Michael Omi and Howard Winant, *Racial Formation in the United States, from the 1960s to the 1990s*, 2nd ed. (New York and London: Routledge, 1994).

54 See Eric Williams, *From Columbus to Castro: The History of the Caribbean, 1492–1969* (New York: Vintage, 1970); Edward Braithwaite, *The Development of Creole Society in Jamaica* (Boston: New Beacon, 1971); Robin Blackburn, *The Making of New World Slavery: From the Baroque to the Modern 1492–1800* (London: Verso, 1997).

55 Bonilla-Silva, *Racism without Racists*, loc. 189 of 254, Kindle.

56 Bonilla-Silva, loc. 190 of 254, Kindle.

57 Krista Johnson, "It Matters How We Define the African Diaspora," Africa in Transition and Africa Program (Washington, DC: Council on Foreign Relations), April 5, 2023, https://tinyurl.com/2ak9xfu9/.

58 See Katie Walker Grimes, *Christ Divided: Antiblackness as Corporate Vice* (Minneapolis: Fortress Press, 2017).

59 While same-sex relationships are no longer widely criminalized, sixty-eight nations in the Americas, Asia, including the Middle East, Africa, and Oceania do so: these nations include Dominica, Jamaica, and St. Lucia; Iran, Iraq, Myanmar, Qatar, Saudi Arabia, and the United Arab Emirates; Ghana, Kenya, Morocco, Nigeria, Tanzania, and Uganda; Papua New Guinea, Samoa, and Tonga. See Erasing 76 Crimes, "About," https://tinyurl.com/4cukr76w.

60 See Cannon, "Sexing Black Women," in Pinn and Hopkins, eds., *Loving the Body*, 11–30; Rita Nakashima Brock and Susan Brooks Thistlethwaite, *Casting Stones: Prostitution and Liberation in Asia and the United States* (Minneapolis: Fortress Press, 1996).

61 Dwight Hopkins, "The Construction of the Black Male Body," in Pinn and Hopkins, eds., *Loving the Body*, 186–88, 185; see also Robert C. Young, *Colonial Desire: Hybridity in Theory, Culture and Race* (London: Routledge, 1995).

62 Recall the senseless murders of lesbian, gay, and transgender persons—Matthew Shepherd, 1998; Saskia Gunn, Shani Baraka, and Rayshon Holmes, 2003; Angie Zapata, 2008; Eric Garner, Tamir Rice, and Michael Brown, 2014; Freddie Gray Jr., 2016; the forty-nine women and men in Orlando, Florida, at the Pulse Night Club, including Stanley Almodóvar, Amanda Alvear, Antonia Davon Brown, Luis Daniel Conde, Anthony Laureano Disla, Mercedez Marisol Flores, Eddie Justice, and Christopher Andrew Leinonen, 2016.

63 See Patrick S. Cheng, *Radical Love: An Introduction to Queer Theology* (New York: Seabury Books, 2013); Patrick S. Cheng, *Rainbow Theology: Bridging Race, Sexuality, and Spirit* (New York: Seabury Books, 2013); Marvin M. Ellison and Kelly Brown Douglas, eds., *Sexuality and the Sacred: Sources for Theological Education*, 2nd ed (Louisville, KY: Westminster John Knox Press, 2010); Pamela Lightsey, *Our Lives Matter: A Womanist Queer Theology* (Eugene, OR: Pickwick Publications, 2015); Robert Shore-Goss, Thomas Bohache, Patrick S. Cheng, and Mona West, eds., *Queering Christianity: Finding a Place at the Table for LGBTQI Christians* (Santa Barbara, CA: Praeger, 2013); Scott Bader-Saye, "The Transgender Body's Grace," *Journal of the Society of Christian Ethics* 39, no. 1 (Spring/Summer 2019): 75–92; Sarah Coakley, *God Sexuality and the Self: An Essay "On the Trinity"* (Cambridge: Cambridge University Press, 2013).

64 *Homosexualitatis problema*, "Letter to the Bishops of the Catholic Church on the Pastoral Care of Homosexual Persons," October 1, 1986, https://tinyurl.com/2waxzmnr; *The Catechism of the Catholic Church*, #2358.

65 *Persona Humana*, "Declaration on Certain Questions Concerning Sexual Ethics," CDF, December 29, 1975, #8; see also "Considerations Regarding Proposals to Give Legal Recognition to Unions between Homosexual Persons," March 28, 2003.

66 *The Catechism of the Catholic Church*, #2357.

67 Scanlon, "Postmodernism and Theology," 18.

68 *Homosexualitatis problema*, #12.

69 Paul G. Crowley, "Homosexuality and the Counsel of the Cross," *Theological Studies* 65, no. 3 (September 2004): 500–29.

70 Paul G. Crowley, *Unwanted Wisdom: Suffering, the Cross, and Hope* (New York: Continuum, 2005), 109.

71 Xavier John Seubert, "'But Do Not Use the Rotted Names': Theological Adequacy and Homosexuality," *The Heythrop Journal* 40, no. 1 (January 1999): 74, n23.

72 James Alison, *Faith beyond Resentment: Fragments Catholic and Gay* (New York: Crossroad Publishing, 2001), 94. In "Nicodemus and the Boys in the Square," 209–35, Alison critiques Catholic teaching on sexuality and homosexuality; also see Sebastian Moore, "A Word for Sexual Desire: Order Is in Things Not Over Them," in *Lonergan's Openness: Polymorphism, Postmodernism, and Religion, Lonergan Workshop*, vol. 18, ed. Fred Lawrence (Chestnut Hill, MA: Boston College, 2005), 203–24.

73 Stephen J. Pope, "The Magisterium's Arguments against 'Same-Sex Marriage:'
    An Ethical Analysis and Critique," *Theological Studies* 65, no. 3 (September
    2004): 550.

74 Pope, "The Magisterium's Arguments against 'Same-Sex Marriage,'" 550.

75 For a critique of Black Church teaching on homosexuality, see Victor Anderson,
    "The Black Church and the Curious Body of the Black Homosexual," in Pinn and
    Hopkins, eds., *Loving the Body*, 297–312; Alton B. Pollard, III, "Teaching the Body:
    Sexuality and the Black Church," in Pinn and Hopkins, eds., *Loving the Body*, 315–46;
    Douglas, *Sexuality and the Black Church*; Kelly Brown Douglas, *Black Bodies and
    the Black Church: A Blues Slant* (New York: Palgrave Macmillan, 2012).

76 Seubert, "'But Do Not Use the Rotted Names,'" 65.

77 "Bishops in Belgium Authorize Prayer for Committed Gay Couples," *National
    Catholic Reporter*, September 20, 2022, https://tinyurl.com/4tdytjxc.

78 Luke Coppen, "German Synodal Way Backs Same-Sex Blessings," *The Pillar*, March
    10, 2023, https://tinyurl.com/mptr9wtk. The German bishops issued a five-page
    document, "Blessing Ceremonies for Couples Who Love Each Other," which report-
    edly was passed by 176 votes for, 14 against, and 12 abstentions.

79 James Martin, *Building a Bridge: How the Catholic Church and the LGBT Community
    Can Enter into a Relationship of Respect, Compassion, and Sensitivity* (New York:
    HarperCollins, 2017), loc. 2 of 190, Kindle. New Ways Ministry is a national ministry
    located in Mount Rainier, Maryland, that acts as a Catholic outreach to educate about
    and advocate for equitable inclusion and justice for LGBTQ+ persons in church and
    civil society. New Ways was founded in 1977 by Father Robert Nugent, SDS, and
    Sister Jeannine Gramick, SSND, who took inspiration from a 1976 pastoral letter,
    "Sexuality: God's Gift" (February 11, 1976), written by Bishop Francis Mugavero
    of Brooklyn, New York. In the letter, Bishop Mugavero offered encouragement to
    lesbian and gay people and pledged to them "to try to find new ways to communicate
    the truth of Christ," https://tinyurl.com/3tstuet2.

80 "*Responsum* of the Congregation for the Doctrine of the Faith to a *dubium*
    Regarding the Blessings of Unions of Persons of the Same Sex," March 15, 2021,
    https://tinyurl.com/2ahmujyf.

81 The declaration carries papal assent. It is difficult to correlate the assent of the
    present pontiff to this declaration with the welcoming attitude and public he seems
    to extend to lesbian and gay persons.

82 Thomas Bohache, "Embodiment as Incarnation: An Incipient Queer Christology,"
    Theology and Sexuality 10, no. 1 (2003): 12.

83 Althaus-Reid, *Indecent Theology*, 111. As a hermeneutical or interpretative lens, queer
    theory seeks to destabilize social and cultural constructions of gender binaries and
    identity politics rooted in fixed performative notions of "gay" or "lesbian." Queer
    theory foregrounds sexuality in order to uncover heretofore unexamined assump-
    tions about sexuality and challenge heterosexist normativity in mainstream feminist
    analysis. Queer theory charges not only "traditional" theologies regarding these
    assumptions but also the various theologies of liberation. Major theorists include:
    Michel Foucault, *The History of Sexuality: An Introduction*, vol. 1, trans. Robert
    Hurley (New York: Vintage, 1990); Judith Butler, *Gender Trouble: Feminism and
    the Subversion of Identity* (London and New York: Routledge, 1990); Judith Butler,
    Bodies That Matter: On the Discursive Limits of "Sex" (London: Routledge, 1993); Eve
    Kosofsky Sedgwick, *Epistemology of the Closet* (Berkeley: University of California

Press, 1990); Rachel Alsop, Annette Fitzsimons, and Kathleen Lennon, *Theorizing Gender* (Oxford: Blackwell, 2002).

84 Sarah Coakley, "Living into the Mystery of the Holy Trinity: Trinity, Prayer and Sexuality," *Anglican Theological Review* 80, no. 2 (Spring 1998): 230. Coakley cautions, "no language of eros is safe from possible nefarious application . . ." (231).

85 Engelbert Mveng proposed the notion of anthropological impoverishment to account for the assault by Western colonialism on Africa's languages, cultures, traditions, and human beings; see his *L'Afrique dans l'Eglise, Paroles d'un Croyant* (Paris: L'Harmattan, 1985) and "Impoverishment and Liberation: A Theological Approach for Africa and the Third World," in *Paths of African Theology*, ed. Rosino Gibellini (Maryknoll, NY: Orbis Books, 1994), 154–65; cf. Achille Mbembe, *On the Postcolony* (Berkeley: University of California Press, 2001).

86 Lonergan, *Insight*, 715.

87 Robert Goss, *Jesus Acted Up: A Gay and Lesbian Manifesto* (San Francisco: HarperCollins, 1993).

88 Goss, *Jesus Acted Up*, 83.

89 Timothy K. Beal, "Opening: Cracking the Binding," in *Reading Bibles, Writing Bodies: Identity and the Book*, ed. Timothy K. Beal and David M. Gunn (London: Routledge, 1997), 1–12.

90 Goss's book appeared in the same year (1993) as that of womanist theologian Delores S. Williams. In *Sisters in the Wilderness* (Maryknoll, NY: Orbis Books, 1993), Williams compared the coerced surrogacy of Jesus to the coerced surrogacy of Black women in the contexts of enslavement and post-enslavement.

91 Goss, *Jesus Acted Up*, 83.

92 Goss, 83.

93 Goss, 83, 84.

94 Goss, 83, 84.

95 Christological reflection from the perspectives of Black, Mexican American, Asian, African, Latin American, feminist, *mujerista*, and womanist makes this same appeal to particularity.

96 Coakley, "Living into the Mystery of the Holy Trinity," 224. Coakley writes: "[I]n any prayer of the sort in which we radically cede control to the Spirit there is an instant reminder of the close analogue between this ceding (to the trinitarian God), and the *ekstasis* of human sexual passion. Thus it is not a coincidence that intimate relationship is at the heart of both these matters. . . . [T]he early Fathers were aware of this nexus of associations" (between Trinitarian conceptuality, prayer of a deep sort, and the—to them—dangerous connections with issues of sex and gender) (224).

97 Moore, "A Word for Sexual Desire," 210, 213, 205.

98 Alison writes: Jesus is a "sign of the possibilities of unscandalised human desire," in "Nicodemus and the Boys in the Square," 215.

99 This proximate fulfillment admits of proper, i.e., nonutilitarian, nonmanipulative, nondominative sexual relations and intimate friendship. The final fulfillment or complete fulfillment of the body is its resurrection.

100 Alison, "Nicodemus and the Boys in the Square," 214.

101 Goss, *Jesus Acted Up*, 169.

102 The phrase comes from Jean-Marie Roger Tillard, *Flesh of the Church, Flesh of Christ: At the Source of the Ecclesiology of Communion* (1992; Collegeville, MN: Pueblo/Liturgical Press, 2001).

103 Gregory of Nyssa, "On the Making of Man," 13, 1049B-1052A, in *Gregory of Nyssa, Dogmatic Treatises*, ed. Philip Schaff and Henry Wace (Grand Rapids, MI: William B. Eerdmans, 1979), cited in Graham Ward, *Cities of God* (London: Routledge, 2000), 116.

104 Ward, *Cities of God*, 116, emphasis mine.

CHAPTER 5

This chapter was first published as "The New Anthropological Subject at the Heart of the Mystical Body of Christ," *Proceedings CTSA* (November 1998): 25–47. It is used with permission and has been revised.

1 Philippians 2:6–8.

2 Negro Spiritual.

3 Jean-Luc Nancy, "Corpus," in his *The Birth to Presence*, trans. Brian Holmes et al. (Stanford, CA: Stanford University Press, 1993), 196.

4 The phrase, "turn to the subject," signals the shift in Christian theology that adverts to the challenges of modern philosophy initiated by Descartes, Locke, Hume, and Kant. These philosophers shifted discourse toward speech about human subjectivity and its role within human knowledge and religious belief. For some discussions of issues basic to theological anthropology see Lieven Boeve, Yves De Maeseneer, and Ellen Van Stichel, eds., *Questioning the Human: Toward a Theological Anthropology for the Twenty-First Century* (New York: Fordham University Press, 2014), especially essays by Anthony J. Godzieba, Michelle E. Gonzalez, and Rosemary P. Carbine; David G. Kirchhoffer, with Robyn Horner and Patrick McArdle, *Being Human: Groundwork for a Theological Anthropology for the 21st Century* (Eugene, OR: Wipf & Stock, 2013); Jawanza Eric Clark, *Reclaiming Stolen Earth: An Africana Ecotheology* (Maryknoll, NY: Orbis Books, 2022); Wendy Farley, *Gathering Those Driven Away: A Theology of Incarnation* (Louisville, KY: Westminster John Knox Press, 2011); Melanie L. Harris, *Ecowomanism: African American Women and Earth-Honoring Faiths* (Maryknoll, NY: Orbis Books, 2017); Mary Ann Hinsdale and Stephen Okey, eds., *T & T Clark Handbook of Theological Anthropology* (London: Bloomsbury, 2021); Cheryl Kirk-Duggan, *The Sky Is Crying: Race, Class, and Natural Disaster* (Nashville: Abingdon Press, 2011); Shelly Rambo, *Spirit and Trauma: A Theology of Remaining* (Louisville, KY: Westminster John Knox Press, 2010); Mayra Rivera, *Poetics of the Flesh* (Durham, NC, and London: Duke University Press 2015); Michelle Voss Roberts, *Body Parts: A Theological Anthropology* (Minneapolis: Fortress Press, 2017); Michele Saracino, *Being about Borders: A Christian Anthropology of Difference* (Collegeville, MN: Liturgical Press, 2011); Michele Saracino, *Christian Anthropology: An Introduction to the Human Person* (Mahwah, NJ: Paulist Press, 2015); Todd A. Salzman and Michael G. Lawler, *The Sexual Person: Toward a Renewed Catholic Anthropology* (Washington, DC: Georgetown University Press, 2008); Phillis Isabella Sheppard, *Self, Culture and Others in Womanist Practical Theology* (New York: Palgrave Macmillan, 2011); Eboni Marshall Turman, *Toward a Womanist Ethic of Incarnation* (New York: Palgrave Macmillan, 2013).

5   Enrique Dussel, *The Invention of the Americas, Eclipse of "the Other" and the Myth of Modernity* (New York: Continuum, 1995), 20.

6   Immanuel Kant, "An Answer to the Question: 'What Is Enlightenment?'" in *Kant's Political Writings*, trans. H. B. Nisbet, ed. Hans Reiss (1970; Cambridge: Cambridge University Press, 1979), 54.

7   Charles Long, *Significations: Signs, Symbols, and Images in the Interpretation of Religion* (1986, 1995; Aurora, CO: Davies Group Publishers, 1999); Cornel West, *Prophesy Deliverance! An Afro-American Revolutionary Christianity* (Louisville, KY: Westminster John Knox Press, 2002), especially 47–65; David Theo Goldberg, *Racist Culture: Philosophy and the Politics of Meaning* (Oxford: Blackwell, 1993); Emmanuel Eze, *On Reason: Rationality in a World of Cultural Conflict and Racism* (Durham, NC: Duke University Press, 2008); Michelle Wright, *Becoming Black: Creating Identity in the African Diaspora* (Durham, NC: Duke University Press, 2004); Michelle Wright, *Physics of Blackness: Beyond the Middle Passage Epistemology* (Minneapolis: University of Minnesota Press, 2015); Sylvia Wynter, "Unsettling the Coloniality of Being/Power/Truth/Freedom: Towards the Human, after Man, Its Overrepresentation: An Argument," *CR, The New Centennial Review* 3, no. 3 (Fall 2003): 257–337.

8   Michael Hardt and Antonio Negri, *Multitude: War and Democracy in the Age of Empire* (New York: Penguin, 2004), loc. 2 of 359, Kindle.

9   Lonergan, "Third Lecture: The Ongoing Genesis of Methods," in *Collected Works*, vol. 16, *A Third Collection*, ed. Robert M. Doran and John D. Dadosky (Toronto: University of Toronto Press, 2017), 141.

10 Frantz Fanon, *The Wretched of the Earth*, trans. Constance Farrington (1961; New York: Grove, 1963), 311.

11 Dussel, *The Invention of the Americas*, 9. Dussel argues that, while modernity is a European occurrence, it arose in dialectical relation with the so-called "new" and "third" worlds—Africa, North America, South America, and Asia. North American and European thinkers, however, rarely acknowledge this relation; for some examples, see Charles Taylor, *The Sources of the Self: The Making of the Modern Identity* (Cambridge, MA: Harvard University Press, 1989); Stephen Toulmin, *The Hidden Agenda of Modernity* (New York: Macmillan, 1990); Jürgen Habermas, *The Philosophical Discourse of Modernity*, trans. Frederick Lawrence (1985; Cambridge, MA: MIT Press, 1987); Zygmunt Bauman, *Modernity and the Holocaust* (Ithaca, NY: Cornell University Press, 1989); Richard Bernstein, *The New Constellation: The Ethical-Political Horizons of Modernity/Postmodernity* (Cambridge, MA: MIT Press, 1992).

12 Metz, *Faith in History and Society*, 75.

13 Political theologies in Europe and North America and liberation theologies in Africa, Asia, Central and Latin America, and North America have never escaped suspicion. The Vatican's Sacred Congregation for the Doctrine of the Faith (CDF) issued "Instruction on Certain Aspects of the Theology of Liberation," August 6, 1984, https://tinyurl.com/2pj7cv2j. This document rebuked theologies of liberation for the use of Marxist analysis. The "Instruction" charged that these theologies risked the "subversion of the meaning of truth and violence," "localiz[ed] evil principally or uniquely in bad social, political, or economic structures," reduced the gospel to temporal salvation, and demonstrated a "misunderstanding [of] the entire meaning of the Kingdom of God and the transcendence of the person"

(§IV #15; §VII #9; §VIII; §XI #11). For some criticisms of political and liberation theologies, see Alfredo Fierro, *The Militant Gospel: A Critical Introduction to Political Theologies* (Maryknoll, NY: Orbis Books, 1975); Paul L. Lehmann, "Black Theology and 'Christian' Theology," *Union Seminary Quarterly Review* 31 (1975): 31–37; Daniel M. Bell, *Liberation Theology: After the End of History: The Refusal to Cease Suffering* (London: Routledge, 2001); Alistair Kee, *The Rise and Demise of Black Theology* (Burlington, VT: Ashgate, 2006); Ivan Petrella, *Beyond Liberation Theology: A Polemic* (London: SCM Press, 2008).

14   United Nations, International Day of Persons with Disabilities, Facts and Figures, December 2022, https://tinyurl.com/33vrtdk7; see Mary Jo Iozzio, *Disability Ethics and Preferential Justice: A Catholic Perspective* (Washington, DC: Georgetown University Press, 2023), Mary Jo Iozzio, with Mary M. Doyle Roche and Elsie M. Miranda, *Calling for Justice throughout the World: Catholic Women Theologians on the HIV/AIDS Pandemic* (New York: Continuum, 2009).

15   Joe Hasell, Max Roser, Esteban Ortiz-Ospina, and Pablo Arriagada, "Poverty," OurWorldinData.org, 2022, https://tinyurl.com/3vx45s2b.

16   Gustavo Gutiérrez, *A Theology of Liberation: History, Politics, and Salvation*, trans. and ed. Sister Caridad Inda and John Eagleson (1971; Maryknoll, NY: Orbis Books, 1973), 8.

17   Jürgen Moltmann, *The Spirit of Life: A Universal Affirmation*, trans. Margaret Kohl (Minneapolis: Fortress Press, 1992), 130. Because the cross of Jesus of Nazareth has been used to justify social oppression and intrapersonal violence as the will of God, it remains for many theologians a challenge. For some examples, see William R. Jones, *Is God a White Racist? A Preamble to Black Theology* (1973; Boston: Beacon Press, 1998); Joanne Carlson Brown and Carole R. Bohnn, "For God So Loved the World," in *Christianity, Patriarchy, and Abuse: A Feminist Critique*, ed. Joanne Carlson Brown and Carole R. Bohnn (Cleveland, OH: Pilgrim Press, 1989), 36–59; Anthony B. Pinn, *Why Lord? Suffering and Evil in Black Theology* (New York: Continuum, 1995).

18   Moltmann, *The Spirit of Life*, 130–31.

19   Moltmann, 130–31.

20   This was exposed in the analyses of female ethicists, theologians, and scholars from Africa, Asia, Central and Latin America, and North America.

21   There has been a good deal of literature on these concerns. For a brief sample, see Gloria Anzaldúa, ed., *Borderlands/La Frontera: The New Mestiza*, 5th ed. (San Francisco: Aunt Lute Books, 2022); Trinh T. Minh-Ha, *Woman Native Other* (Bloomington: Indiana University Press, 1989); bell hooks, *Black Looks: Race and Representation* (Boston: South End Press, 1992); Henry Giroux, *Border Crossings* (London: Routledge, 1992); Tzvetan Todorov, *On Human Diversity* (Cambridge, MA: Harvard University Press, 1992); Cornel West, *Race Matters* (Boston: Beacon Press, 1993), 9–20, 81–91, 93–105; M. Jacqui Alexander and Chandra Talpade Mohanty, eds., *Feminist Genealogies, Colonial Legacies, Democratic Futures* (New York: Routledge, 1997).

22   Enrique Dussel, "Domination—Liberation," in *Beyond Philosophy, Ethics, History, Marxism, and Liberation Theology* (Lanham, MD: Rowman & Littlefield, 2003), 41.

23   With this focus on the humanity of women of color, I intend neither to replace poor men of color with the women of their communities and cultures nor to rank-order oppressions. At the same time, I do not dismiss the oppression of White women, particularly poor White women. Women of color are *overdetermined* in their flesh—they

can in no way represent or stand-in for White men or White women or even men of color. This may be mistaken for naive empiricism on my part, but the abusive suffering that is meted out because of their indelible difference is neither naive nor merely empirical. Further, global statistics reveal that these women are the most exploited and impoverished. Despised for their race and their sex, they have no one to care for them as human persons but God.

24 Valerie Saiving, "The Human Situation: A Feminine View" (1960), reprinted in *Womanspirit Rising: A Feminist Reader in Religion*, ed. Carol Christ and Judith Plaskow (San Francisco: Harper & Row, 1979), 25–42.

25 What follows is very small sample of book-length works that demonstrate how these theological issues have been treated by critical White feminist, womanist, *mujerista, mestiza, minjung* biblical scholars, theologians, and ethicists. On biblical studies, hermeneutics: Phyllis Trible, *God and the Rhetoric of Sexuality* (Philadelphia: Fortress Press, 1978); Trible, *Texts of Terror: Literary-Feminist Readings of Biblical Narratives* (Philadelphia: Fortress Press, 1984); Elisabeth Schüssler Fiorenza, *In Memory of Her: A Feminist Theological Reconstruction of Christian Origins* (New York: Crossroad Publishing, 1983); Schüssler Fiorenza, *Bread Not Stone: The Challenge of Feminist Biblical Interpretation* (Boston: Beacon Press, 1984); Schüssler Fiorenza, *Jesus: Miriam's Child, Sophia's Prophet: Critical Issues in Feminist Christology* (New York: Continuum, 1994); Schüssler Fiorenza, *Miriam's Jesus and the Politics of Interpretation* (New York: Continuum, 2000); Renita J. Weems, *Battered Love: Marriage, Sex, and Violence in the Hebrew Prophets* (Minneapolis: Fortress Press, 1995). On the doctrine of the Triune God: Sally McFague, *Models of God: Theology for an Ecological, Nuclear Age* (Philadelphia: Fortress Press, 1987); Catherine Mowry LaCugna, *God for Us: The Trinity and Christian Life* (San Francisco: Harper, 1991); Elizabeth Johnson, *She Who Is: The Mystery of God in Feminist Theological Discourse* (New York: Continuum, 1993); Rebecca S. Chopp, *The Power to Speak: Feminism, Language, God* (New York: Crossroad Publishing, 1989). On Christology: Rita Nakashima Brock, *Journeys by Heart: A Christology of Erotic Power* (New York: Crossroad Publishing, 1988); Jacquelyn Grant, *White Women's Christ and Black Women's Jesus: Feminist Christology and Womanist Response* (Atlanta, GA: Scholars Press, 1989); Kelly Brown Douglas, *The Black Christ* (Maryknoll, NY: Orbis Books, 1994). On ecclesiology: Letty M. Russell, *Church in the Round: Feminist Interpretation of the Church* (Louisville, KY: Westminster John Knox Press, 1993); Rosemary Radford Ruether, *Women-Church: Theology and Practice of Feminist Liturgical Communities* (San Francisco: Harper & Row, 1985); Elisabeth Schüssler Fiorenza, *Discipleship of Equals: A Critical Feminist Ecclesia-logy of Liberation* (New York: Crossroad Publishing, 1995). On ethics: Barbara Hilkert Andolsen, *Racism and American Feminism: "Daughters of Jefferson, Daughters of Bootblacks* (Macon, GA: Mercer University Press, 1986); Margaret Farley, *Personal Commitments: Beginning, Keeping, Changing* (San Francisco: Harper & Row, 1980); Farley, *Just Love: A Framework for Christian Ethics* (New York: Continuum, 2006); Cannon, *Black Womanist Ethics*; Cannon, *Katie's Canon*; Emilie M. Townes, *Womanist Justice, Womanist Hope* (Atlanta, GA: Scholars Press, 1993); Townes, *In a Blaze of Glory: Womanist Spirituality as Social Witness* (Nashville: Abingdon Press, 1995); Townes, *Womanist Ethics and the Cultural Production of Evil* (New York: Palgrave Macmillan, 2006); Sally B. Purvis, *The Power of the Cross: Foundations for a Christian Feminist Ethic of Community* (Nashville: Abingdon Press, 1993); Ada María

Isasi-Díaz, *En La Lucha/In the Struggle: A Hispanic Women's Liberation Theology* (Minneapolis: Fortress Press, 1995); Marcia Y. Riggs, *Awake, Arise, Act: A Womanist Call for Black Liberation* (Cleveland, OH: Pilgrim Press, 1995); Christine Firer Hinze, *Comprehending Power in Christian Social Ethics* (Atlanta, GA: Scholars Press, 1995); Anne E. Patrick, *Liberating Conscience: Feminist Explorations in Catholic Moral Theology* (New York: Continuum, 1996); Michelle A. Gonzalez, *Created in God's Image: An Introduction to Feminist Theological Anthropology* (Maryknoll, NY: Orbis Books, 2007).

26 See Max Scheler, *Ressentiment*, ed. Lewis A. Coser, trans. William W. Holdheim (1915; New York: The Free Press of Glencoe, 1961). The word *ressentiment* is borrowed from the French and was introduced into philosophy by Friedrich Wilhelm Nietzsche. *Ressentiment* is a reactive emotional state related to *re-feeling* or reliving a particular conflict or moment, when a vulnerable or powerless person (or group) feels hurt or is made to feel shame. *Ressentiment* is usually directed against powerful persons or groups in a society. Hostility appears with *ressentiment* and may take the forms of envy, malice, hatred, revenge. Scheler defines *ressentiment* as psychic self-poisoning. This refeeling or reliving damages and spoils the human spirit.

27 Thomas Merton, *New Seeds of Contemplation* (New York: New Directions, 1961), loc. 72 of 298, Kindle.

28 Edward Schillebeeckx employs the term "humanum" to speak of the vision of a full humanity that, while not antecedently given by God, presents as a goal to be achieved through justice; see his *Jesus: An Experiment in Christology*, trans. Hubert Hoskins (New York: Crossroad Publishing, 1995), 49.

29 Schillebeeckx, "The Role of History in What Is Called the New Paradigm," in *Paradigm Change in Theology*, ed. Hans Küng and David Tracy, trans. Margaret Kohl (New York: Crossroad Publishing, 1989), 318.

30 For some feminist treatments of Christian theological anthropology see Kari Elisabeth Børrensen, *Subordination and Equivalence: The Nature and Role of Woman in Augustine and Thomas Aquinas*, trans. Charles H. Talbot (1968; Washington, DC: University of America Press, 1981); Sheila D. Collins, *A Different Heaven and Earth: A Feminist Perspective on Religion* (Valley Forge, PA: Judson Press, 1974); Mary Daly, *The Church and the Second Sex* (New York: Harper & Row, 1968); Rosemary Ruether, ed., *Religion and Sexism: Images of Women in the Jewish and Christian Traditions* (New York: Simon & Schuster, 1974); Ruether, *New Woman/New Earth: Sexist Ideologies and Human Liberation* (New York: Seabury Press, 1975); Mary Aquin O'Neill, "Toward a Renewed Anthropology," *Theological Studies* 36 (1975): 725–36; O'Neill, "The Mystery of Being Human Together," in *Freeing Theology: The Essentials of Theology in Feminist Perspective*, ed. Catherine Mowry LaCugna (San Francisco: Harper Collins, 1993), 139–60; Sara Butler, ed., *CTSA Research Report: Women in Church and Society* (Mahwah, NJ: Catholic Theological Society of America, 1978); Mary Buckley, "The Rising of the Women Is the Rising of the Race," *Proceedings CTSA* 34 (1979): 48–63; Anne Carr, "Theological Anthropology and the Experience of Women," *Chicago Studies* 19 (1980): 113–28; Carr, *Transforming Grace: Women's Experience and Christian Tradition* (San Francisco: Harper & Row, 1988), 117–33; Ann O'Hara Graff, ed., *In the Embrace of God: Feminist Approaches to Theological Anthropology* (Maryknoll, NY: Orbis Books, 1995); Michelle Gonzalez, *Created in God's Image: An Introduction to Feminist Theological Anthropology* (Maryknoll, NY: Orbis Books, 2007).

31 O'Neill, "The Mystery of Being Human Together," 150.

32 For some instances of Lonergan's treatment of this topic, see *Insight*, 346–52, 410–12, 451–52; *Method in Theology*, 78–82; *A Second Collection*, 13, 19, 20, 27, 28, 113, 162, 191; "Doctrinal Pluralism," in *Collected Works*, vol. 17, *Philosophical and Theological Papers, 1965–1980*, ed. Robert C. Croken and Robert M. Doran (Toronto: University of Toronto Press, 2004), 70–104.

33 While this description approximates what Mary Buckley called a "transformative, person-centered model" in opposition to dual and single-sex anthropologies, it goes beyond Buckley's model by emphasizing the importance of community, difference, and interdependence; see Buckley, "The Rising of the Woman Is the Rising of the Race," 48–65; also Edward Schillebeeckx, *Christ: The Experience of Jesus as Lord* (New York: Seabury Press, 1980), 731–43; Elizabeth Johnson, "The Maleness of Christ," in *The Special Nature of Women? Concilium*, ed. Anne Carr and Elizabeth Schüssler Fiorenza (Philadelphia: Trinity Press, 1991), 108–16; and Hinsdale, "Heeding the Voices: An Historical Overview," in Graff, ed., *In the Embrace of God*, 22–48, at 29.

34 Marie Vianney Bilgrien, *Solidarity: A Principle, an Attitude, a Duty? Or the Virtue for an Interdependent World* (New York: Peter Lang, 1999), 32–35. This is a very helpful study of the literature, history, and development of the notion of solidarity in Catholic social thought, with detailed analysis of the work of Pope John Paul II, who began writing on this theme in 1969, and, in that context, "*Sollicitudo Rei Socialis*" (December 30, 1987) denotes a culmination.

35 Mike Davis, *Planet of Slums* (London and New York: Verso, 2006), 135. For two important studies of progress, see Robert Nisbet, *History of the Idea of Progress* (New York: Basic Books, 1980) and Christopher Lasch, *The True and Only Heaven: Progress and Its Critics* (New York: W. W. Norton, 1991).

36 For some general discussions of solidarity, see Karl Rahner and Herbert Vorgrimler, eds., "Solidarity," in *Dictionary of Theology*, 2nd ed. (New York: Crossroad Publishing, 1990), 481; René Coste, "Solidarité," in *Dictionnaire de Spiritualité*, vol. XVI (Paris: Beauschene, 1990), 999–1006; Matthew Lamb, "Solidarity," in *The New Dictionary of Catholic Social Thought*, ed. Judith A. Dwyer (Collegeville, MN: Liturgical Press, 1993), 908–12; Roberto Goizueta, "Solidarity," in *The New Dictionary of Catholic Spirituality*, ed. Michael Downey (Collegeville, MN: Liturgical Press, 1993), 906–7; Ada María Isasi-Díaz, "Solidarity," in *Dictionary of Feminist Theologies*, ed. Letty M. Russell and J. Shannon Clarkson (Louisville, KY: Westminster John Knox Press, 1996), 266–67.

37 Walter Rauschenbusch, *A Theology for the Social Gospel* (1917; Louisville, KY: Westminster John Knox Press, 1997), 102–3.

38 Coste, "Solidarité," 999–1006; cf. Edmund Arens, *Christopraxis, A Theology of Action*, trans. John E. Hoffmeyer (1992; Minneapolis: Fortress Press, 1995), 162–64. Arens argues that while contemporary papal teaching underscores the subjective, intersubjective, societal, international, and global levels of solidarity, it remains a toothless appeal, a moralism.

39 Benedict XVI, *Deus Caritas Est* (December 25, 2005); *Spe Salvi* (November 30, 2007); Francis, *Laudato Si'* (May 24, 2015), *Fratelli Tutti* (October 3, 2020).

40 For political theology, see Metz, *Faith in History and Society*; Dorothee Sölle, *Political Theology*, trans. John Shelley (1971; Philadelphia: Fortress Press, 1974); Matthew L. Lamb, *Solidarity with Victims: Toward a Theology of Social Transformation*

(New York: Crossroad Publishing, 1982); Helmut Peukert, *Science, Action and Fundamental Theology: Toward a Theology of Communicative Action*, trans. J. Bohman (Cambridge, MA: MIT Press, 1984); Gregory Baum, *Compassion and Solidarity: The Church for Others* (Mahwah, NJ: Paulist Press, 1990). For various theologies of liberation, see Gutiérrez, *A Theology of Liberation*; Jon Sobrino and Juan Hernández Pico, *Theology of Christian Solidarity* (Maryknoll, NY: Orbis Books, 1985); Albert Nolan, *Jesus before Christianity* (1978; Maryknoll, NY: Orbis Books, 1987); Nolan, *God in South Africa: The Challenge of the Gospel* (Maryknoll, NY: Orbis Books, 1988); Sharon D. Welch, *Communities of Resistance and Solidarity: A Feminist Theology of Liberation* (Maryknoll, NY: Orbis Books, 1985); Welch, *A Feminist Ethic of Risk* (Minneapolis: Fortress Press, 1990); my "Toward a Critical Christian Feminist Theology of Solidarity," in *Women and Theology*, ed. Mary Ann Hinsdale and Phyllis H. Kaminski (Maryknoll, NY: Orbis Books, 1995), 3–38; Anne Clifford, "When Being Human Becomes Truly Earthly: An Ecofeminist Proposal for Solidarity," in *In the Embrace of God*, 173–89; Pontifical Commission *Justitia et Pax*, "The Church and Racism: Towards a More Fraternal Society" (Vatican City, 1988), nos. 17–33. For some theological reflections on solidarity, see Hadewych Snijdewind, "Ways towards a Non-Patriarchal Christian Solidarity," in Metz and Schillebeeckx, eds., *God as Father? Concilium* (1981): 81–89; Gerhard Hoffmann, "Solidarity with Strangers as Part of the Mission of the Church," *International Review of Mission* 78 (1989): 53–61; Peter J. Henriot, "The Challenge of Global Prosperity: Social Justice and Solidarity," *Journal of Ecumenical Studies* 24 (Summer 1987): 382–93; Norbert Mette, "Solidarity with the Lowliest: Parish Growth through the Witness of Practical Service," in *Diakonia: Church for Others: Concilium* (1988): 76–83; Pastoral Statement of the Zimbabwe Catholic Bishops' Conference, "Solidarity and Service," *African Ecclesial Review* 32 (1990): 51–58; Daniel A. Helminiak, "Human Solidarity and Collective Union in Christ," *Anglican Theological Review* 70 (January 1988): 34–59.

41 Lonergan, "Third Lecture: The Ongoing Genesis of Methods," in *A Third Collection*, 155.

42 Lonergan, 155.

43 See Lonergan, *Method in Theology*, 74–78; cf. Davies, *A Theology of Compassion*, 17–18.

44 John Phillips, "Racists Jeer at Roadside Birth," *The Times* (London), February 12, 1992, 8. Jodi Dean begins her study, *Solidarity of Strangers: Feminism after Identity Politics* (Berkeley: University of California Press, 1996), 13–17, with this news report. She does not name the woman and she makes a detailed analysis of the response of the Italians.

45 Lewis Gordon, *Fanon and the Crisis of European Man: An Essay on Philosophy and the Human Sciences* (New York: Routledge, 1995), 70.

46 Italy joined the other Western powers in the partition and colonization of Africa between 1880 and 1900; see A. Adu Boahen, *African Perspectives on Colonialism* (Baltimore: The Johns Hopkins University Press, 1987).

47 See Max Roser, "Human Development Index (HDI)," OurWorldinData.org, 2014, https://tinyurl.com/y3tcmaby.

48 Ada María Isasi-Díaz works out the meaning of *lo cotidiano* (the everyday) in various essays, including "Mujerista Theology: A Challenge to Traditional Theology," in her *Mujerista Theology* (Maryknoll, NY: Orbis Books, 1996), 66–73, and *En La Lucha/ In the Struggle: A Hispanic Women's Liberation Theology* (Minneapolis: Fortress Press, 1995).

49 Lamb, *Solidarity with Victims*, 4; Lonergan, *Insight*, 191–244.

50 Gordon, *Fanon and the Crisis of European Man*, 44.

51 The sight of a lone woman giving birth by the side of a road calls out to basic intersubjective spontaneity, i.e., simple human care and human feeling. The refusal of the crowd to assist Fatima Yusif demonstrates how bias chokes the spontaneous demands of intersubjectivity, in this case, the natural and spontaneous impulse to help another human being, simply because she (or he) is another human being suffering. Critical attention to intersubjective spontaneity uncovers the way bias seeps into and disrupts the desires and aversions of competing individuals and groups within a social order.

   Lonergan's treatment of bias is found in *Insight*, chaps. 6 and 7. Individual bias is distortion in the development not only of a person's intelligence but also of affective and experiential orientation. This distortion comes from the egoistic pursuit of personal desire at the expense of *humanum* as well as human relations, social cooperations, and solidarity. Group bias sacrifices intelligent, responsible discernment in the bringing about of the common human good in the social order to the blind pursuit of the interests of a particular class or racial or social group to the exclusion and repression of "other" classes, racial or social groups. Individual bias overcomes intersubjective feeling. Group bias is kindled by the frustration, resentment, and bitterness of a group and reinforces these feelings in individual persons.

52 Miroslav Volf, *Exclusion and Embrace: A Theological Exploration of Identity, Otherness, and Reconciliation* (Nashville: Abingdon Press, 1996), 24.

53 Peukert, *Science, Action, and Fundamental Theology*, 206.

54 See Segundo Galilea, "Liberation as an Encounter with Politics and Contemplation," in *The Mystical and Political Dimension of the Christian Faith: Concilium*, ed. Claude Geffré and Gustavo Gutiérrez (New York: Herder & Herder, 1974), 23.

55 Lonergan sets forth a theory of the unity of the human race: "[Humanity] is one reality in the order of the intelligible. It is a many in virtue of matter alone. Now any right and any exigence has its foundation only in the intelligible. Matter is not the basis of exigence but the basis of potentiality. The one intelligible reality, man, humanity, unfolds by means of matter into a material multiplicity of men [humans], that the material multiplicity may rise, not from itself, but from the intelligible unity, to an intelligible multiplicity of personalities," Lonergan, "Philosophy of History," in *Collected Works*, vol. 25, *Archival Material: Early Papers on History*, ed. Robert M. Doran and John D. Dadosky (Toronto: University of Toronto Press, 2019), 26.

56 Iris Marion Young, in her *Justice and Politics of Difference* (Princeton, NJ: Princeton University Press, 1990), identifies and analyzes five specific forms of oppression: exploitation, marginalization, powerlessness, cultural imperialism, and violence.

57 Javier Jiménez Limón, "Suffering, Death, Cross, and Martyrdom," in *Mysterium Liberationis: Fundamental Concepts of Liberation Theology*, ed. Ignacio Ellacuría and Jon Sobrino (1990; Maryknoll, NY: Orbis Books; North Blackburn, Vic.: Collins Dove, 1993), 706.

58 Because humanity is one reality, Lonergan argues, "that the [humans of the] present should suffer for the past is not unjust, for humanity is not an aggregation of individuals. . . . Men [and women] become from man [and woman] as grapes from the one vine; if the vine corrupts, so do the grapes; but the grapes suffer no injustice from the vine; they are but part of the vine," Lonergan, "Philosophy of History," in *Archival Material*, 26.

59 Lonergan, "The Mystical Body of Christ," in *Collected Works*, vol. 20, *Shorter Papers*, ed. Robert C. Croken, Robert M. Doran, and H. Daniel Monsour (Toronto: University of Toronto Press, 2007), 106.

60 For some general discussions, see Rahner and Vorgrimler, eds., "Body of Christ," in *Dictionary of Theology*, 53–54; Bernard Lee, "Body of Christ," in *New Dictionary of Spirituality*, 100–104; John A. T. Robinson, *The Body: A Study in Pauline Theology* (Philadelphia: The Westminster, 1952); John C. Haughey, "Eucharist at Corinth: You Are Christ," in *Above Every Name: The Lordship of Christ and Social Systems*, ed. Thomas E. Clarke (Ramsey, NJ: Paulist Press, 1980) 107–33; Dorothy A. Lee, "Freedom, Spirituality and the Body: Anti-Dualism in 1 Corinthians," in *Freedom and Entrapment: Women Thinking Theology*, ed. Maryanne Confoy, Dorothy A. Lee, and Joan Nowotny (North Blackburn, Vic.: HarperCollins, 1995), 42–62.

61 Pope Pius XII, "Mystici Corporis Christi," June 29, 1943. The encyclical treated the relation of head and members in juridical and hierarchical terms, which confined membership in the mystical body of Christ to membership in the Catholic Church. The document also called attention to the interior operation and reality of grace and the role of the Holy Spirit. This teaching was moderated by the Second Vatican Council with the introduction of biblical themes in understanding the church (e.g., "Lumen Gentium," nos. 7–9).

62 See Émile Mersch, *Le Corps Mystique du Christ: Études de Théologie Historique*, 2nd ed (Paris: Desclée de Brouwer, 1936). An abridged English translation of this work is found in *The Whole Christ: The Historical Development of the Doctrine of the Mystical Body in Scripture and Tradition*, trans. John R. Kelly (Milwaukee: Bruce Publishing Co., 1938). In an examination of the use of the mystical body of Christ by John LaFarge and Paul Hanley Furfey in the service of interracial justice, Bradford Hinze points up their precritical limiting of the mystical body to a homogeneous (White and Catholic) group; see Hinze, "Ethnic and Racial Diversity and the Catholicity of the Church," in *Theology: Expanding the Borders*, ed. María Pilar Aquino and Roberto S. Goizueta (Mystic, CT: Twenty-Third Publications, 1998), 162–99, especially 179–83.

63 Lonergan, "The Mystical Body of Christ," in *Shorter Papers*, 106.

64 Lonergan, 107.

65 Lonergan, 107–8.

66 Lonergan, 107–8.

67 Lonergan, 109.

68 Lonergan, 109.

69 Lee, "Body of Christ," 104.

70 Lonergan, "Finality, Love, Marriage," in *Collection*, 27.

71 Marcella Althaus-Reid, "Demythologizing Liberation Theology: Reflections on Power, Poverty and Sexuality," in *The Cambridge Companion to Liberation Theology*, ed. Christopher Rowland (Cambridge: Cambridge University Press, 2008), 125.

72 Lonergan, "Third Lecture: The Ongoing Genesis of Methods," in *A Third Collection*, 147.

73 Merton, *New Seeds of Contemplation*, loc. 74 of 304, Kindle.

CHAPTER 6

1   Isaiah 62:1.

2   Negro Spiritual.

3   "Give Your Hands to Struggle," words and music by Bernice Johnson Reagon, 1969, recorded 1992 by Sweet Honey in the Rock, *Give Your Hands Struggle* (Smithsonian Folkways Recordings, 1997).

4   Saidiya Hartman, *Lose Your Mother: A Journey along the Atlantic Slave Route* (New York: Farrar, Straus, & Giroux, 2007), 6.

5   Markus Rediker in *The Slave Ship, A Human History* (New York: Viking, 2007) includes an illustration of ship's crewmen hoisting a young captured African girl by her ankle; whips lie on the deck of the ship, *Recovery*, and an officer leers. Rediker cites Isaac Cruikshank, "The Abolition of the Slave Trade, Or the inhumanity of dealers in human flesh exemplified in Captain John Kimber's treatment of a young Negro girl of 15 for her virgin modesty," 1792, Library of Congress, British Cartoon Collection (434). Rediker writes: "[Kimber] was brought to trial and acquitted, not because it was proven that the alleged killing did not happen but because the two members of the crew who reported it were shown to have a grudge against him" (see this volume, page 12).

   Hartman offers a plaintive and searing (fictional) account of the death of this young girl, see *Lose Your Mother*, 136–53. Regarding Kimber's trial and the involvement of member of the British Parliament William Wilberforce, Hartman writes, "The Committee for the Abolition of the Slave Trade first brought the case to the attention of the public. On April 2, 1792, William Wilberforce immortalized the girl in a speech delivered before the House of Commons and the world lent its attention, at least for a few days. When the trial ended, so did any interest in the girl. No one has thought of her for at least two centuries, but her life still casts a shadow," *Lose Your Mother*, 138.

6   For some treatments of Black women who took up the challenge to enflesh struggle, see Rosetta E. Ross, *Witnessing and Testifying: Black Women, Religion, and Civil Rights* (Minneapolis: Fortress Press, 2003); Cheryl Townsend Gilkes, *If It Wasn't for the Women: Black Women's Experience and Womanist Culture in Church and Community* (Maryknoll, NY: Orbis Books, 2001); Marcia Riggs, *Can I Get a Witness? Prophetic Religious Voices of African American Women: An Anthology* (Maryknoll, NY: Orbis Books, 1997); Townes, *Womanist Justice, Womanist Hope*; Townes, *In a Blaze of Glory*.

7   Walter Benjamin, "Theses on the Philosophy of History, VIII," in *Illuminations: Essays*, trans. Harry Zohn (New York and Boston: Houghton Mifflin Harcourt, 2018), loc. 110 of 110, Kindle.

8   Angela D. Sims, *Lynched: The Power of Memory in a Culture of Terror* (Waco, TX: Baylor University, 2016), 23.

9   Sims, *Lynched*, 96.

10 Jacquelyn Grant, "Womanist Theology: Black Women's Experience as a Source for Doing Theology, with Special Reference to Christology," in *Black Theology: A Documentary History, Vol II: 1980-1992*, ed. James H. Cone and Gayraud S. Wilmore (Maryknoll, NY: Orbis Books, 1993), 284.

11 Kimberlé Williams Crenshaw, Andrea J. Ritchie, Rachel Anspach, Rachel Gilmer, and Luke Harris, "Say Her Name: Resisting Police Brutality against Black Women" (New York: African American Policy Forum, July 2015), loc. 138 of 1038, Kindle.

12 See Black Lives Matter, Herstory, https://tinyurl.com/ypvhhmmy (accessed May 8, 2023).

13 Lori D. Patton and Nadrea R. Njoku, "Theorizing Black Women's Experiences with Institution-Sanctioned Violence: A #BlackLivesMatter Imperative toward Black Liberation on Campus," *International Journal of Qualitative Studies in Education* 32, no. 9 (September 2019): 1162–82, at 1164.

14 Crenshaw et al., "Say Her Name," loc. 665 of 1038, Kindle.

15 Crenshaw, "Demarginalizing the Intersection of Race and Sex: A Black Feminist Critique of Antidiscrimination Doctrine, Feminist Theory and Antiracist Politics," *University of Chicago Legal Forum*, Article 8 (1989): 139–67; Crenshaw, "Mapping the Margins: Intersectionality, Identity Politics, and Violence against Women of Color," *Stanford Law Review* (1991): 1241–99; Crenshaw, "Twenty Years of Critical Race Theory: Looking Back to Move Forward," *Connecticut Law Review* 43, no. 5 (July 2011): 1253–1352.

16 Vivian May, *Pursuing Intersectionality, Unsettling Dominant Imaginaries* (New York: Routledge, 2015), 19.

17 Deborah Gray White, *Ar'n't I a Woman? Female Slaves in the Plantation South*, rev. ed. (New York: W. W. Norton, 1999), 176, 12.

18 Gray White explains that as a mythical stereotype, "Sapphire is a domineering female who consumes men and usurps their role. Her persona is not sexual but is as indomitable as Jezebel's. Jezebel emasculates men by annulling their ability to resist her temptations, and thus her manipulations, Sapphire emasculates men by usurping their role," *Ar'n't I a Woman?* 176.

19 Michelle S. Jacobs, "The Violent State: Black Women's Invisible Struggle against Police Violence," *William & Mary Journal of Women and the Law* 24 (2017): 39–100, at 46.

20 Cannon, "Sexing Black Women," in Pinn and Hopkins, eds., *Loving the Body*, 11–12.

21 Monique W. Morris, *Pushout: The Criminalization of Black Girls in Schools* (New York: New Press, 2016), 34; see Rebecca Epstein, Jamilia J. Blake, and Thalia González, "Girl Interrupted: The Erasure of Black Girls' Childhood" (Washington, DC: Georgetown Law Center on Poverty and Inequality, 2017).

22 See Edward Phillip Antonio, "Desiring Booty and Killing the Body: Toward 'Negative Erotics,'" in Pinn and Hopkins, eds., *Loving the Body*, 279.

23 See *Time* Magazine: "An *NPR/PBS NewsHour*/Marist poll released Oct. 3, 2018 found that 45% of respondents thought Ford was telling the truth, compared to 33% who believed Kavanaugh. That's a marked shift from 1991, when Americans sided with then Supreme Court nominee Clarence Thomas after Anita Hill accused him of sexual harassment. . . . In 2016, when [Donald J.] Trump was facing several sexual-misconduct allegations, 62% thought such allegations were not a deal breaker. The nation might agree: two-thirds of voters thought Ford's allegations, even if they were true, were not necessarily enough to force Kavanaugh to withdraw from consideration, according to Quinnipiac," October 15, 2018 (with reporting by Alana Abramson, Philip Elliott and Abby Vesoulis/Washington; Ciara Nugent/London; Suyin Haynes and Aria Chen/Hong Kong), https://tinyurl.com/8bpfz6rd.

The literature on both Hill and Ford is quite extensive; only a few examples can be included here: Toni Morrison, ed., *Race-ing Justice, En-Gendering Power: Essays on Anita Hill, Clarence Thomas, and the Construction of Social Reality Ford* (New York: Pantheon, 1992); Leslie Dorrough Smith, *Compromising Positions: Sex, Scandals, Politics, and American Christianity* (New York: Oxford University Press, 2020); Sarah E. Heck, "From Anita Hill to Christine Blasey Ford: A Reflection on Lessons Learned," *Equality, Diversity and Inclusion* 39, no. 1 (January 2020): 101–8.

24 Patricia Hill Collins, *Black Sexual Politics: African Americans, Gender, and the New Racism* (New York: Routledge, 2004), 216, author's emphasis.

25 Collins, *Black Sexual Politics*, 217, emphasis mine. Androcentrism reinforces the focus on men, White men in particular, and places them at the center of societal structures. The needs, concerns, actions, desires, and values of men dominate these structures, and are integral to their formation. Men, in particular White men, instantiate normative humanity and rank as the gender-neutral norm. Women are gender-specific, an afterthought. It ought not to be surprising that, as a group, Black people are influenced by the androcentrism of the larger dominant White society.

26 The Combahee River Collective, "A Black Feminist Statement," in *All the Women Are White, All the Blacks Are Men, But Some of Us Are Brave: Black Women's Studies*, ed. Gloria T. Hull, Patricia Bell Scott, and Barbara Smith (Old Westbury, NY: Feminist Press, 1982), 18, emphasis mine.

27 Jelani Cobb, "The Matter of Black Lives," *The New Yorker Magazine*, March 14, 2016, https://tinyurl.com/bdd77ek9.

28 See Patrisse Khan-Cullors and Asha Bandele, *When They Call You a Terrorist: A Black Lives Matter Memoir* (New York: St. Martin's Griffin, 2017).

29 Olga M. Segura, *Birth of a Movement: Black Lives Matter and the Catholic Church* (Maryknoll, NY: Orbis Books, 2021), 4.

30 Black Lives Matter, "The Creation of a Movement," https://tinyurl.com/ypvhhmmy (accessed May 8, 2023).

31 Ransby, *Making All Black Lives Matter*, loc. 245 of 3854.

32 Black Lives Matter, "The Creation of a Movement."

33 Ransby, *Making All Black Lives Matter*, loc. 986 of 3854.

34 Black Lives Matter, "Guiding Principle," https://blacklivesmatter.com/guiding/ principles (last accessed March 17, 2016).

35 Julie Bosman and Joseph Goldstein, "Timeline for a Body: 4 Hours in the Middle of a Ferguson Street," *New York Times*, August 23, 2014, https://tinyurl.com/2s3wym8y; see Jamala Rogers, *Ferguson Is America: Roots of Rebellion* (St. Louis: Mira Digital, 2015).

36 Crenshaw et al., "Say Her Name," loc. 47 of 1038.

37 Associated Press, "Detroit Police Officer to Face Retrial over Killing of Girl, 7, in Raid," *The Guardian*, September 14, 2014, https://tinyurl.com/3wu2sy8t; see also Charlie Leduff, "What Killed Aiyana Stanley-Jones?" Mother Jones, November/ December 2010, https://tinyurl.com/mvrzfe5f.

38 Jacobs, "The Violent State: Black Women's Invisible Struggle against Police Violence," 52.

39 Crenshaw et al., "Say Her Name," loc. 111 of 1038.

40 Crenshaw et al., loc. 98 of 1038.

41 The African American Policy Forum, About #SayHerName, https://tinyurl. com/mrx8tjn9 (accessed May 8, 2023).

42 Crenshaw et al., "Say Her Name," loc. 65 of 1038.

43 Crenshaw et al., loc. 129 of 1038.

44 The African American Policy Forum, Our Demands, https://tinyurl.com/2hdmxzav (accessed May 8, 2023).

45 Frank Leon Roberts, "How Black Lives Matter Changed the Way Americans Fight for Freedom," ACLU, Speaking Freely, July 13, 2018, https://tinyurl.com/2pa7u957; see also Connor Friedersdorf, "How to Distinguish between Antifa, White Supremacists, and Black Lives Matter," *The Atlantic*, August 31, 2017, https://tinyurl.com/3hvvaftw.

46 Barbara Ransby, *Making All Black Lives Matter: Reimagining Freedom in the Twenty-First Century* (Oakland: University of California Press, 2018), loc. 211 of 3854, Kindle.

47 Juliana M. Horowitz and Gretchen Livingston, "How Americans View the Black Lives Matter Movement," Pew Research Center, July 8, 2016, https://tinyurl.com/4muc6z4z. At that time, 65% of Blacks, 33% of Hispanic/Latinos, and 40% of Whites supported the movement; 22% of all Americans opposed the group, 12% of Blacks, 11% of Hispanic/Latinos, and 28% of Whites opposed BLM.

48 Palash Ghosh, "A Year after George Floyd Killing, Fewer Americans Support Black Lives Mater Movement, Poll Finds," *Forbes*, May 25, 2021, https://tinyurl.com/66amc4f2.

49 Jemar Tisby, *The Color of Compromise: The Truth about the American Church's Complicity in Racism* (Grand Rapids, MI: Zondervan, 2019), 183; see also Christopher Cameron and Phillip Luke Sinitiere, ed., *Race, Religion, and Black Lives Matter: Essays on a Moment and a Movement* (Nashville: Vanderbilt University Press, 2021).

50 Anthea Butler, *White Evangelical Racism: The Politics of Morality in America* (Chapel Hill: University of North Carolina Press, 2021), loc. 132 of 164, Kindle.

51 CNA (Catholic News Agency) Staff, "Spokane Bishop Responds to Catholic Charities Racism Video," July 6, 2020, https://tinyurl.com/mr3h835n; see also, Megan Carroll, "Spokane Catholic Bishop Says Black Lives Matter Movement Is 'in Conflict with Church Teaching,'" Krem2, July 9, 2020, https://tinyurl.com/3489x9m3. The provocation for the bishop's remarks occurred on June 19, 2020, when layman Robert McCann, CEO and president of Catholic Charities of Eastern Washington, posted a video acknowledging personal and corporate racism in the church.

52 Rhina Guidos, "After 'Taking a Knee' Border Bishop Gets Call from Pope, Releases Statement," *Angelus News*, June 4, 2020, https://tinyurl.com/yjek27ep.

53 Bob D'Angelo, Cox Media Group National Content Desk, quotes Fr. Theodore Rothrock, who, according to the *Indianapolis Star*, wrote in his weekly message: "The only lives that matter is their own and the only power they seek is their own. They are wolves in wolves clothing, masked thieves and bandits, seeking only to devour the life of the poor and profit from the fear of others. They are maggots and parasites at best, feeding off the isolation of addiction and broken families, and offering to replace any current frustration and anxiety with more misery and greater resentment," "Priest in Indiana Calls Black Lives Matters Protesters 'Maggots and Parasites,'" Boston 25 News, June 30, 2020. See also Sebastian Morello, "Misdirected Religion and the Motives of the 'Black Lives Matter' Movement," *The Catholic World Report*, June 30, 2020, https://tinyurl.com/5yjtkbzz.

54 Fr. Matthew Hawkins, "A Catholic Understanding of Black Lives Matter," *The Pittsburgh Catholic*, June 30, 2020.

55 Robert D. Putnam and David E. Campbell, *American Grace: How Religion Divides and Unites Us* (New York: Simon & Schuster, 2010), 319.

56 Richard Kearney, *Poetics of Imagining: Modern to Post-Modern* (New York: Fordham University Press, 1998), 8, 9.

57 Iris Marion Young, *Justice and the Politics of Difference* (Princeton, NJ: Princeton University Press, 1990), 119.

58 Young, *Justice and the Politics of Difference*, 41.

59 Freire Institute, Concepts Used by Paulo Freire, https://tinyurl.com/yc84vc6j (accessed May 8, 2023).

60 "Conscience is a judgment of reason whereby the human person recognizes the moral quality of a concrete act that [they are] going to perform, are in the process of performing, or has [sic] already completed," *Catechism of the Catholic Church* (Liguori, MO: Liguori Publications, 1994), #1778.

61 *Catechism of the Catholic Church*, #1779. On Bernard Lonergan's assessment, the realm of interiority is a distinct world of its own where the eros of the human spirit unfolds in yet another way, different from the developments of the mind in the world of common sense or the world of theory. Yet, says Lonergan, "related to, important for, and connected" with them. It is the realm that each one can discover for himself by an examination of one's consciousness and its operations. For one enters the realm of interiority only by a process of self-appropriation. Self-appropriation means that one adverts to immediate internal experience, to oneself as a conscious operator, to one's conscious operations, and to the dynamic structure that relates the operations to one another.

62 Rebecca Chopp, "Reimagining Public Discourse," *Journal of Theology for Southern Africa* 103 (March 1999): 33–48 at 39–40.

63 Mari Evans, "Speak the Truth to the People," in her *I Am a Black Woman* (New York: William Morrow, 1970), 91.

64 Thomas A. Hoyt, "Testimony," in *Practicing Our Faith: A Way of Life for a Searching People*, 2nd ed., ed. Dorothy C. Bass (San Francisco: Jossey-Bass, 2010), 89–101; see also Craig Dykstra and Dorothy C. Bass, "Times of Yearning, Practices of Faith," in *Practicing Our Faith*, 1–12: "Christian practices are things Christian people do together over time in response to and in light of God's active presence for the life of the world in Christ Jesus. Practices address fundamental needs and conditions through concrete human acts. Practices are done together over time. Practices possess standards of excellence," 5, 6, 7.

65 Hoyt, "Testimony," in *Practicing Our Faith*, 92.

66 Hoyt, "Testimony," 93. The Black Church continues this practice and it has proved salvific, therapeutic, and prophetic.

67 Lonergan, *Method in Theology*, 41.

68 Chopp, "Reimagining Public Discourse," *Journal of Theology for Southern Africa* 103 (March 1999): 33–48 at 40.

69 bell hooks, *Writing Beyond Race: Living Theory and Practice* (New York: Routledge, 2013), 192.

70 Chielozona Eze, "Open Wounds of Being: The Poetics of Testimony in the Works of Patricia J. Wesley," *Interdisciplinary Literary Studies* 16, no. 2 (2014): 282–306 at 290.

71   William T. Cavanaugh, *Torture and Eucharist: Theology, Politics, and the Body of Christ* (Oxford: Blackwell, 1998), 237.

CHAPTER 7

This chapter was published as "Body, Race, and Being: Theological Anthropology in the Context of Performing and Subverting Eucharist," in Serene Jones and Paul Lakeland, eds., *Constructive Theology: A Contemporary Approach to Classical Themes* (Minneapolis: Fortress Press, 2005), 97–101, 103–13, 115–16. This chapter is used with permission and has been substantively revised.

1   John 5:53, 55.
2   Mellon, *Bullwhip Days*, 18.
3   Jean-Luc Marion, *God without Being: Hors-Texte*, trans. Thomas A. Carlson (Chicago and London: University of Chicago Press, 1991), 3–4.
4   Johannes Betz, "Eucharist," in Rahner, *Encyclopedia of Theology*, 448.
5   Betz, "Eucharist," 448.
6   Maurice Godelier, *The Enigma of the Gift* (Oxford: Blackwell, 1999), 32–33, cited in Douglas J. Davies, *Anthropology and Theology* (Oxford and New York: Berg, 2002), 195.
7   James Boggs in *Racism and the Class Struggle* (New York: Monthly Review, 1970) offers a comprehensive definition of racism as "systematized oppression of one race of another. In other words, the various forms of oppression within every sphere of social relations—economic exploitation, military subjugation, political subordination, cultural devaluation, psychological violation, sexual degradation, verbal abuse, etc.—together make up a whole of interacting and developing processes which operate so normally and naturally and are so much a part of the existing institutions of society that the individuals involved are barely conscious of their operation," 147–48.
8   I employ here Lonergan's technical denotation of bias as the more-or-less conscious refusal of insight, of further and potentially correcting questions, see *Insight*, chaps. 6, 7.
9   Ruy O. Costa, "Introduction," in *Struggles for Solidarity: Liberation Theologies in Tension*, ed. Lorine M. Getz and Ruy O. Costa (Minneapolis: Fortress Press, 1991), 21.
10 Evelyn M. Simien, "Introduction," in *Gender and Lynching: The Politics of Memory*, ed. Evelyn M. Simien (New York: Palgrave Macmillan, 2011), loc. 5 of 185, Kindle.
11 Cone, *The Cross and the Lynching Tree*, 30.
12 Cavanaugh, *Torture and Eucharist*, 251.
13 Lonergan, "Third Lecture: The Ongoing Genesis of Methods," in *A Third Collection*, 160.
14 Crossan, *God and Empire*, 122.
15 The Africans belonged as they do today to specific, particular linguistic-cultural groups, e.g., Igbo, Yoruba, Fulani, Tiv, BaKongo, Akan, Twi, etc. Valentine Y. Mudimbe, in his *The Idea of Africa* (Bloomington: Indiana University Press; London: James Currey, 1994), revisits the "discovery" of Africa and, while acknowledging the injurious fifteenth-century encounter with Europeans as well as the late

nineteenth-century "scramble" for Africa, reconsiders evidence that indicates prior to the sixth century BCE, according to Herodotus, a Phoenician crew worked for the Egyptian pharaoh and circumnavigated the continent (17–37, at 17–18); see also his *The Invention of Africa: Gnosis, Philosophy, and the Order of Knowledge Africa* (Bloomington: Indiana University Press; London: James Currey, 1988).

16   Stephanie E. Smallwood, *Saltwater Slavery: A Middle Passage from Africa to American Diaspora* (Cambridge, MA, and London: Harvard University Press, 2007), 58.

17   Orlando Patterson, *Slavery and Social Death: A Comparative Study* (Cambridge, MA, and London: Harvard University Press, 1982).

18   An example of such circularity may be found among the BaKongo people, who, on some estimates, accounted for about one-third of Africans enslaved in the United States. Robert Farris Thompson, in *Flash of the Spirit: African and Afro-American Art and Philosophy* (New York: Random House/Vintage, 1984), writes that the BaKongo world "was profoundly informed by a cosmogram—an ideal balancing of the vitality of the world of the living with the visionariness of the world of the dead," 106. And John M. Jantzen and Wyatt MacGaffey comment in *An Anthology of Kongo Religion: Primary Texts from Lower Zaire* (Lawrence: University of Kansas Press, 1974) that the "BaKongo believe and hold it true that man's [sic] life has no end, that it constitutes a cycle. The sun, in its rising and setting, is a sign of this cycle, and death is merely a transition in the process of change." Thus, if man or woman lived a good life, he or she could expect to "return within another dawn, emerg[e] from the midnight world, [and be] carried back into the mainstream of the living, in name or body of grandchildren or succeeding generations," 34.

19   Smallwood, *Saltwater Slavery*, 61.

20   Patterson, *Slavery and Social Death*, 46.

21   Smallwood, *Saltwater Slavery*, 63.

22   Johnson, *Soul by Soul*, 4.

23   The best-known symbols of this frightful departure are the House of Slaves on Goree Island, Senegal, and the Cape Coast Castle, Ghana.

24   Johnson, *Soul by Soul*, 5.

25   Johnson, 118, 120.

26   William Wells Brown, *From Fugitive Slave to Free Man: The Autobiographies of William Wells Brown* (1847; Columbia and London: University of Missouri Press, 1993), 43.

27   Johnson, *Soul by Soul*, 138.

28   Mellon, *Bullwhip Days*, 291.

29   Yetman, *Voices from Slavery*, 36.

30   Mellon, *Bullwhip Days*, 287–88.

31   Brown, *From Fugitive Slave to Free Man*, 83.

32   Page duBois, *Slaves and Other Objects* (Chicago and London: University of Chicago Press, 2003), 220.

33   Johnson, *Soul by Soul*, 116.

34   Patterson, *Slavery and Social Death*, 196.

35   Mellon, *Bullwhip Days*, 18.

36   Mellon, 180.

37   Belinda Hurmence, ed., *Before Freedom: When I Just Can Remember* (Winston Salem, NC: John F. Blair, 1989), 83.

38   Yetman, *Voices from Slavery*, 53.

39   Mellon, *Bullwhip Days*, 59.
40   Mellon, 18.
41   Blassingame, *Slave Testimony*, 341, 342–43.
42   Blassingame, 341, 342–43.
43   Spillers, "Mama's Baby, Papa's Maybe," 207.
44   See Beverly E. Mitchell, *Plantations and Death Camps: Religion, Ideology, and Human Dignity* (Minneapolis: Fortress Press, 2009).
45   Negro Spiritual.
46   Achille Mbembé, "Necropolitics," trans. Libby Meintjes, *Public Culture* 15, no. 1 (Winter 2003): 21.
47   Martin Hengel, *The Cross of the Son of God*, trans. John Bowden (London: SCM Press, 1976/1977, 1981), 114.
48   Cited in David M. Carr, *Holy Resilience: The Bible's Traumatic Origins* (New Haven, CT, and London: Yale University Press, 2014), 157.
49   Hengel, *The Cross of the Son of God*, 180, 138–39, 143–55. Generally, members of the nobility and Roman citizens were exempt from this penalty.
50   Carr, *Holy Resilience*, 157.
51   Carr, 158. Death by suffocation was quick, almost merciful, but sometimes the victim's agony was prolonged by offering a drink.
52   Cited in Hengel, *The Cross of the Son of God*, 118.
53   Anthony S. Pitch, *The Last Lynching: How a Gruesome Mass Murder Rocked a Small Georgia Town* (New York: Skyhorse, 2016), Kindle; see also Laura Wexler, *Fire in a Canebrake: The Last Mass Lynching in America* (New York: Scribner, 2003).
54   George M. Frederickson, *The Black Image in the White Mind: The Debate on Afro-American Character and Destiny, 1817–1914* (1971; Middletown, CT: Wesleyan University Press, 1987), 272. For some literature on lynching, see Ashraf H. A. Rushdy, *American Lynching* (New Haven, CT: Yale University Press, 2012); Amy Louise Woods, *Lynching and Spectacle: Witnessing Racial Violence in America, 1890–1940* (Chapel Hill: University of North Carolina Press, 2009); Anne P. Rice, ed., *Witnessing Lynching: American Writers Respond* (New Brunswick, NJ: Rutgers University Press, 2003); James Allen, with essays by Hilton Als, John Lewis, and Leon F. Litwack, *Without Sanctuary: Lynching Photography in America* (Santa Fe, NM: Twin Palms, 2000). For the most important early work on American lynchings in the post-Reconstruction era, see Ida B. Wells-Barnett, *On Lynchings* (New York: Humanity, 1892, 2002).
55   Hengel, *The Cross of the Son of God*, 117.
56   Cited in Hengel, *The Cross of the Son of God*, 117.
57   David W. Chapman, *Ancient Jewish and Christian Perceptions of Crucifixion* (Grand Rapids, MI: Baker Academic, 2008), 69, 70; Hengel, *The Cross of the Son of God*, 118.
58   Ida B. Wells-Barnett, *Southern Horrors: Lynch Law in All Its Phases* (1892), *A Red Record: Tabulated Statistics and Alleged Causes of Lynchings in the United States, 1892–1893–1894* (1895), and *Mob Rule in New Orleans: Robert Charles and His Fight to the Death* (1900); Ralph Ginzburg, *100 Years of Lynchings* (Baltimore: Black Classic Press, 1962/1988), 38, 68; see also James E. Cutler, *Lynch-Law: An Investigation into the History of Lynching in the United States* (New York: Longmans, Green, & Co., 1905), 192; Trudier Harris, *Exorcising Blackness: Historical and Literary Lynching and Burning Rituals* (Bloomington: Indiana University Press, 1984), 7, 10.

59   See John Johnson Jr., "How Los Angeles Covered Up the Massacre of 17 Chinese," *LA Weekly*, March 10, 2011.

60   Orlando Patterson, *Rituals of Blood: Consequences of Slavery in Two American Centuries* (New York: Basic Civitas, 1998), 173–75.

61   Frederickson, *The Black Image in the White Mind*, 272. For some treatments of lynching, see W. Fitzhugh Brundage, ed., *Under Sentence of Death: Lynching in the South* (Chapel Hill: University of North Carolina Press, 1997); Rice, *Witnessing Lynching*; Philip Dray, *At the Hands of Persons Unknown: The Lynching of Black America* (New York: Random House, 2002); Allen et al., *Without Sanctuary* (this collection of photographs also contains essays by James Allen, Hilton Als, Congressman John Lewis, and Leon Litwack).

62   James R. McGovern, *Anatomy of a Lynching: The Killing of Claude Neale* (1982; Baton Rouge: Louisiana State University, 1992), 5.

63   Frederickson, *The Black Image in the White Mind*, 272.

64   Ginzburg, *100 Years of Lynchings*, 38.

65   Leon F. Litwack, *Trouble in Mind: Black Southerners in the Age of Jim Crow* (New York: Vintage, 1999), 290; Simien, "Introduction," in *Gender and Lynching*, loc. 2 of 185.

66   Ginzburg, *100 Years of Lynchings*, 68.

67   "A Typical Southern Crucifixion," *Chicago Whip* vol. III, no. 25, June 18, 1921.

68   Jacqueline Goldsby, *A Spectacular Secret: Lynching in American Life and Literature* (Chicago and London: University of Chicago Press, 2006), loc. 62 of 418, Kindle. Goldsby is quoting Ida B. Wells-Barnett's chronicle of a lynching.

69   The name of the man lynched was Sam Hose. The newspaper account misreported his name as Sam Holt.

70   *Springfield (Massachusetts) Weekly Republican*, April 28, 1899, cited in Ginzburg, *100 Hundred Years of Lynching*, 12.

71   Simien, "Introduction," in *Gender and Lynching*, loc. 4 of 185.

72   Allen, *Without Sanctuary*.

73   Patterson, *Rituals of Blood*, 169.

74   Litwack, *Trouble in Mind*, 290.

75   *St. Louis Argus*, November 25, 1921, quoted in Ginzburg, *100 Hundred Years of Lynching*, 156.

76   Julie Buckner Armstrong, "Mary Turner, Hidden Memory, and Narrative Possibility," in *Gender and Lynching*, loc. 15 of 85; also see her *Mary Turner and the Memory of Lynching* (Athens: University of Georgia Press, 2011).

77   Litwack, *Trouble in Mind*, 288.

78   Armstrong, "Mary Turner, Hidden Memory, and Narrative Possibility," loc. 15 of 185, Kindle; Litwack, *Trouble in Mind*, 288–89; see also Rachel Marie-Crane Williams, *Elegy for Mary Turner: An Illustrated Account of a Lynching* (London: Verso, 2021), Kindle.

79   Christopher C. Meyers, "'Killing Them Wholesale': A Lynching Rampage in South Georgia," *Georgia Historical Quarterly* 90, no. 2 (Summer 2006): 214–35 at 224.

80   Armstrong, "Mary Turner, Hidden Memory, and Narrative Possibility," loc. 15 of 185.

81   Wells-Barnett, *A Red Record*, reprinted in *Selected Works of Ida B. Wells-Barnett*, comp. Trudier Harris (New York: Oxford University Press, 1991), 138–252; Wells-Barnett, *Southern Horrors*, reprinted in Harris, comp., *Selected Works of Ida B.*

Wells-Barnett, 14–45. See also Paula J. Giddings, *Ida, A Sword Among Lions: Ida B. Wells and the Campaign against Lynching* (New York: HarperCollins, 2008). James Cutler estimated that, between 1882 and 1903, 2,060 Blacks were lynched, that is, roughly one person every other day for twenty years, and in 1892 alone there were 235 lynchings.

82 Angela Davis, *Blues Legacies and Black Feminism: Gertrude "Ma Rainey," Bessie Smith, and Billie Holiday* (New York: Pantheon Books, 1998), 189.

83 Civil Rights Congress, "We Charge Genocide: The Historic Petition to the United Nations for Relief from a Crime of the United States Government against the Negro People" (New York, 1951).

84 Debra Walker King, *African Americans and the Culture of Pain* (Charlottesville and London: University of Virginia Press, 2008), 57, 58.

85 In 2017, historian Timothy B. Tyson interviewed Carolyn Bryant Donham, the White woman who accused Emmett Till of grabbing her hand, her waist, and proposition-ing her (Chuck Johnston, "Grand Jury Declines to Indict Carolyn Bryant Donham, the Woman Whose Accusations Led to the Murder of Emmett Till," CNN, August 10, 2022, https://tinyurl.com/7jrr2t7e). Tyson reexamined the lynching of Emmett Till and declared that Carolyn Bryant Donham recanted her original testimony against him. But, further investigation was unable to corroborate Tyson's claim, since Bryant Donham's comments were missing from the recorded interview.

86 These formal measures overturned Black enslavement, corrected Black exclusion from the body politic, and conferred formal equality. As political liberalism would have it, the freed people now held the same opportunities as other citizens since they now possessed the natural liberty that had been denied them. However, the granting of basic civil rights and equal protection under the law made little or no difference in the daily lives of Black people.

87 Walton M. Muyumba, *The Shadow and the Act: Black Intellectual Practice, Jazz Improvisation, and Philosophical Pragmatism* (Chicago and London: University of Chicago Press, 2009), 64.

88 Angela D. Sims, *Lynched: The Power of Memory in a Culture of Terror* (Waco, TX: Baylor University Press, 2016), 96.

89 Sims, *Lynched*, 97.

90 M. Shawn Copeland, "Listening to the Struggle of Cincinnati," *CTSA Proceedings* 58 (2003): 83–86. This is a summary of a workshop that I organized and facilitated for the Catholic Theological Society of America (CSTA) in June 2003. Registrants for the workshop participated in two sessions: the first day, Thursday, June 5, 2003, CTSA member Jamie T. Phelps, OP, moderated the session; speakers were Angela Leisure, the mother of Timothy Thomas, and Monica McGloin, representing the Intercommunity Justice and Peace Center, a coalition of faith-based organiza-tions and individuals who collaborate to educate the public about justice issues on local, national, and international levels; CTSA members Christine Firer Hinze and Bryan Massingale responded. On the second day, Friday, June 6, CTSA work-shop registrants participated in an informal brown bag lunch at Christ Church Episcopal Cathedral to learn more about the underlying condition of the economic boycott in downtown Cincinnati and the status of anti-black racism. Presenters were Attorney Paul DeMarco of the law firm of Waite, Schneider, Bayless, and Chesley, and former member of the Citizen Police Review Panel (CPRP) and the

Rev. Dr. Calvin A. Harper, Pastor of Morning Star Baptist Church and President of the Baptist Ministers Conference of Cincinnati, Southern Ohio, and Northern Kentucky. See also Howard Wilkinson, "It's Been 20 Years since the 2001 Civil Unrest in Cincinnati," https://tinyurl.com/5bjwxev7.

91 Richard Stewart and Steven Lash, *The Houston Chronicle*, Friday, June 12, 1998, https://tinyurl.com/3j89mpm2.

92 Patterson, *Rituals of Blood*, 172.

93 Cited in Ross, *Witnessing and Testifying*, 117.

94 See Billie Holiday, *The Billie Holiday Songbook*, compact disc, PolyGram Records, 1986, track 11. Abel Meeropol wrote the lyrics under the name of Lewis Allen and Holiday recorded "Strange Fruit" in 1939. See David Margolick, *Strange Fruit: Biography of a Song* (Philadelphia: Running Press, 2000) and Davis, *Blues Legacies and Black Feminism*, 181–97.

95 Davis, *Blues Legacies and Black Feminism*, 187.

96 Countee Cullen, *On These I Stand: An Anthology of the Best Poems of Countee Cullen* (New York: Harper & Row, 1947); Langston Hughes, *The Collected Poems of Langston Hughes*, ed. Arnold Rampersad (New York: Vintage Books, 1995), "Scottsboro," 142–43, "Christ in Alabama," 143, and "The Bitter River," 242–44. Hughes dedicated this last poem to the memory of Charlie Lang and Ernest Green, two fourteen-year-olds who were lynched together beneath the Shubuta Bridge over the Chicasawhay River in Mississippi, October 12, 1942. Claude McKay, "The Lynching," in Nathan Irvin Huggins, *Voices from the Harlem Renaissance* (New York: Oxford University Press, 1976), 354–55. W. E. B. Du Bois wrote at least three pieces on lynching: a prose poem, "A Litany at Atlanta," 14–16, the poem "The Prayers of God," 145–48, and the short story, "Jesus Christ in Texas," 70–77, in *Darkwater: Voices from within the Veil* (Mineola, NY: Dover Publications, 1999). There is a variant of "Jesus Christ in Texas," with small changes entitled "Jesus Christ in Georgia," *The Crisis* (December 1911): 70–74.

97 Cone, *The Cross and the Lynching Tree*, 31.

98 Douglas, *What's Faith Got to Do with It?* 7.

99 Litwack, *Trouble in Mind*, 185–97.

100 Patterson, *Rituals of Blood*, 214.

101 Patterson, 216.

102 Patterson, 217.

103 Leon Litwack, "Hellhounds," in *Without Sanctuary*, 21.

104 Wells-Barnett, *A Red Record*, 251.

105 Cone, *The Cross and the Lynching Tree*, xv.

106 Douglas, *What's Faith Got to Do with It?* 5.

107 Douglas, 27.

108 Douglas, 38.

109 Douglas, 37.

110 Douglas, 105. Douglas is insistent that "Jesus Christ . . . renders a platonized tradition and all that issues forth from it antithetical to the 'truth' of Christianity," 105.

111 Cone, *The Cross and the Lynching Tree*, 37.

112 Cone, 161–62.

113 Delores Williams in *Sister in the Wilderness* (Maryknoll, NY: Orbis Books, 1993) rightly and sharply criticizes substitutionary arguments derived from atonement

theories to justify Black women's suffering and abuse in the name of the cross. Williams has been accused, quite inaccurately, of discarding the cross altogether, but what she is calling for is a *new way of thinking and speaking* about the meaning of the death of Jesus. For other notable womanist treatments of Christology and soteriology, see Grant, *White Women's Christ, Black Women's Jesus*; Douglas, *The Black Christ*; JoAnne Marie Terrell, *Power in the Blood? The Cross in the African American Experience* (Maryknoll, NY: Orbis Books, 1998).

114 Augustine, Sermon 272, PL 38: 1246–48, cited in Louis-Marie Chauvet, *Symbol and Sacrament*, trans. Patrick Madigan and Madeline Beaumont (Collegeville, MN: Liturgical Press, 1995), 313.

115 David Power, "Sacraments," in *The New Dictionary of Catholic Spirituality*, ed. Michael Downey (Collegeville, MN: Liturgical Press, 1993), 836.

116 Davis, *Blues Legacies and Black Feminism*, 194–95.

117 Andrea Bieler and Luise Schottroff, *The Eucharist: Bodies, Bread, and Resurrection* (Minneapolis: Fortress Press, 2007), 142.

118 Cavanaugh, *Torture and Eucharist*, 12.

119 Cavanaugh, 279.

120 It will come as no surprise to some readers that my exposition here follows on Lonergan's analysis, see his *Method in Theology*, especially 125–27, 223–30. As embodied praxis, conversion is "existential, intensely personal, and utterly intimate," 126. As cognitive, conversion overcomes the ocular myth of knowing according to which all knowing is looking and objectivity is seeing what is there to be seen. The African American adage, "a heap see, but a few know," cautions against rash judgment or making judgments only on partial and or unreflected upon evidence. Of course, it is possible to be satisfied with what is given. But this adage invites thoughtful, critical questioning that refuses to ignore other and relevant questions that crop up. It presses for reflection on, then verification of, evidence, and refuses to repress contradictory or new insights that emerge or call for revision. Then, and only then, does this adage call for judgment. Moral conversion changes the standards by which we choose and take decisions. True value, the truly good, supplants simple satisfaction. Where value and satisfaction conflict, moral conversion adheres to value. Religious conversion is falling in love with God, it is "other-worldly falling in love," 240. This love is a dynamic state that precedes, grounds, and directs all our decisions, choices, and acts. And although each of these conversions is a different type of event, they overlap and compenetrate one another.

121 Leela Fernandes, *Transforming Feminist Practice: Non-Violence, Social Justice and the Possibilities of a Spiritualized Feminism* (San Francisco: Aunt Lute Books, 2003), 18.

EPILOGUE

1 Negro Spiritual.

2 Vincent W. Lloyd, *Black Dignity: The Struggle against Domination* (New Haven, CT, and London: Yale University Press, 2022), loc. 182 of 210, Kindle.

3 Jean-Luc Marion, *God without Being: Hors-Texte*, 2nd ed., trans. Thomas A. Carlson (Chicago: University of Chicago Press, 2012), 1.

4 Spillers, "Mama's Baby, Papa's Maybe," 207.

5 Dorothee Soelle writes that political theology "is rather a theological hermeneutic, which holds open an horizon of interpretation in which politics is understood as the comprehensive and decisive sphere in which Christian truth should become praxis," *Political Theology*, trans. John Shelley (1971; Philadelphia: Fortress Press, 1974), 59.

6 Ralph Ellison, "Richard Wright's Blues," in *Shadow and Act* (New York: Random House, 1972), 78–79.

7 Marion, *God without Being*, 1.

Index

Emancipation Proclamation 35
Empire/imperialism xiv; bodies in xv,
    42, 43, 54, 55; critique of 43; and
    homosexuality 64, 66; and Jesus
    43, 44, 46, 51; racism of 55; and
    sexuality 63, 64
Employment, decreasing 81
Enlightenment, European 2–4, 75, 78,
    80, 91
Eros 50, 51, 69, 70, 73, 78
Ethnocentrism 8
Eucharist: aesthetics of 72; and cross/
    lynching tree xvi; and freedom
    130; gift of 112; meaning of
    111, 112; and mystical body
    112; and racism 111, 112, 113;
    and solidarity 114, 132, 133; as
    symbol 112
Existence and divine revelation 15
Eze, Emmanuel 13, 75

Falls, Robert 34
Fancy, use of term 25
Fanon, Franz 8–11, 76
Ferguson, Mary 21, 22
Fetishization 6, 42, 69
Flesh, warnings about 16. See also
    bodies
Floyd, George xii, 104, 126
Foucault, Michel 147n.13
Fourteenth Amendment 125
Fox-Genovese, Elizabeth 27, 33
Francis (pope) 82
Frederickson, George 122
Freedom: Black religious 27; and
    Black women's bodies 17, 19,
    28, 36, 37; for community 36;
    enfleshment of xiii, 130, 133;
    essential 1, 2, 16, 35, 80; and
    Eucharist 130; for healing 37;
    and literacy 27; and martyrdom
    27; and memory of slavery
    xiii; of mind 28, 29; practical
    demands of 34; from slavery

18; of spirit 27, 33; statutory
    35; of thinking 30. See also
    emancipation
Fugitive Slave Law 118

Galilee 43–46
Gambling 22
Garlic, Delia 21, 30
Garrison, William Lloyd 131
Garza, Alicia 94, 96, 99, 100
Gender: and embodied spirituality
    49; of Jesus 49; performance 43,
    48, 49; and race 54; roles and
    sexuality 48
Genocide charge 124
Genuineness. See Law of Genuineness
Gift: of Eucharist 112; of grace 79, 90;
    and Jesus 111, 112; of life 64,
    111; and love 71
Gildersleeve, Basil Lanneau 144n.7
Gilroy, Paul 8
Globalization 53, 55–57, 63, 64
God: Anawim 49; as author 27, 30;
    and creativity xi; desire for 70;
    desire of 71; and freedom 30;
    freedom for 34; in history 76,
    80; imago Dei xiv, 15, 17, 136,
    143n.4; love of 89, 91, 112; reign
    of 40, 43, 46, 48, 51, 69, 77; and
    victims 77, 88; YHWH as king
    46
Goldberg, David Theo 75
Goodell, William 20, 21
Gospel and change xvi, 69
Goss, Robert 69, 70
Gould, Stephen Jay 4
Grace 14, 38, 49, 65, 66, 68, 79, 80, 90,
    136
Grandberry, Mary Ella 29
Grandy, Moses 35
Grant, Jacquelyn 95
Great Banquet parable 47
Gregory of Nyssa 71, 72
Grief 36